"An essential manual to promote leadership skills for any group seeking to ensure a free, just, and sustainable future. Without competent leadership, activism is virtually doomed to fail, and this book is a critical first step in building it."

- Michael Carter, author of *Kingfisher's Song: Memories Against Civilization*

Leading Communities of Resistance

A Manual and Workbook for Community Activists, Radical Community Builders, and Elders

Dr. Fred Gibson

Leading Communities of Resistance: A Manual and Workbook for Community Activists, Radical Community Builders, and Elders
© 2024 by Fred Gibson

Edited and published by Boris Wu
BabylonApocalypse.org

ISBN: 9783759736710
Herstellung und Verlag: BoD – Books on Demand, Norderstedt

Cover photo courtesy of Appalachians Against Pipelines
(appalachiansagainstpipelines@protonmail.com)

Back cover photo of the Colorado River courtesy of author

ACKNOWLEDGMENTS

It doesn't necessarily take a Community to raise a book, but it sure helped in this case. Comrades aided in this production in several stages and in several ways.

Jennifer Murnan and Jules Kirk are the Core of Communities that Protect and Resist. There's not a better, more committed, and supportive Cadre of comrades in the resistance. Let's keep this thing moving forward.

Along with Jennifer and Jules, Salonika Neupane and Suresh Balraj encouraged me to design the original course this book is based on, and cautioned me not to make it one that students in a business course would likely run across.

Boris Wu encouraged me to write this book, and stepped up to offer himself as a publisher without even being asked. That's leadership. My comrades mentioned above also cajoled me into making the course into this book. They told me, "No, really." when I wasn't sure this would work.

Michael Carter reviewed an earlier version of the book and gave me excellent advice as to how to proceed.

Elisabeth Robson generously offered her time and expertise to review the manuscript and provide much-needed guidance and editing suggestions. Whatever faults remain in the book are there despite Beth's inputs.

Participants in the Leading Communities of Resistance (LCOR) course offered interesting, wise, and perceptive comments and feedback to the material and the way it was structured. Thank you for helping me find my voice, and continued success in finding yours!

> Bastou Bacharach, Ewelina Bajda, Sue Breen, Sarah Gardam, Trinity La Fey,
> Lancia Flores, Daniel Sterk, Liam Griffith, Susan Hyatt, James Mante,
> Michelle Martin, Jeffrey Reyes, and Niraj Tamrakar, I'm looking at you.

DEDICATION

**For Teresa, who shows again and again that
Resistance is Love.**

Table of Contents

PREFACE

Purpose of the book

This book is for all the Deep Green activists, radical feminists, Elders, and those who aspire to taking on leadership roles in service of a living planet.

I wrote this book for those activists who understand the dominant culture must be dismantled, and replaced by just and sustainable forms of social collectives.

I also mean to equip those who see social and environmental collapse as a real and impending danger with the means to protect themselves and their collectives from, and resist, the dominant culture. This aim applies also to those who recognize that radical Community and its related forms are perhaps the basic standalone means of such resistance. I try to provide the knowledge and best-practice actionable items resistance-based Community builders can leverage.

What prompted the book

Leading Communities of Resistance (LCOR) was not originally intended to be a book. It began as a training program, responding to a perceived need for developing leadership capacity that is not as prevalent in the resistance as it needs to be.

To the extent that resistance warriors and activists develop leadership capacity, it's generally a result of one of two avenues:
- **Attending the School of Hard Knocks**: Taking on leadership roles or positions, doing what one thinks is the best way to proceed, and hoping for the best.
- **Reading the leadership literature** put out by the business, military and / or academic worlds. Yes, we need to develop the same sorts of skills used by those worlds, but at the same time, we need to frame those works about the leadership process in a resistance context. Learning about leadership from the military or business worlds enables the development of useful skills, but often at the cost of a worldview that doesn't work for us in building just and sustainable societies for the future planet. I try to point out these departures here and there in the ensuing chapters.

I've been a leadership scholar, executive coach, team leader, and organizational leader for over 40 years, and an activist for nearly 10 of those years. My hope is to translate the mainstream knowledge into a more useful Community-of-Resistance form, as well as to create new knowledge to help Community builders build and leverage the resulting power to protect and resist. LCOR is that attempt.

Given that philosophical backdrop, I must mention that the original LCOR course is the capstone of a 3-course sequence offered by Communities that Protect and Resist (CPR).

- **Leadership for Resistance** is an introduction to leadership, at the interpersonal level.
- **Leading Resistance Cadres** expands the sphere of influence of the resistance leader to resistance cadres (generally called "teams" in the mainstream literature; here, teams with a resistance purpose). These are the small groups you will work most closely with to build your Community, to build a campaign and so on.
- **Leading Communities of Resistance** caps off the sequence by expanding the sphere of influence of the resistance leader. Here, leaders build a strong collective, and use the resulting power and capacity in a strategic form to protect the collective and resist incursions and threats posed by the dominant culture.

I'm proceeding a bit out of order by publishing LCOR first, but the demand for this work obliged me to start here. My plan is to publish separate texts on Leadership for Resistance, and Leading Resistance Cadres (prequels if you will) in the coming year or two. However, so as not to leave the reader with large gaps in knowledge leading up to Community building, the first two chapters serve as primers on interpersonal and Cadre leadership respectively.

LCOR the book is the cumulative result of my research and analysis, and of the insights and experiences of two cohorts of course participants. Talking with activists from across various states, countries and continents has humbled me, and allowed me to test my thoughts and propositions against others' worldviews and best practices. The book is all the better for that.

Structure

My aim in this book is to help activists develop their skills as leaders, and to foster development and clarification of values and worldviews to prepare them to be, or become, Community builders and Elders.

First, though, I need to give you a **structure for developing your leadership**, in whatever leadership context we discuss.

To introduce this structure, consider that one of the most common myths of leadership is that leaders are born, not made. Actually, leaders need **opportunities** to develop. The best way to do that is from a combination of **study and learning from experience**.

The "AOR" Model (Action, Observation, Reflection) (Hughes, Ginnett & Curphy, 2002) is an excellent way for leaders to learn from experience.

- Developing your leadership depends not just on the **kinds** of experiences you have, but how you **use them** to foster your growth.
- How? We learn more from our experiences when we spend time thinking about them.
- If you **Act** (or monitor another's actions), but don't <u>Observe</u> the consequences of those actions or **Reflect** on their significance and meaning, you haven't really learned from that experience. Just "doing" doesn't necessarily lead to growth.
- Good leaders see all leadership experiences as learning opportunities – but insights only come from reflection and analysis.

Unexamined Experiences Yield no Lessons.

The AOR Model involves three processes:

- **Action**: what did you do, or see someone else do? And were these actions consistent with a valid model of leadership (which I introduce in the next chapter), or at odds with effective leadership practices? We grow from our mistakes too, and from others'. Experience is the most important opportunity for learning. It's necessary but not sufficient for growth. Monitoring others is valuable, too. You won't live long enough to make all the mistakes yourself. Look for models of leadership you want to emulate, and those you don't.
- **Observation**: What happened as a result? What were the results? What behaviors, events, feelings, etc. ensued? What was the impact on comrades, the leader, the project, campaign, or collective?
- **Reflection**: How do you look at things now? Can you frame the event in the perspectives provided by the model I'll introduce? Were the leadership behaviors consistent, inconsistent, or at odds with effective leadership? How

do you feel about your leadership (or others'), the behaviors or styles you witnessed? What would you do better, or differently?

The result of practicing the AOR model kind of looks like this over time. That is, each time you work your way through the Action / Observation / Reflection cycle, your experience level increases.

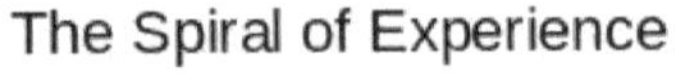

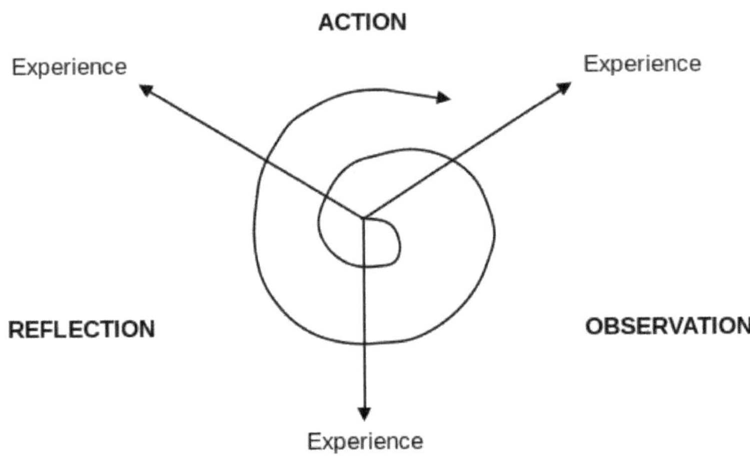

In other words, as you work your way through this process over time:
    Your Actions become more effective;
    Your Observations become more perceptive and nuanced; and
    Your Reflections become more sophisticated and grounded, in best practices and in this model.

Pretty simple, really. However, it can be difficult to "get out of your own head" regarding Observations and Reflections. What to do? Trusted comrades can help you:

- **Act.** They can coach you, train you, and facilitate you with respect to the best practices we'll explore later in this book.
- **Observe.** They are more likely to see your blind spots, and can spot things from different perspectives in the Cadre or collective, for example.
- **Reflect.** They can help bypass your tendency to make attributions, and can share the "real" reasons for how leadership scenarios play out and the results you might have missed yourself.

If you have access to trusted comrades, consider asking them to help you in your leadership development. It's an investment in the future for all of you.

I'd make the case that Reflection is possibly the most important component of the model. Effective reflection challenges your thinking and helps you become more conscious about how well you're engaging in aspects of your leadership. This discipline can provide you with a variety of insights / perspectives about how to frame problems differently, look at situations from multiple perspectives, and better understand yourself or others.

- For this to happen effectively, you can't always reflect in isolation. You need to seek feedback from others to provide alternate perspectives, confront your biases or fundamental ideas, etc. (see above).
- It's also valuable to use thinking frames to organize thinking and construe meaning to events. But the frames need to be good ones (valid perspectives on leadership). Don't worry – I provide such a model in the next chapter.

Given this AOR perspective, we can think of leadership development as the process of developing more complex and differentiated frames to organize our thinking and action about leadership. This achievement can be one of the most valuable contributions made in the course of your leadership development. You don't have to invent the whole field of leadership theory yourself.

How does this discussion of the AOR model relate to the structure of this book? I baked in elements that will help you engage in the three facets of the model.

- **Narrative descriptions** of best practices and "theory" components help you Observe and Reflect.
- **Reflection questions** after most chapters aid in actively processing the material and Reflecting on your leadership.
- **Action Items** after most chapters help you use the principles and practices. As an added benefit of sorts, by working your way through these questions, you'll be well on your way to crafting a plan for your development, and your Community's. Don't dismiss them as busy work or administrative red tape.

- - - - - - - - - - - - - - - - -

This somewhat lengthy preamble leads us to the overall structure of the book.

LCOR chapters are organized into four sections:
<u>Primers on Interpersonal Leadership and Leading Resistance Cadres</u>. The first two chapters give you a brief overview of leadership from these two perspectives. While not a comprehensive treatise on either topic, each Primer offers a useful introduction to the topic, and enough detail (including Action Items) for you to begin to take stock of your leadership capacity at the moment, and to begin your development journey if you haven't embarked on one yet.

<u>Understanding Radical Community</u>. This chapter contains my thoughts on what a radical Community is, and how it differs from mainstream views of community.

<u>Building Community Power.</u> These chapters explore the essential components of an effective radical Community. Included in each chapter are sections on cultivating the various Community components. I also discuss Community building as a process.

<u>Leveraging Community Power.</u> Building a strong Community is commendable for its own sake, but building Community Power is more important in the drive to Protect and Resist. This section talks about how to think strategically in a Community context. I include a discussion of how to conduct an effective campaign using my "EDS" campaign model, how to devise and choose tactics, and how to choose a resistance target.

- - - - - - - - - - - - - - - - -

As a whole, these chapters trace a progression in **scope** or **sphere of influence** for the resistance leader. It's probably not surprising that we can trace a related progression in the **role(s)** resistance leaders are asked to take on in each level.

It's not really as simple as scaling up or down. There are qualitative and cumulative differences between the roles you play as leader in the contexts we explore. The graphic below relates how scope and role relate.

The Changing Role(s) of Resistance Leader			
Context	Role(s)		
Basic Leadership for Resistance (LFR)	Model / Modeler		
Leading Resistance Cadres (LRC)	Model / Modeler	Professional / Linchpin	
Leading Communities of Resistance (LCOR)	Model / Modeler	Professional / Linchpin	Land Defender / Protector / Elder

I'll flesh out these roles in the chapters devoted to each "level" of resistance leadership. One thing to note, again, is that these roles are cumulative:

- The "basic" resistance leader is a model for comrades (of core values) and a modeler (she or he builds and maintains an effective culture).
- A Cadre leader should also be versed as a linchpin and professional, as well as model and modeler.
- The Community leader takes on the mantle of Land Defender and/or Protector and Elder on top of all these roles.

These skills profiles might differ somewhat from one context to another, but the themes seem robust. There is also overlap among the skills required at the various "organizational" levels, as you'd expect. I consider this a matter of relative emphasis. For example, skill in crafting and communicating a compelling vision is essential at pretty much all levels, but the *scope* of the vision might vary depending on the scope of your leadership.

As a preview of the issues we'll explore, here's a visual "map" of the aspects of leadership we'll explore, some more briefly than others. I'll revisit this map with "you are here" reminders from time to time, to help give you a sense of perspective.

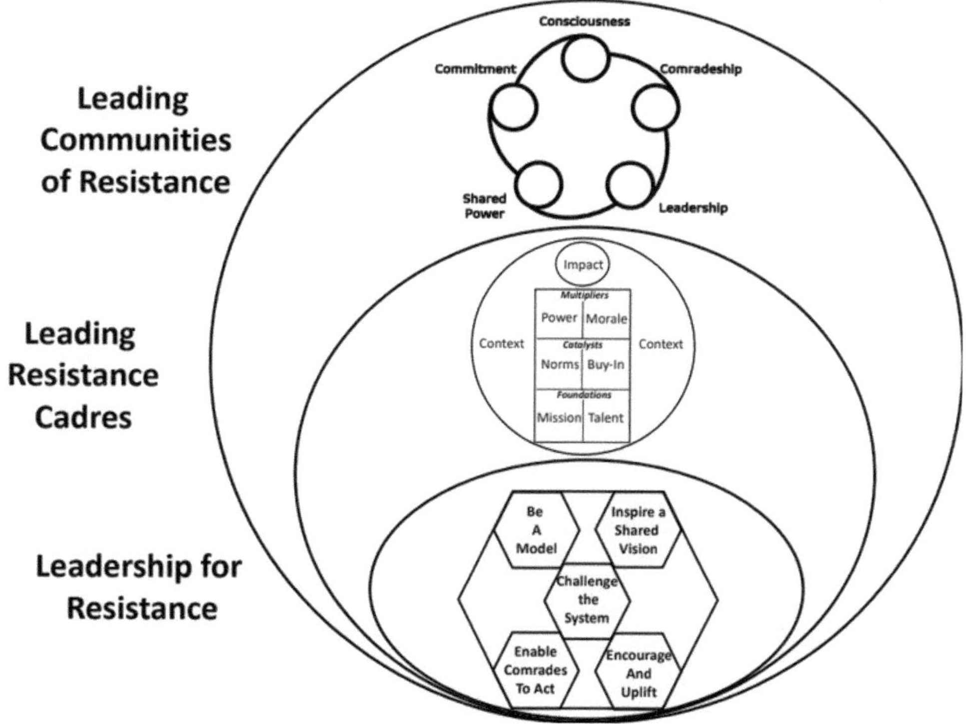

Reflecting on this model of leadership roles, and its cumulative nature leads me, and I hope you, to understand why the "Elders" notion embodied by so many indigenous Communities makes sense – it takes time to grow into all these roles. All the more motivation for you to not skip any chapters – you need to absorb them all!

Just as Plato asserted that it takes 30 years to "grow" a senator, so too does it take time to "grow" an Elder. But by working through the models and practices in this work, you can speed up that process significantly. And we need you to because your leadership in resistance is sorely needed. Now.

FIRST PRINCIPLES:
Leadership Basics

CHAPTER 1

First Principles, Part 1: Leadership for Resistance (Interpersonal Leadership)

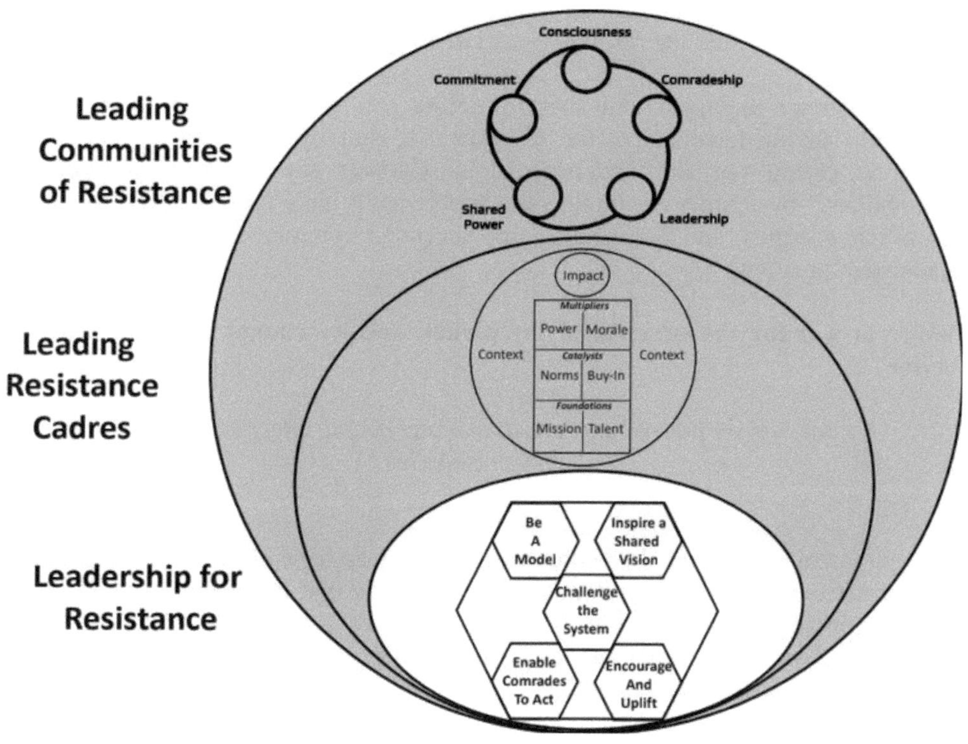

Why Leadership?

It's no secret that resistance to industrial civilization isn't winning. The planet is still dying, and injustice and oppression are rampant. You might say we in the resistance are getting our asses kicked.

Our struggles are in part due to the enormity of the problem, and in part our small numbers. We have no control over the former, but we do have control over the latter.

Consider these issues for a moment:
- Do we have problems with recruitment? Turnover? Commitment?
- Are we all, even within the same collective, on the same page regarding purpose, direction, and / or strategy?
- Do we experience drama or horizontal hostility within our ranks, or across resistance collectives?
- Do we want comrades to struggle with us, to take risks, or to take direct action, but find the response underwhelming?

It's not a stretch to suggest that these questions can be addressed by more effective leadership among members of the resistance. It isn't hyperbole to declare that the planet is crying out for leadership. John Gardner says, "we are anxious but immobilized" by immensely threatening problems. What's needed is the capacity to focus our energies, and a capability for sustained commitment. This is a call for leadership, of course.

We're at war for the survival of the planet, and we cannot afford not to fight better.

No one has yet figured out how to manage people effectively into battle;
they must be led.

John Kotter[1]

The corporate world and the military invest heavily in leadership development, as they understand the payoff in competitive advantage that leadership capacity brings. They're organized: we need to be, too. We have to compete and win without traditional leverage (rewards, authority) over others. Comrades need to be led – not managed, coerced, or manipulated.

Organizer Aric McBay offers that leadership skills are critical for the long-term success of any movement.[2] Movements need leaders, according to McBay. So do Communities of resistance.

---

[1]   Kotter, John P. What Leaders Really Do. Harvard Business Review. (May—June 1990).

[2]   McBay, A. (2019a). Full Spectrum Resistance, Volume One: Building Movements and Fighting to Win. New York: Seven Stories Press.

What is Leadership?

A challenge for us is to choose a conceptualization of leadership to work with. Why? Because embedded in each definition are assumptions, about:
- The agency followers or peers possess;
- The perceived relative worth or value of comrades vis a vis leaders;
- The acceptability of a hierarchy or power differential; and so on.

McBay's approach is that leadership is the "ability to engage and mobilize people for collective action".[3] This perspective aligns well with what we'll adopt.

A conceptualization that fits our requirements comes from Kouzes and Posner:
Leadership is the art [and practice] of mobilizing others to
want to struggle for shared aspirations.[4]

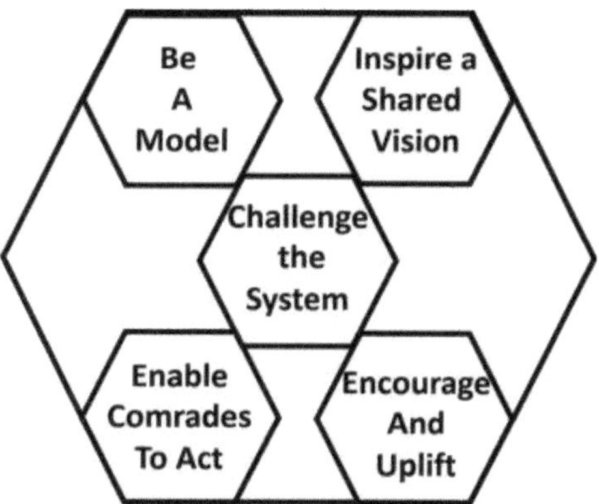

This approach to leadership fits nicely for us in resistance work. Leadership is not a position, or about power; instead, the leadership process (and leadership role) can and should be shared among comrades. To the extent we rely on power, it is the power of a shared vision to inspire and sustain efforts, and the power of mutually complementary talents blended together in single purpose. This notion of leadership also suggests a process of mutual influence, not coercion or manipulation.[5]

For resistance members, this relatively egalitarian view should be more palatable than mainstream management-oriented approaches. At the same time, when we view leadership as a process shared by all we avoid a tendency for resistance groups to

---

[3]   McBay, A. (2019a). Full Spectrum Resistance, Volume One: Building Movements and Fighting to Win. New York: Seven Stories Press, p. 180

[4]   Kouzes, J.M., & Posner, B.Z. (2012). The Leadership Challenge: How to Make Extraordinary Things Happen in Organizations (Fifth Ed.). San Francisco: Wiley.

[5]   Gibson, F.W. & Pason, A. (2003). Levels of Leadership: Developing Leaders Through New Models. Journal of Education for Business, Vol 79, Issue 1.

devolve into cults of personality, which not only limit the existence of the collective to the lifetime of the cult leader, but also tend toward abuse and misogyny.

How then can we practice leadership consistent with this approach? By incorporating five "practices" that enable leaders to inspire comrades to get extraordinary things done. (I borrow substantially from the Leadership Practices described by Kouzes & Posner.)

Be a Model and a Modeler.

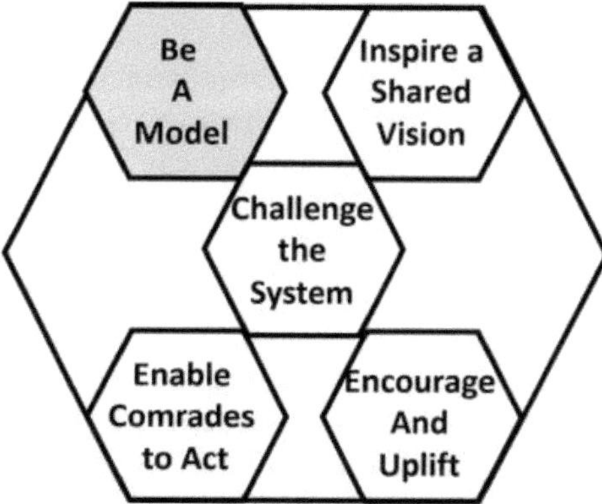

Effective leaders first **"find their voice"** – they discover, prioritize, and clarify their values, both personal and organizational. Leaders take time to reflect on what is really important to themselves, to their collectives, and to the living planet.

This may not be as easy as it seems. For one thing, we often default to a long list of values we claim to adhere to. I recently saw a list of values (labeled "virtues") posted from a well-respected resistance collective. There were 30 values on the list. I don't care how cognitively complex you are, but it's going to be really hard to keep all 30 in your head all the time. It's even more difficult to live by 30 values simultaneously. If everything is important, nothing is important. Long lists of values serve more to confuse and overwhelm than focus our work. So, the clarification process needs to involve a winnowing down of your values list to the 3-5 essential, core values you want to subscribe to, commit to, and communicate to your comrades.

Realize, too, that in your values hierarchy, you should be willing to sacrifice values lower on your list to those higher. For example, in much of the business world, managers say they value workers, but they value profits more, and are therefore willing to sacrifice worker well-being for the sake of profit. They value profit over the natural world, too, and we know how the rest of that story goes.

The process of values clarification is arguably the most effective way to allow leaders to "find their voice". Once a leader's values are identified and clarified, she can more effectively resolve potential conflicts between her values and those of whatever collective she is part of. Once they have found their voice, leaders are also better able to speak and act consistent with their values and those of the larger collective. Generally, they can do this by constantly engaging in dialogue with others about what is important, what is not, and why the shared values are necessary for the collective to survive and thrive.

At a larger level, clarity regarding and commitment to these values are essential prerequisites for leaders to establish core principles concerning the way comrades, constituents, and allies should be treated and the way goals should be pursued. We'll talk more about this "culture work" later.

Leaders serve as **models** – they set the example by behaving in ways consistent with their voiced values, and with values shared by the collective. By acting as an exemplar for shared values, leaders help comrades see how the values play out in behavioral terms – they teach. It's one thing to declare that you value a diversity of perspectives, and quite another to somehow wind up with a senior leadership staff made up entirely of your friends. Don't let things like this happen to you or your collective.

By **modeling and teaching**, leaders establish and maintain a healthy culture for the group. "Culture work" is a critical leadership function, and the practices I describe here play a role in influencing the culture of the group. Effective leaders are therefore *modelers*, as well as models.

Applying the AOR Model: Be a Model / Modeler

What's important to you in creating a climate in the collective you want to be part of, or lead?

Do you know what your collective's core values are?

How clearly would your comrades be able to describe what's important to you?

What can you do to demonstrate the importance of your shared values to comrades?
P.S. you're building culture when you do these sorts of things!

Inspire a Shared Vision.

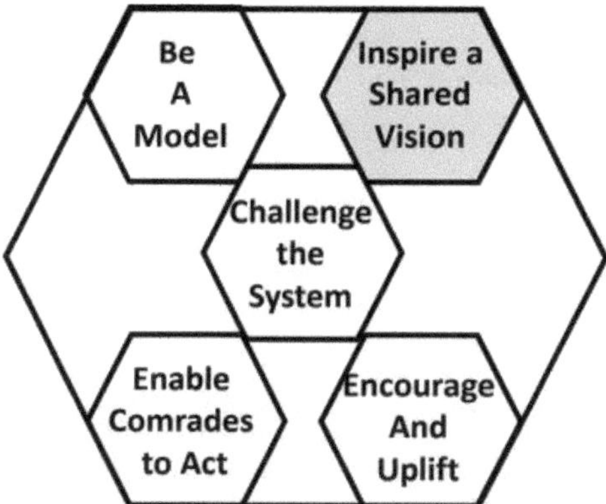

Resistance leaders need to answer the question, "What are we struggling for?"

Collective struggle is fueled by a shared vision of the future – of a realistic, credible, attractive future, an ideal and unique image of the future for a group, organization or larger collective. Leaders envision the future (often in concert with comrades) and paint a clear picture for the group to comprehend. Without a vision for the collective or movement, little can happen. If resistance leadership is going to take people places they haven't been before, comrades need to have a sense of direction. This is the function an effective vision provides.

Here's an example, from Communities that Protect and Resist:
> *"CPR strives for a planet of resilient, self-directed, self-governing communities thriving in mutually regenerative relationships with their landbases; a planet without empires; a planet where inhabitants are **Bonded** (by healthy interrelation among other community members), not **Bound** (by constraints, restrictions, or controls imposed by others in service to the dominant culture); where work is meaningful and jobs are meaningless; where the sights, smells and feelings enrich, instead of toxify. These communities, as diverse as the lands that give rise to them, recognize and guarantee the rights of all creatures of the living world (including air, rocks, bodies of water, and soil) to exist, thrive, evolve and flourish."*[6]

This paints a realistic, credible, attractive future – that ideal and unique image of the future that members of CPR and their allies want to struggle for. But visions seen only by the leader aren't enough to make things happen; effective leaders show others how

---

[6]   https://ctpr.home.blog/

the collective's shared values and interests will be served by a long-term vision of the future.

The visioning process is enabled by laying the groundwork of shared values. If you've engaged in the values clarification process I talked about above, you'll be better prepared for this practice.

A vision …doesn't just reveal itself in a flash of light or a brilliant dream!
It evolves from knowledge of ourselves, our values, and our desires.

Laraine Matusak[7]

The process of creating a shared vision isn't mystical or limited to the charismatic or eloquent individual; in fact, it's pretty straightforward. Know yourself and your collective. And know the past. Visit the past of your group or your movement to better understand the possible futures. Talk with Elders and do your research. I'll give you a chance to do that in the Community Walk exercise, later in the book.

- Get in touch with your collective's values, not just your own. Determine what you want to fight for.
- Let yourself dream, and get creative. An effective (inspiring) vision works on the heart more than the head, so you may need to concentrate less on numbers and narratives and more on emotions, senses, and feelings.
- Engage others in the vision - attract comrades to a common purpose. Discuss it, articulate it, repeat it, and ask for feedback as part of your repetitions, appealing to shared aspirations. Demonstrate your belief and confidence in the vision, and in the ability of your comrades to achieve it.

Maybe your collective already has a vision in place. That doesn't imply you can't undertake this important work for whatever part of the organization you're leading. You can also craft a vision for your **part** of the collective (e.g., your Cadre). Your comrades may be hungry for direction and meaning – feed that need. In the process of doing this, you may find yourself challenging how the collective does business.

You can contribute to an effective update or revision of that vision, as appropriate. Which brings us to the next leadership practice.

---

[7] Matusak, Larraine R. (1997). Finding Your Voice: Learning to Lead…Anywhere You Want to Make a Difference. San Francisco: Jossey-Bass, P. 23

Applying the AOR Model: Inspire a Shared Vision

What is your vision, for your own leadership, for your Cadre, or for your Community? Write your vision statement using what you know and feel.

What future trends (demographics, technological, environmental, governmental, etc.) are likely to influence the direction of your vision for you or your collective, and what you aspire to achieve? The results can give you an "audit" you can use to craft your vision.

What medium do you feel most comfortable with to communicate your values and picture of the future for your group? Are you best suited to communicating in writing, song, pictures, or something else? How might you incorporate that into your vision statement?

Who do you need to talk with about your vision, to get feedback, or to begin to create buy-in?

Challenge the System, Not Just the Dominant Culture.

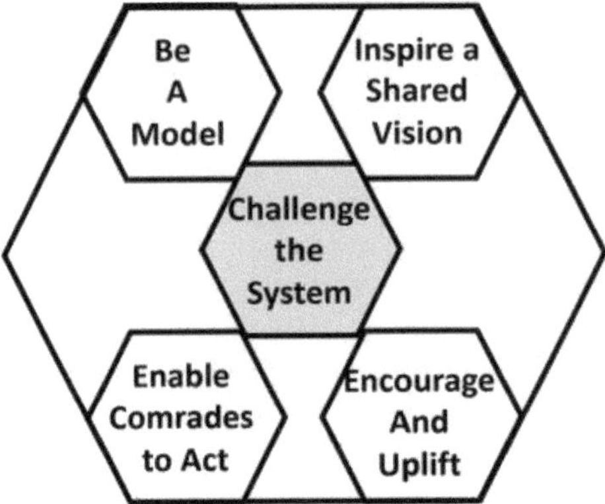

I don't need to tell resistance warriors they need to challenge the status quo (dominant culture), as that's likely the path that led them to resistance work in the first place. Continue to do that! It's less likely, though, that these same advocates for fundamental, radical change in the world apply that analysis internally, to their own collectives. I know I'm occasionally guilty of that.

Earlier I gave you permission (which you hopefully do not need or want) to lead. There's another, related license you should offer: **Give yourself permission to voice the need for changes, wherever they might be needed.**

I doubt your collective is perfect, so do yourself and the collective a favor and help them move in the direction of improvement and evolution. Let me repeat that, for those who might dismiss this as focused on someone else. I'm looking at you. Voice the need for change. You are allowed - obliged, even - to question not just the dominant culture, but the way your collective operates, even if you're not in charge. It's the only way things will get better.

Challenging the System isn't screaming, "burn it down!" – and certainly not regarding your collective! How then do we go about this challenge process? Here are some approaches.

Be open and alert for opportunities to change your status quo, because comrades do their best when there's a chance to change the way things are. Look for challenging opportunities to test *your* abilities, and motivate others to exceed *their* self-perceived limits while you're at it. Maybe you can lead an initiative to change your newsletter, or ask a comrade in your group to do that with you. How about driving a change to the way your Cadre plans for protests or direct-action campaigns? Let others know what your innovative ideas or wise thoughts are.

We're not going to make a dent in the dominant culture by doing business as usual, in the larger society or in our respective collectives. We must be vigilant for chances to change our comrades, our groups, and ourselves. Look for innovative ways to change, grow and improve.

Get out of your own head. One technique to find ways of doing things better is to take stock of what other activists and leaders have done. You don't have to reinvent the wheel. What can you do to get fresh, new perspectives, or discover best practices?

- Make use of "consultants". We're not getting fancy here – just ask for help from comrades who know about areas you may not, or who have more experience than you do in a particular area. We in CPR received very valuable help from a comrade in another collective who knew about setting up and maintaining our blog.
- **Brainstorm** within your group. You'd be surprised at what comes from a well-led session.
- Attend conferences or collective **gatherings** to learn what the friendlies are up to. Or the enemy.
- Do some "benchmarking" by spending time with comrades or other collectives. Make a list of questions beforehand to make sure you get the specific information you need to get smart in the areas you want to improve in.
- Do your own research. Read up on areas you think can help you further your mission. Check out a book on political or community organizing, perhaps, or watch videos on planning direct actions.
- Reflect on successes and failures of leadership (your or others'), and incorporate them into your aspirations going forward.

To maintain energy and momentum as part of the change process, one thing leaders can do is treat every task as an adventure, not just another routine. Even in the resistance world, there are lots of tasks that are less than romantic. Have you been tasked with updating mailing lists, drafting a press release, or operating the merchandise store? Is there something you could do to make these activities or similar ones more engaging, even rewarding? Look for ways to keep yourself and comrades engaged as much as possible, and open to suggesting change.

Another broad category of action items clusters around the notion of continuing the drive to change and evolve by **experimenting and taking risks**, trying new ways of reaching toward your mission and purpose. Take your comrades on these trips/experiments, too!

- Start an intentional community.
- Organize an advocacy campaign.
- Survey activists on a particular topic, and publish the results.
- To this end, constantly create small wins (incremental successes linked to innovations being tried) and learn from the mistakes, too. Make sure comrades who take risks are recognized and rewarded, even if they don't succeed. Build a culture of constructive questioning, risk-taking and experimentation.

Alas, you might feel you're not the creative one in the batch. That doesn't mean you can't contribute in this important leadership practice. You don't have to be the creator or innovator yourself - you can recognize and support the good ideas of comrades, and challenge the system to get them adopted.

- You can **be a champion** of risk takers. Encourage others to take risks, try new things and drive for better ways to run your collective or to resist. This can be as simple as providing praise, or you might offer them resources to allow them to pursue the improvements they are advocating for. In the next section, I discuss the linchpin aspect of the Cadre leader role. Serving as a champion is one way in which the linchpin function can benefit your Cadre or larger collective.
- While you're in culture-building mode (and you always are), create a climate for learning, taking risks, and changing.

Applying the AOR Model: Challenge the System

Do you feel like you have permission to question or challenge in your Cadre, Collective, or Community? You should! Is this something you want to have a conversation about with others?

What can you do differently to make your organization, Cadre or Community better? Who do you need to talk to, to make this change?

What sources can you make use of to get out of your own head or discover better ways of operating?

Are your comrades taking initiative? How can you encourage them to do so?

What small wins could you engineer for your group, to build momentum?

Enable Comrades to Act (Help Comrades Resist).
Warning: You may need to "decolonize" your mind.

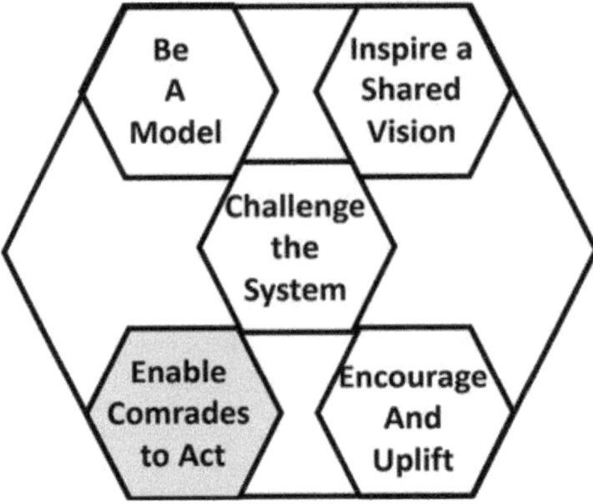

Effective resistance efforts won't be led by the strong loners of our neoliberal movie mythology; they will be led by activists who encourage comrades (and help them) to thrive in their resistance work. Leaders can't succeed alone (this is leadership, after all, not good citizenship). They create and maintain trustworthy relationships, and build cohesive Cadres (teams). But while good leaders don't try to do everything by themselves, they don't just delegate, either; they involve comrades in planning and give them discretion.

Enabling Comrades to Act is not any more complicated than ensuring comrades are willing **and** able **to do what's necessary for the collective to succeed.**

Let's look at things that way. First and foremost, leaders facilitate relationships and **build trust**. Trust is a core component of collaboration and nurturing effective groups. It's the central issue in human relationships. Without trust you cannot lead. Those who are unable to trust others fail to become leaders, precisely because they can't bear to be dependent on the words and works of others.

On the other hand, a climate of trust fosters effective teamwork. Trust allows cadre members to stay problem-focused (rather than on who has their back, and who doesn't). Trust promotes more efficient communication and coordination. Finally, trust leads to comrades compensating for mistakes or deficiencies in comrades.

From the comrades' perspective, why should a fellow resistance warrior work hard or take on risk for someone she or he doesn't trust? Make sure you create a climate of trust. Be the first to trust. Be a model!

This is the CPR model of building trust, which lays out the requirements in a bit more detail (Duckworth & Gibson, 1996).[8]

Trust-Building & Maintaining Model

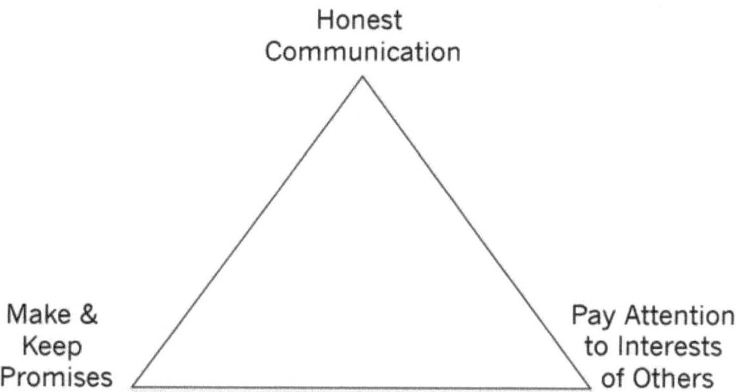

Here are some commitments you can make to build and maintain trust in your collective:

Use Honest Communication
- Use open, sincere statements to clearly state your personal position ("I" statements).
- Provide explanations for your actions.
- When you make a mistake, admit it - But don't dwell.
- Take time to think through your answers instead of responding too quickly.
- Share important information – don't withhold, hoard, etc.

Make Realistic Promises and Keep Them
- Activists often tend to overcommit, particularly when the fate of the planet is involved.
- Follow through on commitments. Be on time for meetings, complete assignments and be on schedule.
- Explain changes in your plans, as early as possible.
- Close the loop: communicate completion or lack thereof (early, again).
- Resist the urge to make empty promises to keep others off your back or to buy yourself time. Voice your concerns or reservations.

---

[8] Duckworth, S. & Gibson, F. (1996). Building Trust. In Coaching Workshop, developed for OppenheimerFunds.

Pay Attention to the Interests of Others – comrades, for example, who aren't present regarding tasks, interpersonal issues, and so on. Decline to participate in 3rd party shenanigans. Instead, ask those who broach such issues to you, "Have you talked to ___________ about this?"

Show compassion. Avoid blaming comrades for failures. Display your appreciation for lack of understanding, and differences between comrades.

Is there more involved in ensuring comrades are willing to support the resistance mission? Yes, but cultivating a climate of trust and relationships is a solid start.

- - - - - - - - - - - - - - - -

To enable comrades to act, effective resistance leaders complement trust-building to enhance comrades' **willingness** with cultivating their **ability** - leaders continually develop comrades and nurture their confidence and self-efficacy. Leaders strengthen comrades by sharing power and decision-making agency, and by delegating with development and challenge in mind. A comrade may not be as good as you in a particular area, but that doesn't mean you can't delegate that task to her! Recently, CPR was joined by a new member, who voiced the opinion that she was not a good facilitator. Although we had several members already experienced in meeting facilitation, we delegated the role of facilitating our weekly meetings to her. After a few weeks, she was much more confident in her ability to engage in this task, and my sense is that she would be more likely to take on that role in other context down the road.

Let comrades do their best and grow from the practice and feedback. Sharing builds competence and confidence as well as trust. It's a powerful practice.

Resistance leaders can generate a learning climate and educate others in other ways, too. **Be a coach (not a judge).**
- Give constructive feedback, especially when a comrade completes something you delegated to her / him.
- Probe a comrade for his understanding, reflection and learning following a challenge. Engage in Socratic questioning to further a comrade's ability to reason and reflect.
- Teach.

Don't try to do everything yourself. Spoiler – you can't. Develop others. While sometimes time consuming, it's an investment in your movement that pays huge dividends. When leaders coach, educate, enhance self-determination and otherwise share power, they demonstrate profound trust in and respect for others' abilities.

Applying the AOR Model: Enable Comrades to Act

Are you experiencing trust issues with comrades? If there are issues, what aspects of the Trust model do you need to emphasize? Who can you talk to, to work on this?

What aspects of the trust model can you use to give comrades feedback on their trust issues?

What can you delegate to a comrade to help with their confidence and development?

Do you have difficulty delegating? Why is that? What can you do about that?

How effective are you in giving constructive feedback to others? How do you know? Ask trusted comrades, and act on their feedback.

Are your comrades confident in their ability to do what needs to be done?

Encourage and Uplift (Keep Comrades Moving Forward).

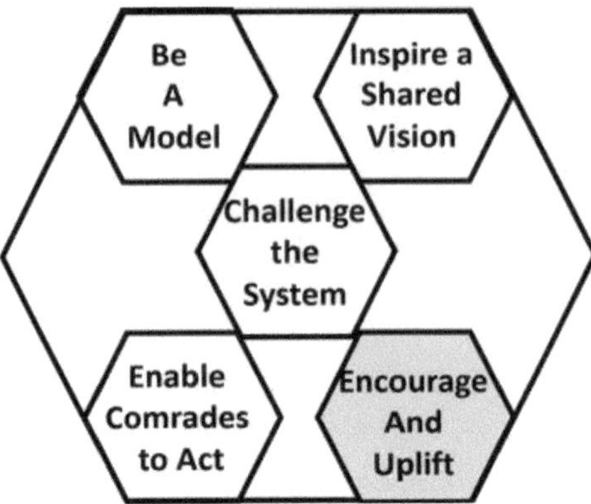

Activist work, particularly direct action, is difficult, isolating, stressful, and fraught with risks. Few people share our worldview, and those that do often live far away. We're also beset by parties that want to harm us as well as the planet, incarcerate us, take away our livelihood, and/or shame and berate us. It's hard to maintain motivation, energy, and a sense of purpose in these circumstances. Comrades need encouragement to function at their best and to persist. They need emotional fuel to replenish their spirits. At the same time, no one is likely to persist for very long when they feel ignored or taken for granted.

Often the best, or only, way to keep comrades going is through your demonstrated appreciation, pride, and affection for them and what they're doing. And when comrades experience wins, small or large, these occasions should be all the more celebrated, given the challenges. So, make sure your leadership practice includes encouraging and uplifting your comrades.

Encouraging leaders recognize the contributions comrades make. They communicate that they believe in the abilities of their comrades to help them achieve their purpose. Belief in others is crucial because positive expectations influence comrades' efficacy and aspirations. They really do. But don't just *tell* comrades you believe in them – *show* them by how you behave toward them.
- Offer reinforcement for the right behaviors, for effort, for innovation, and for perseverance. Make sure you recognize these in public when you can, and make sure the recognition is personal, and personalized. Form letters and the like don't cut it.
- Be a good, active listener.
- Provide support and resources as you're able. (Another example of the importance and effectiveness of being a good linchpin.)

To do these things well, you'll need to get close to comrades. Be out and about or at least in regular contact with them, and be attentive to what they're doing, feeling, and needing.

There's another perspective on feedback to mention here. Make sure your comrades get regular, useful feedback concerning their activist work and assignments. Comrades need to know if they're making progress toward the goal. I've seen volunteers in large resistance collectives fall by the wayside and move on after just a few months. In their "exit interviews" a common theme is that they felt lost, lacked focus or direction, and never heard from anyone other than "do what you think needs to be done." That's not effective leadership – it's not even good management.

Now for the fun part. Here's a question: When is a party not a party? Feeling they're part of a Community often keeps activists going even in the dire circumstances we all experience to one extent or another. Resistance leaders can create this "spirit of Community" by being mindful and creative about **celebrations**. We already talked about the importance of celebrating comrades' hard-won victories, even if they are small wins. These events should also **celebrate the collective's values**. Celebrations are among the most significant way people display respect and gratitude, renew a sense of Community, and recall shared values and traditions. They're important ways leaders communicate what's important to them and the collective.

But be careful what you celebrate! There's a basic principle in organizational psychology that "you get what you reward", so when you take time for a celebration:
- Be planful about the event – incorporate some narrative about what you are celebrating and how your event / recognition pays tribute to purpose, vision and core values in your collective.
- While you may all just need a break from the stress, also take time to reinforce the culture you want.
- You may only need a minute or so up front, before the dancing begins, to make your comments and frame the rest of the event.

This is an investment you really should take advantage of.

A final word about keeping activists going, apart from celebrations *per se*. Leaders can also provide **social support** themselves, and champion systems that enable support for all comrades. Supportive relationships among comrades are critical to maintaining energy and hope. Social support networks are essential for sustaining motivation and work as an antidote to burnout. One collective I know of holds "church" every week or so, where comrades come together virtually to talk about personal accomplishments, challenges and setbacks, and where everyone can share in offering happy comments, resources, condolences, and just an ear. How would you organize a support system for your collective?

Keep your comrades on the road, as they say, by supporting them.

Again, invest in fun. In a difficult climate for activists, people need to have a sense of personal well-being (which fun can contribute to) to sustain their commitment. And leaders set the tone.
- Be yourself (don't try too hard to be funny if that's not your personality), but build fun into the work itself, celebrations, or personal / cadre recognition.
- It helps if you're a clown, but be a clown with a purpose.

Applying the AOR Model: Encourage and Uplift

Do you recognize or reward comrades in ways that will motivate them? How? What else can you do in this regard?

Why don't you celebrate more? Why?! Seriously, what opportunities should you take to celebrate successes, perseverance, natural cycles, or something that draws the collective together and keeps them moving forward?

What would a social support network look like in your collective?

What can you do in your group to reward behavior or values exemplification?

Do you think the comrades in your group know you appreciate them? You could ask.

<u>Leadership is a Role. Be Ready to Play It.</u>
You may not be "the person in charge" in your collective. That doesn't imply this chapter, or this book, is for someone else. If you're working to save the living planet, we need your leadership in whatever form it takes, regardless of formal position, title, or assignment. Read on.

It's exceedingly difficult for resistance organizations or the movement writ large to function without a broad spectrum of individual activists taking on leadership roles. Characterizing leadership as a role is important, because such a representation emphasizes that anyone can assume leadership, depending on circumstances and task. This realization also de-emphasizes the importance of organizational position and hierarchy, too – in fact, our movement is more likely to be effective when leadership is widely dispersed, not limited to the charismatic, most experienced, or traditionally privileged, for example.

When leadership roles are widely dispersed and shared, we leverage better the diverse talents and experiences at our disposal. We also generate better "bench strength" so when a leadership position or new role emerges, we have the capacity on board to meet that challenge.

When we accept that leadership is a role, we also free ourselves from the assumption (myth) that some people are "gifted" with leadership ability, while others are not.

Everyone possesses leadership potential, and as resistance warriors we are obligated to develop our skills and clarify our values to sharpen our capacity to lead. In this way, "leadership" is wholly consistent with our collective identity.

Anyone can take on the mantle of leadership, depending on the circumstances and the makeup of the group she or he find himself or herself part of. Depending on your task-relevant skills or passion, you may be asked to take the lead. And if you're not asked, **step up anyway**. We need more of you to do that.

You might be thinking you can't use your leadership skills because you're new to resistance or to your collective, or maybe you're not a top staff member. Think again. You're likely a member of some team, task force or committee that can benefit from leadership. You're also part of some community that needs leadership to deepen, evolve, or thrive.

Don't wait for an invitation to lead.

- - - - - - - - - - - - - - - -

Becoming a better leader

Reading through this primer, and even checking out other resources, will not make you a better leader any more than reading about becoming a better baseball hitter will get you to the major leagues. So how can you improve your leadership? Same way you get to Carnegie Hall; you know, practice.

There's good news, though. We know leadership consists of observable and learnable behaviors. If you're new to leadership, or if you've struggled with that in the past, you can improve in any and all the Leadership Practices we outlined. In the Preface, we talked about a simple model you can use to make the most of your leadership experiences (and those of others): the Action Observation Reflection (AOR) Model. The AOR model is a good way to use the book to bring about your own Spiral of Experience.

We can take that one step further. Even if you're an experienced leader with a track record of some success, you can improve your ability to lead if you commit to this expanded development process:
- Adopt a model of leadership to aspire to, with a behavioral basis. Otherwise, you're just guessing about what to observe and practice. You have that model – the one I introduced here.
- Observe positive and negative models of those behaviors.
- Try your hand at some of the Practices yourself.
- Get feedback on your present use of the desired behaviors based on this model.
  This can be via written feedback, discussions with peers, or working with a mentor or coach.
- Reflect on the results.
- Set goals for yourself and / or build a development plan.
- Practice the behaviors.
- Ask for and receive updated feedback on your performance.
- Set new goals.
- Repeat.

You don't need to take this trip alone, and in fact you'll find it much easier with others. Consider getting a mentor or coach, or joining a leadership support group. You may have to recruit, perhaps with the promise that you are working to improve, but the results can be enriched substantially. You might also enroll in a resistance leadership course we offer in CPR.

<u>Final Thought</u>

If your Mom was dying, you'd do anything to save her. Well, she is, and you will. Resistance is risky, and direct action scary, but learning to be a better leader and maybe occasionally being uncomfortable? C'mon! You can do it.

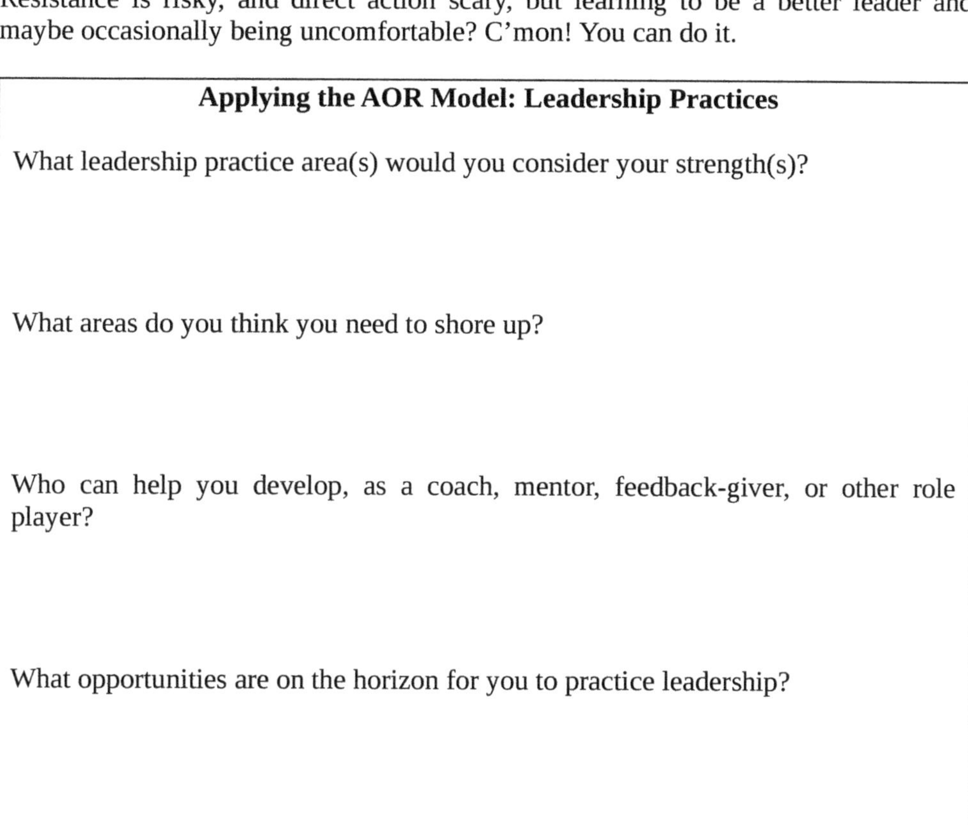

CHAPTER 2

First Principles, Part 2:
Leading Resistance Cadres

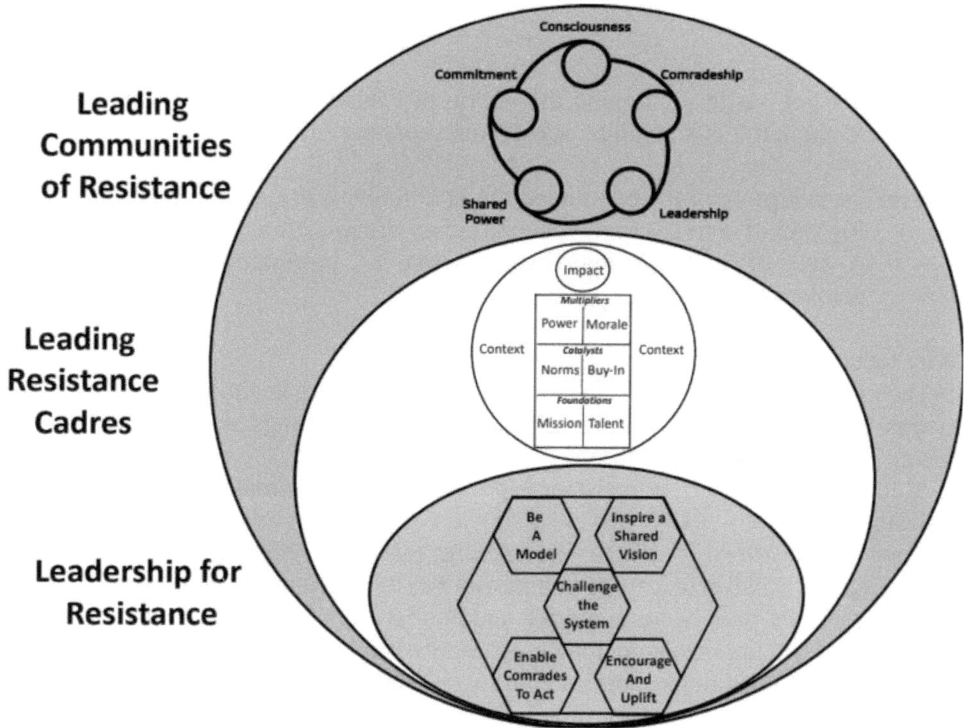

A recent survey conducted by Gallup Poll asked Americans, **"What do you think is the most important problem facing the country today?"**[9] "Environment / Pollution / Climate change" came in at roughly 17th place, with 2% endorsing that response.

We are truly screwed.

We're never going to be able to materially effect the attitudes and worldviews of many in our culture, and certainly not in time to save the planet. We can only work to dismantle this culture, and replace it with just and sustainable social forms.

---

[9] https://news.gallup.com/poll/1675/most-important-problem.aspx [Accessed Nov 5, 2022]

This you know. How though does this happen? Several years ago, Derrick Jensen, co-founder of Deep Green Resistance, was asked what it would take to dismantle industrial civilization. His answer, more or less, was 1,000 dedicated cadres. Makes sense! I can't argue that numerous cadres are indeed critical to the resistance dismantling industrial civilization. I'd add that **effective, well-led Cadres** are also critical to building radical Communities (more in a moment).

- - - - - - - - - - - - - - - -

We'd better get our heads around the notion of Cadres and how they are best built, cultivated, and led. Let's begin by addressing some basics:

Cadre: a small group of people trained for a particular purpose or profession.
- A group of activists in a… revolutionary organization.
- A cell of indoctrinated leaders active in promoting the interests of a revolutionary party.[10]

Why focus on Cadres?
1. The mainstream stuff, to begin with. There is lots of organizational scholarship that asserts that teams can be highly effective in getting things done. Let's adapt the "team" literature for our purposes.
2. Cadres (teams with a resistance purpose) are the smallest material unit of resistance.
3. They are an effective structure for getting resistance work done, and because of their relatively small size, can be nimble and flexible in terms of operations.
4. Although they need to be supported and nourished by radical Communities, cadres are where the rubber meets the road in resistance work.
5. Unfortunately, although cadres are pretty commonplace, they are often under-led.

Cadres are also critical components in building radical Communities and leveraging their power. Cadre leadership is an important building block, maybe even a prerequisite, for Community Leadership.

As a preview, let's go back to the future – later we'll cover how to begin strategically leveraging Community power. Here's an excerpt from the topic Getting Ready to Work:

> *Now that you've crafted your strategy, how do you make it happen?*
> *We'll find there are four areas of preparation you should consider. Mattesich & Monsey, and Murphy & Cunningham suggested a list like this in*

---

[10] [Google Dictionary, accessed Nov 8, 2022)

discussing the characteristics of the Community building process.[11] *We feel the wisdom in that list bears discussion from our viewpoint.*

Components of Creating Readiness to Work
1: Form a Core (Cadre) [emphasis added]
2: Cultivate Community awareness of the Issues
3: Ensure a good system of communication
4: Guarantee early involvement & support from existing Indigenous Organizations

One of the critical aspects of leveraging Community power, as we will see, is to be able to form (and lead!) resistance cadres.

Why?
You need a focused, cohesive group that collectively is able to commit to on-the-ground work, planning and/or executing on important Protect & Resist tasks.
- *These cadre will provide the 'E','D', & 'S' [Energize, Direct and Sustain functions] for a campaign.*
- *Of course, they can do that for more than one campaign at a time, and depending on the size of your Community, you might have several Cadre involved in various campaigns.*

Building, contributing to, and leading resistance Cadres aids resistance work in and of itself through the independent work of these "cells", and by empowering Cadres to contribute to the leveraging of Community power.

<table>
<tr><td>

Worksheet: Planning to Lead Your Cadre

Before we launch into the conversation, reflect on this question: In broad terms, what do you see as your overall Cadre leadership challenge?
- Build / begin a new Cadre.
- Maintain the effectiveness of my current Cadre.
- "Fix" a Cadre that is experiencing difficulties.
- Provide leadership to my Cadre, even though I'm not "in charge".

</td></tr>
</table>

---

[11] See Mattesich, P., & Monsey, B. (1997). Community Building: What Makes it Work. Saint Paul, MN: Amherst H. Wilder Foundation, and Murphy, P. & Cunningham, J. (2003). Organizing for Community Controlled Development: Renewing Civil Society. Thousand Oaks: Sage Publications.

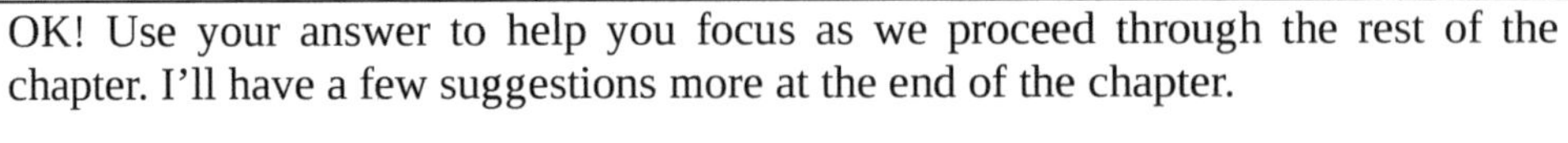

OK! Use your answer to help you focus as we proceed through the rest of the chapter. I'll have a few suggestions more at the end of the chapter.

- - - - - - - - - - - - - - - -

What's involved in Cadre leadership, then? I'll first approach this by considering the **role** of cadre leaders, and then examining a **model** for building effective Cadres.

The Role(s) of the Cadre Leader

I showed you the "hierarchy" of leadership roles you're likely to take on as you become a resistance leader in various and expanding contexts. The Resistance Leader (the basic role of leaders), as I detailed in the last chapter, models core values, helps shape culture, and contributes to a collective's effectiveness, whether she is "in charge" or not.

We may find from time to time that we are indeed "in charge" of a relatively small group of comrades, focused on a particular task, function, region, and/or product. Maybe you're tasked with leading the Social Media Team for your resistance collective, or you're heading up a squad organizing and executing a mountaintop protection campaign, or perhaps you've been encouraged by comrades to set up and take the reins of a band of comrades recruiting for the larger collective in a particular region of your country.

OK, you're "it" – now what?

We already know you can and should be a model of your larger collective's values and culture, and work to strengthen that. Now you'll be asked to do a bit more.

A central role you function in now is to be a professional.
What's involved in being a professional in the context of resistance leadership? Here's a working list of things to address. As you work your way through these role demands, take stock of where you are right now. This is an excellent way for you to begin to assemble a development plan for yourself. There are lots of perspectives on this notion, but these characteristics seem most appropriate to our work:

Dedication to a Mission. There's a planet that needs saving, as a start. But how does your larger collective aim to realize that mission, and more specifically, how does your Cadre contribute to the mission of the larger collective? This is the "line of sight" notion. You should always be aware of this, and working to clarify it with comrades. It's why we fight, and this line of sight should be fresh in everyone's mind, and refreshed as necessary.

Expert Knowledge. Strive to be competent or skilled in a particular activity. You don't need to be the expert in the specific function of your cadre, but you should be able to display competence. That competence, by the way, could even be in leadership skills. Simply being an effective, trusted leader allows you to provide guidance in a wide variety of contexts, and you can often learn the details of the tasks as you go.

The very word professional implies that you are competent.
- Become adept in the skills and tools necessary to do your cadre's work, as we mentioned.
- Keep your knowledge up to date. Get help from coaches, Elders and others.
- Know about, and commit to learning, best practices in your Cadre's essential functions and as a leader.

"Be a professional. Know your shit."

Max Wilbert[12]

Integrity. Do what you say and say what you can do. Being a professional implies an emphasis on integrity. If your larger collective doesn't already have one, consider advocating for a Code of Conduct. At the least, feel confident enough to declare your personal code. Make efforts to live up to it, and be strong enough to own up to it when you fall short – no one is expecting perfection from you.

Professionals deliver on their promises. Be thoughtful about what you promise. Don't overpromise to impress others, to try to fill competence gaps in your cadre, or to get others to leave you alone. This is a recipe for bad news. By delivering what you promise, you will also be building a climate of trust.

Accountability. If you make a mistake, own up to it and try to fix it if possible. Resist the temptation to place blame on a comrade.

Knowledge Sharing. Information isn't a limited resource. Your mind won't be emptied by giving away wisdom or experience. Think of knowledge as an ocean of facts, not a stream of data. Help your comrades as you can.

---

[12]   Max Wilbert, commenting on Lessons Learned from the Thacker Pass Campaign

"Lack of effective leadership is the common thread running through these…reasons why groups and teams fail. Far too often, leaders are either unwilling to take action or do not know how to improve the functioning of their [comrades]."[13]

As a resistance professional, you owe it to your comrades to develop competence in cadre leadership. This is what we discuss in the rest of this Primer.

- - - - - - - - - - - - - - - -

A complementary role to that of professional is the linchpin notion.
It's an effective practice Cadre leaders should emulate. Cadre leaders, when they do their best work, serve as linchpins between their Cadre and the rest of the larger collective they're part of. This includes being an advocate, but there's more to it than that. For your Cadre to be most effective, your comrades will occasionally need access to resources, decision-making agency, information, and other assets. Your obligation is to make sure your Cadre receives what they need in this regard, without doing the larger collective a disservice or causing other Cadres to go without. Advocate for your Cadre, but not to the detriment of others. Beware the fiefdom trap, in which you're so obsessed with protecting your little group or functional area you often work against the larger collective and compete for resources for example, with comrades who might need them more than you. This occurs often in academia, where department heads ferociously protect their departments and serve their interests over those of the larger institution.

One way to conceive of the linchpin role is that you're a Pathfinder and Path-clearer for your cadre. That includes, besides advocate, being a publicist, facilitator, and communicator.

Consider, too, the resulting implications of the linchpin role demands:
- Know what's going on in your larger collective. Ask around. Serve on action groups, etc. Be willing to negotiate on behalf of your Cadre, and / or to manage conflicts arising from your advocacy.
- Find your voice, and speak it.
- Challenge the system (or be ready to do so).

---

[13] Curphy, G. & Hogan, R. (2012). The Rocket Model: Practical Advice for Building High Performing Teams. Tulsa, OK: Hogan Press, p.6

Worksheet: Planning to Lead Your Cadre

How do you stack up against the criteria for being a professional? Is there anything you feel you need or want to work on?

What kinds of activities do you engage in to serve as a linchpin for your cadre, relative to either the larger collective you're in or to the larger Community? What else can you be doing?

An Aside on Mainstream Notions of "Teams".

The mainstream management literature makes a big deal of distinguishing between "teams" and mere "groups". The distinction is supposed to matter a great deal regarding how these collectives are managed and led. I'm tempted to ask, "Is your Cadre a "team" or a "group" in the mainstream sense of the words? That's an unfair question, without me even defining terms. But who cares? As far as we're concerned, most of the best practices concerning how to build, lead and maintain "teams" apply either way. Throw me in that briar patch – what if we learned how to be better Cadre leaders regardless of how management gurus might label our collectives? Maybe our Cadres would act and perform like effective teams if they were well led? Sounds okay to me!

Moreover, we're trying to do something different, and under different circumstances, than business or military teams. Most of us are severely understaffed and under-resourced, as well as outgunned. We also generally work under conditions of rejection by the mainstream culture, and in a context of isolation and anomie. You get the picture. Since we're often limited regarding the number of comrades available to work with, material resources and the like, we need effective leadership practices to address duplication of effort, distractors like conflict, etc. We have no slack, and need effective Cadre leadership practices to make up for that. Because of that, we need our leaders to be, and do things, differently.

> *"Leadership plays a critical role in building high-performance teams."*[14]
> – regardless of whether or not you subscribe to the mainstream distinction.

---

[14] Curphy, G. & Hogan, R. (2012). The Rocket Model: Practical Advice for Building High Performing Teams. Tulsa, OK: Hogan Press, p.8

We're about to work through a model of effective Cadres. We'll discover their critical components. We'll also include best practices, of course, for ensuring your collective measures up in each component. By working your way through the model, engaging in the best practices, and grappling with the worksheets, you'll be building essential Cadre leadership skills and drafting plans for your development and that of your cadre. You can also benefit from this chapter regardless of your Cadre challenge:

- To build a new Cadre.
- To maintain the effectiveness of an existing Cadre.
- To "fix" a Cadre with effectiveness or other problems.

The principles are the same. Looking at the challenges from a slightly different perspective, we want you to be able to frame (understand and put in context) what's going on in your collective to be better able to maintain a high level of functioning, leverage your Cadre's strengths, or respond appropriately to issues that hinder performance.

New activists take note: This primer is not just for current Cadre leaders. You don't have to be the leader at all. You can still shape the Cadre and its functioning by being a good follower.

- You might be leader someday, and this is good practice.
- If you're not part of a Cadre currently, this book can help you prepare and lay plans for starting your own, or joining one as an effective contributor.

Worksheet: Planning to Lead Your Cadre

Here are some introductory questions to keep in mind as we move on:

Does your cadre have a name or title?

What is its function? What is it designed (or supposed) to do?

What's your role in the cadre? What do you want your role to be?

What do you need to be able to lead your cadre more effectively?

Let's explore the model of effective Cadres. To keep you thinking about your collective, take mental stock of the one you're focused on with respect to the model component in question. You may want to check your opinion with others as a sort of informal audit.

**A Model of Effective Resistance Cadres
(Broadly adapted from Curphy & Hogan)**

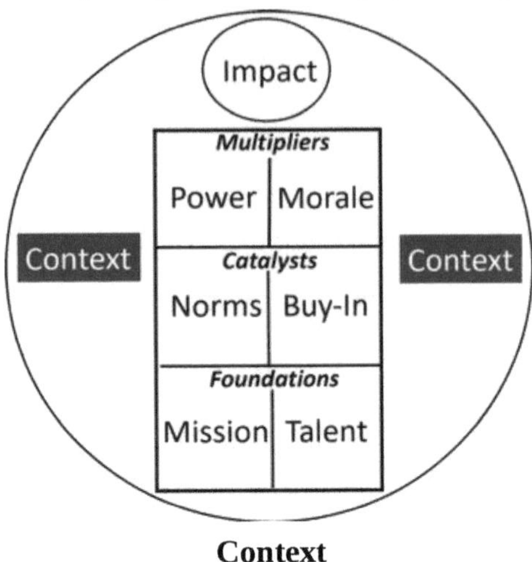

Context

Before we address the model itself, we need to examine the context in which our Cadre must operate. Cadres don't operate in a vacuum – they respond to, or struggle in, a given context. For most of us in the resistance, that context is widely shared – we operate in a toxic culture of patriarchy, capitalism, state repression, and mounting ecological disasters. Keep this context in the forefront of your work.

At the **nation-state / societal level**, what factors or trends do we need to be aware of?
- Does your culture appreciate the living world, or does it worship death?
- Do cultural norms argue strongly against violence in defense of the living, or are they more tolerant, or even encouraging, of that approach?
- An analysis of this sort serves as a strong shaping force in your strategy, and also how you operate.

At levels of **lesser scope**, the details vary more.
- We might be faced with local or regional threats of various types from legislative fiats to issues of water contamination to popular distrust.
- We might also be gifted with opportunities at these levels, not just threats. Be ready to capitalize on these factors. You might notice upticks in the awareness of issues we have been advocating, as with widely shared news stories of water contamination or police brutality.

Narrowing our focus even more, we'd be wise to scrutinize the **larger collective our Cadre operates in,** if any.

- Has funding been a blessing or curse?
- Do the policies of your collective help or hinder what you want to accomplish in your Cadre?
- Is what you offer in the way of Cadre plans supported, ignored or rejected by your larger collective?
- Do other Cadres get priority over yours when it comes to funding, support, staffing, and the like?
- What are the norms regarding how you treat each other across Cadres?

Context matters, and you should engage in scans of your Cadre's environment regardless of scope or your Cadre size, whether you are autonomous or part of a larger collective.

You're less likely to succeed if your strategy isn't formed in response to your circumstances.

Assessing your context (at whatever level or scope) is the beginning of thinking strategically. Blindly crafting plans and tactics, or doing so on the basis of convenient criteria, like doing what you think is cool, might work from time to time, but this is not a recipe for long-term success. My resistance collective, Communities that Protect and Resist, only has three full-time cadre members, but we make sure we hold special sessions several times each year devoted only to discussing our larger context.

Always Be Assessing Context.

We'll talk more in a later chapter about environmental scans and how they feed into effective strategic plans. There is a relatively simple approach to doing this, and I hope you'll find that the whole strategic planning stuff gets demystified.

Examining your context is only the first part of your challenge. It's important to subsequently **check for agreement among Cadre members** regarding that context, and to determine whether there is substantial disagreement. If so, make sure to resolve that through ongoing discussions. Make sure you're all working on the same page.

In other words, ensure everyone has the same assumptions about the larger collective, other Cadres they work with, forces they struggle against or resist, or legal and other challenges. Sometimes these assumptions are implicit and must be drawn out. Have conversations about this. You may notice agreement is greater with respect to the external threats, but less so when it comes to internal relationships, allies and so forth.

When you're able to reach a substantial level of agreement it's easier to clarify and/or articulate your Cadre's purpose and goals and to align the efforts of comrades.

Worksheet: Planning to Lead Your Cadre:

Within your collective or Community, what are the critical context factors that affect how your Cadre operates?

How have you responded to these critical context factors, or how do you need to respond or adapt to them?

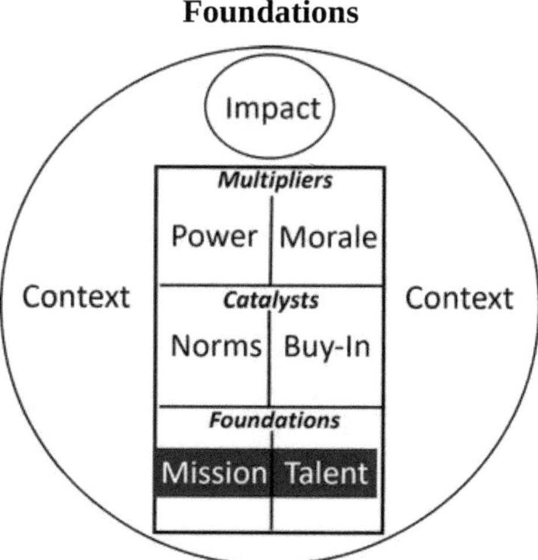

Foundations are essential Cadre components, without which we wouldn't have anything resembling a collective of that nature. If you were assembling a Cadre from scratch, they would be the factors you'd need to concentrate on before anything else. Other model components build on these factors or leverage them, but none are as critical.

Mission:
What the Cadre exists to do, to accomplish. It's your reason for being – your purpose. Mission is the common purpose tying all the comrades in a collective together. You've likely toiled in service to a mission or two in your resistance calling, but in case you're stymied concerning what mission might look like, here are a couple of examples for organizational-level collectives:

> *Communities that Protect and Resist:* "[CPR is] A support group, clearinghouse, resource bank, facilitator of and for activists who want to build, then leverage strong communities to pursue sustainable, just lives, we resist dominant culture, including the forces destroying the planet:*
> - *Patriarchy/Misogyny*
> - *Capitalism/Consumerism*
> - *Racism*
> - *Militarism*
> - *Environmental Destruction*"[15]

---

[15] https://ctpr.home.blog

> *Women's Liberation Front: "WoLF's mission is to restore, protect, and advance the rights of women and girls through legal argument, policy advocacy, and public education."*[16]
>
> *Deep Sea Defenders: "Deep Sea Defenders is an environmental organization dedicated to securing a global ban on Deep Sea Mining. We wish to call attention to the ways in which this industry would threaten ocean life, and therefore all life on the planet."*[17]

A mission, though, is not limited to organizational-level entities. It's totally appropriate, and recommended in fact, that your Cadre create its own mission. What are you in existence to do? What function, product or service do you provide to your larger collective?

As a Cadre leader, you need to work with your comrades to channel your collective energy and passion. Generally, this function consists of identifying key goals, benchmarks, and metrics, and reviewing progress regularly.

Mission development work can be distasteful for some of us, and you can be tempted to charge ahead with more romantic pursuits, energized by emotional vision statements and dramatic gestures, tactics, and campaigns. Resist the urge to pursue the romantic *only* - sometimes we do need to take on "management" tasks to succeed, not just leadership work.

Your Cadre's mission might spring into your head fully formed, and that's ok. If you're struggling to articulate what your mission is, though, or you want to examine your current mission for relevance, there is a technique you can use, called Constituency Analysis. We'll discuss that in the first Strategy chapter.

You might consider mission (or at least a clearly focused one, committed to by comrades) to be the most important component of an effective Cadre. Finally, make sure your mission reflects and responds to your Context. And be ready to adapt your mission as necessary, as the mission of the larger collective changes, or as environmental factors evolve.

---

[16]   https://womensliberationfront.org
[17]   https://www.deepseadefenders.org/about

Worksheet: Planning to Lead Your Cadre:

What is your Cadre's mission? If you don't know what it is, you're in danger of laboring at busywork, or worse, counterproductive activity. Find your focus.

Talent:

It helps to have the right number of comrades, with the right skills, to accomplish your goals / mission. It follows that you won't know what talents you need unless you have a good handle on your Cadre's mission. Do that important foundational work. Recall the mission of **WoLF**. It seems clear that among the skills they look for in cadre members are legal expertise. For **Deep Sea Defenders**, given their emphasis on awareness, social media proficiency might be a priority. In **CPR**, our emphasis on serving as a clearinghouse puts a premium on networking skills and outreach, and our Community building initiative behooves us to bring on board that set of skills. This is the selection approach for ensuring you have the necessary talent.

An alternative philosophy comes from Orlando Behling, organizational psychologist. Behling argues that "Despite years of research designed to match jobs and people, selection decisions are not always based on an exact fit between the person and the job."[18] Instead, he suggests it's sometimes a good idea to look for general intelligence and conscientiousness in potential recruits / new members. This is especially true when the task calls for problem solving, when the member still has a good degree of autonomy, and when the skills the new member will learn on the "job" are more important than those she or he bring to the collective, among other considerations.

This approach makes intuitive sense, and since it's not terribly difficult to gauge the intelligence and conscientiousness of a prospective or current Cadre member if you've spent any amount of time with them in a work situation, you might adopt this tack.

---

[18] Behling, O. Employee selection: Will intelligence and conscientiousness do the job? The Academy of Management Executive; Feb 1998; 12, 1.

It's perhaps an overstatement to conclude that these two approaches create a predicament, but you might get that impression. Can we resolve these apparently conflicting staffing philosophies? Easy. You have four options when it comes to the staffing your cadre with skills/talents in mind:

- **Recruit** comrades who already have the skills. When you recruit, try to be specific about what you need, not just in the way of skills or talents, but also regarding what you want recruits to do.
- Make sure new cadre members have **guidance**, and if possible, a plan for their contributions to the Cadre as well as their development.
- **Train, develop, and coach** your comrades to develop them in the skills areas you need. This approach is particularly important when you find it difficult to identify individuals with skills relevant to your Cadre's effectiveness.
- **[Re]design your Cadre and/or mission** to reflect the assets you have. It's important for you and your Cadre to be nimble, and moreover to capitalize on that as a strength to account for in your strategic planning. We're understaffed and under-resourced, as I've already noted. Lean into these circumstances if you have no other option. Do what you can with what you have or can get, and increase your collective capacity as you're able.

Clearly defined roles are also important. Comrades must know what they are expected to do. I've talked with resistance members who left larger collectives because once they were brought on board, they were left to their own devices, and the implied directive was, "Find something useful you want to do, and do it." It's likely your comrades joined your collective because they want to save the planet or in some way make a real impact. Don't let that commitment fester or rot on the vine - tell comrades what role you need them to play, or at least work with them to define their role.

Keep the Cadre context in mind as you do this. Be careful not to ask more than one person to take on the same role. That creates <u>role overlap</u>, with duplication of effort at best and interpersonal conflict at worst.

You may also find yourself with a particularly talented or energetic comrade, or feel overwhelmed by all that needs to be accomplished. Don't put too much on her / his plate, and thus create **role overload**. Resistance work is difficult enough without adding to the likelihood of burnout of our people. How will you know if a particular comrade is experiencing role overload? Maybe tasks start getting delayed, or lost in the shuffle. Maybe the comrade's attitude takes a turn for the worse. Maybe you ask them! Sometimes the obvious approach is the correct one.

Finally, make sure the role is clear – to the comrades, not just you. Engage in dialogue to make sure they **understand** what is expected, when and how to complete tasks, to what standards, and so on. In the process, you avoid **role ambiguity**. When comrades don't know what they're supposed to be doing, two outcomes are likely, and both are bad. One, they may guess at what they should do, or do just what they want to do, and their guess or preference might lead them to engage in inappropriate or unneeded directions. Two, they might become disillusioned to the point they become behavioral problems or leave the collective entirely – recall the comment on role clarity above.

Worksheet: Planning to Lead Your Cadre:

Do you have enough people on your cadre to make an impact? If not, what will you do? Maybe this becomes part of your Strategic/Tactical Plan going forward.

Are there any signs of role problems (overload, conflict, ambiguity) in your Cadre? Can you plan to address these issues at an upcoming meeting or gathering?

An underappreciated "talent" comrades bring to resistance collectives is their **ability to cooperate**, to work effectively with others. Comrades should be "team players". If you've had the luxury of working with potential Cadre members for a length of time, you should be able to get a bead on this aspect of the potential to contribute to your Cadre. Bad "team players" are often called "team killers". They sap Cadre cohesiveness and morale, and distract from the collective's focus. These comrades can be divisive, too, and left unchecked, their behaviors can result in factions developing within your Cadre. When comrades are pitted against each other, or chose to do so on their own, your ability to make a positive impact is severely damaged. In fact, your group might not survive at all as an entity. These comrades are so dangerous to your collective they must be addressed, strongly and with commitment from you, the leader. In a sense, these noxious comrades are so disruptive because they refuse to or are incapable of following the collective's norms, a topic we turn to now.

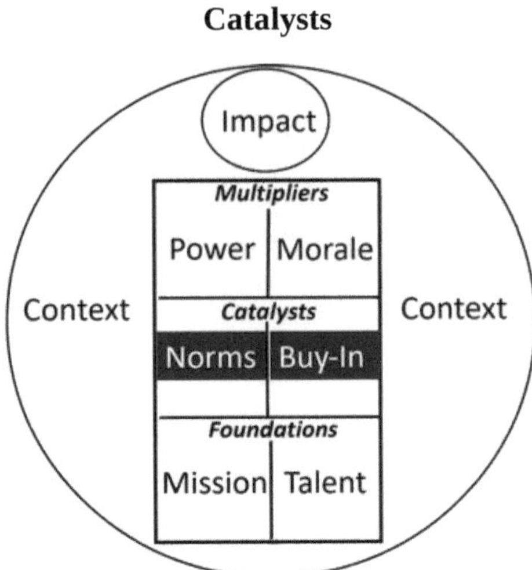

A clear, compelling mission and relevant talent can only carry you so far. Catalysts, in the form of productive norms and strong buy-in, facilitate the focused application of talent toward realizing your collective purpose, and keep comrades engaged in that pursuit.

Norms:
Cadre members need to know what is expected of them, individually and collectively. Expectations go further than just the "job description" or standards for task accomplishment, and they are more pervasive, too. The expectations you need to understand, be aware of, and enforce, are norms.

Norms are **behavioral expectations for a group** – they are often the unwritten rules about working together. We distinguish norms from roles, the behavioral expectations for specific individuals. We might all be expected to show up for weekly cadre meetings on time. This is a norm. We might also all expect Cindy to facilitate these weekly meetings. That's a role.

Norms are usually informal, but the more you can articulate them, the fewer conflicts you're likely to experience and the more effective your Cadre will be. We talk about norms because they impact the performance and cohesiveness of your Cadre. But there's another reason to be aware of them, and that's because a major influence on the development and maintenance of a Cadre's norms is the leader – you. **Leverage your influence** to ensure your Cadre works and interacts in healthy, productive ways. Do this in part by clearly communicating the norms you ask comrades to observe. Check with comrades too, to identify the norms they want to incorporate into your collective interactions.

Norms define and influence a wide range of activities. Consider doing your own audit for your cadre to see if you can articulate norms in areas like these:

- Communication: How we maintain contact with each other, respond to messages, etc.
- Meetings: When we meet, what are rules for how meetings are conducted, etc.
- Decision-making: Who makes decisions (and what types), and under what circumstances?
- Resolving conflicts: How we surface, manage, and resolve issues.
- Interpersonal behavior: How we treat each other, talk to each other.

The process of discovering and articulating your norms might be a great opportunity for you to convene a group discussion with this very focus. Nothing works better to garner commitment than the opportunity for all members of a Cadre to participate in setting the direction for the collective. We'll make use of this when we build Buy-in.

"Norms work" is an opportunity for you to create the culture you want, and this is a central facet of your leadership charter. However, it's neither complicated, nor particularly difficult. Make time for it.

There's a caution to be surfaced, and that is that **norms cut both ways**. They can help the Cadre be more effective and fulfilling, or they can be unhealthy and draining. If there's a prevailing norm that it's ok to make sexist jokes, or that comrades can show up for meetings whenever they feel like it, you'll want to address them soonest.

Simple stuff, really, and pretty intuitive. The issue, among other things, is that norms are so often unspoken we aren't aware of those that help and those that cripple. If you asked me my norms for driving in traffic, I might not be able to tell you too many. But if you spent an hour or so with driving on the highway, we'd be able to discover them as they're violated, because I'd be very verbal about pointing them out to the offending drivers! So, you need to make the implicit explicit. Work with comrades to:

- Identify the Cadre's material norms,
- Reinforce the positive ones (those aligned with cadre goals), and
- Replace the negative ones.

More with the culture work!

In the previous section we introduced the notion of the dreaded "team killer", and indicated that one perspective on these comrades is that they are incapable or unwilling to follow the Cadre norms. How should you handle such individuals? It's never easy to deal with Cadre killers, but the good news is that you have several options. In fact, I suggest a continuum of responses to such behavioral issues, from least to most severe.

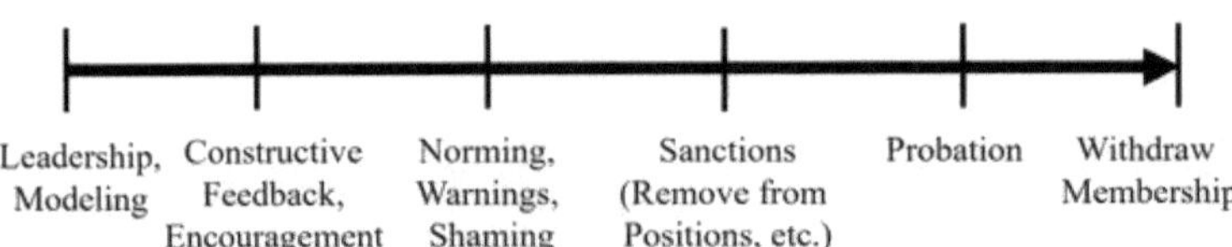

Your task is to choose the option that best fits your circumstance, and summon the courage to follow through with whatever response you choose.

Worksheet: Planning to Lead Your Cadre:

What are the top 2-3 norms you want your cadre to recognize and behave under?

Do your comrades know of these norms? If not, what's your plan to make them known, accepted and enforced?

Have you noticed issues with the norms in your collective? What can you do the address the situation?

Do you see a "social contract" in your Cadre's future? If so, jot down notes here that will serve as the basis for that contract.

Do you have any "Cadre killers" in your collective? How will you respond to this threat to your cadre's work?

Buy-In:
You've done a good job to this point in building your collective. You've taken pains to articulate and clarify your mission, recruited or developed the mission-related (and interpersonal) talents of your comrades, and audited your Cadre for the desired task and interpersonal norms, which you may have assembled with others.

The challenge now is to establish buy-in (commitment) to these elements. Along with effective norms, buy-in transforms the basic elements (mission and talents) into something more. The basic elements of effective Cadres are focused and transformed in part by healthy norms. When comrades hold themselves and others to the Cadre's norms, and commit to what the Cadre is all about, their efforts are not merely directed toward Cadre goals, they are shielded from distracting behaviors and conflicts that weak cultures allow in the door.

Buy-in is essentially **engagement in and commitment** to the goals, roles, processes, and norms of the collective. When comrades buy in to the mission and culture of the Cadre, they readily take on the tasks needed for the Cadre to succeed in pursuit of its focus. Ideally, comrades might even take on more tasks than assigned, and / or pick up slack for others who may be struggling.
- Contrast this turn of events with a Cadre in which some comrades carry the load and others loaf, or do only the bare minimum to stay off everyone's radar. Worse, comrades might do what they want to regardless of the direction the collective has agreed to.
- Even worse (and I hope you've never had to deal with this), a member or two might actively try to distract, delay, or sabotage the Cadre's efforts.

"The degree to which comrades faithfully carry out collective decisions is a good way for leaders to assess buy-in."[19]

Of course you want to avoid the nightmare scenario painted above! But let's focus on the positive for the moment. How can you foster engagement among your comrades? There are more ways to do this than you might have hoped for.
- If you've outlined a **compelling mission** for the collective (and vision), you're part of the way home already. Comrades toil with greater engagement when the Cadre's goals / values are related to something they believe in.
- **Involve comrades** in the creation of goals, roles, and norms. We discussed this when we talked about developing your norms. You're well along the way toward comrade engagement.
- We talked about the **line-of-sight** notion when we explored the components of a professional. That line of sight should be shared with and among your

---

[19]   Curphy, G. & Hogan, R. (2012). The Rocket Model: Practical Advice for Building High Performing Teams. Tulsa, OK: Hogan Press.

comrades - everyone should be able to articulate how their work contributes to the Cadre's goals, and to the goals and mission of any larger collective you're embedded in. In the process, you'll be building professionalism in the resistance, and that definitely is a good thing.

- **Hold everyone accountable** to the same standards: *don't* foster favoritism. This is an occasional issue, even in the resistance.

Hopefully you've been able to recruit and/or develop comrades who share the values and goals of your Cadre. The greater the coherence and fit between a comrade's values and personal goals for resistance and those of your Cadre, the more likely they will engage and commit to the work. It's always recommended you spend time with comrades to assess their fit, buy-in, and needs in order to continue the work. It can be taxing, but few things in leadership are more rewarding.

Worksheet: Planning to Lead Your Cadre:

Are the comrades in your Cadre bought-in and engaged? How do you know - what evidence do you have? If yes, yay! If not, how can you use some or all the practices we discussed to remedy this?

Multipliers

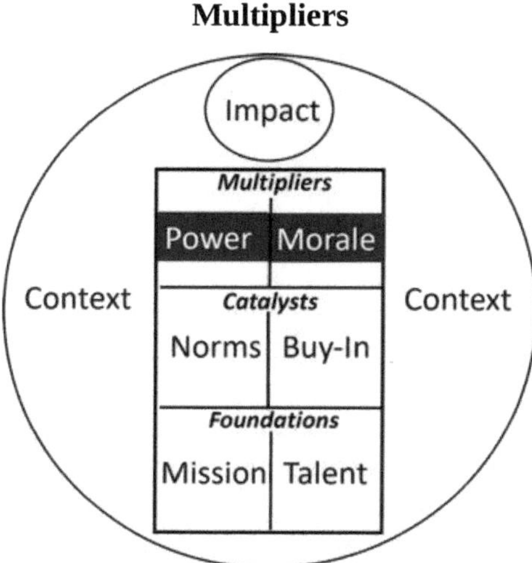

I asserted in the first chapter that effective leadership is a force multiplier. When you cultivate Cadre power and morale, you're exemplifying one aspect of the multiplier construct. Multipliers exert leverage to components of the Cadre model and in the process enable the Cadre to wield greater impact than they might otherwise. Resistance Cadres need the increased effect that multipliers allow them to bring to bear with what they have.

Power:

Think of Power as the capacity of the Cadre to leverage the potential they developed. The talents, focus, and commitment of the members will have little impact unless you're also able to ensure your comrades are **willing and able** to leverage that potential, remember?

Let's address the latter component first. The most talented, committed, and focused Cadre will make little impact if they don't have the resources they need. Whether it's funding, equipment, internet access, land, space to gather, or transportation for example, your leadership task is to first take stock of what these needs are. You should do that by carefully considering your mission and the plans you've developed to realize that mission and its goals. Compare that list to the catalog of what you have now. Bingo, you've got your material needs list.

All teams have material needs.

The leader's role here: help your Cadre identify, acquire, and effectively use their resources. Remember the linchpin notion as part of your leadership role? Here's yet another clear example of how that plays out.

There's a second aspect of this Power notion: that is the capacity for the Cadre to make their own decisions about their functioning, processes, and direction. It's also the Cadre's authority to acquire critical resources. Autonomy, you might say.

What's your role here? To be the linchpin, once more. Advocate with the larger collective if you're part of one on behalf of your Cadre to make sure they can do what they need to do, without undue influence, distraction, or roadblocks.

- Do you have to ask the core leaders of the larger collective for permission to engage in a direct action campaign?
- Does a steering committee have to agree to let you post an article on social media related to your function?
- Is the agenda for your direct action training conference subject to approval from a governing body of some sort? If any or all of these are true, reflect on whether theses situational factors are constraining your Cadre's work.
- If necessary, Challenge the System if it stands in the way of your Cadre doing its job effectively.

The realist might indicate, "If the collective lacks adequate decision-making authority, you must ensure comrades understand what is in and out of scope. Help them understand limitations and appropriate boundaries to their work." True enough. The leader can "stay within bounds" or lobby for additional authority. Your choice.

Now for the "Willing" aspect of Cadre Power.

Resistance work is tough, and not only because of the odds stacked against us: it can also be tough because it often demands skills or actions that are new to us, stressful, illegal, and / or dangerous. Even tasks that are more mainstream, routine, and widely shared can be daunting for some comrades. Trust me: I'd rather provide security for a speaker's group in a hostile crowd than develop a newsletter for social media. Now *that's* scary! Point is, you need to gauge how confident Cadre members are that they can make an impact, even in the face of obstacles. You do that in a number of ways. Building your base of talent is a great start, but there is more.

You can enhance the <u>self-efficacy</u> (SE) of your comrades. Self-efficacy is a comrades' belief he or she can complete the behaviors necessary to performance in a specific behavioral arena.[20] Alternately, think about SE as an individual's belief in their capacity to act in the ways necessary to reach specific goals. SE can influence everything from being able to climb a ladder to making a speech to organizing a campaign.

---

[20]   Bandura, A. (1977). Self-efficacy: Toward a unifying theory of behavioral change. Psychological Review, 84(2), 191-215.

Some tips for developing SE in your comrades:
- Help them engage in **"Mastery Experiences"** when taking on new challenges, and succeeding. A comrade who doesn't think of herself as a skilled event organizer may increase her SE in this area if you ask her to organize increasingly complex events.
- Encourage them to **observe** similar comrades succeeding at activities. Indicate how the observed success is attainable for them, too.
- Use **verbal persuasion**. *"… if people receive realistic encouragement, they will be more likely to exert greater effort and to become successful than if they are troubled by self-doubts."*[21] A few words of encouragement rarely go amiss. You could remind Tim about the practice he's undertaken, and the smaller successes he's racked up as a result.

Worksheet: Planning to Lead Your Cadre:

Does your Cadre have the Power to attain its purpose? Does it lack resources, autonomy, and/or confidence? Start to craft your remedy as part of in your Cadre leadership plan.

Morale:

We talked about buy-in (engagement) above, but your members' commitment should not be limited to the goals and mission of the collective. Comrades' commitment should also be to **each other**. In this risky business, it's particularly relevant and fundamental that we have each other's back, look out for each other, support each other, and help each other through difficult times, both in the work and the interpersonal. In the mainstream culture, toxic individualism, politics, and Social Darwinism are commonplace. We don't care. Our numbers are limited, our resources even more so. We have to leverage every ounce of talent, energy and goodwill possible from ourselves and our comrades. Nurturing Cadre morale is the final lever we can pull to place our comrades in the best position possible to do the work we commit ourselves to.

One result of Cadre leadership (good and bad) is the morale of comrades. Morale is cohesiveness or *esprit de corps*. Strong emotional ties, close relationships, and high levels of trust among comrades are the hallmarks of high morale. Members of high-morale collectives often say they would do anything for their comrades (or would

---

[21] Wood, R., & Bandura, A. (1989). Social cognitive theory of organizational management. Academy of Management Review, 14(3), 361-384.

trust them with their life). On the other hand, low-morale Cadres have members who dislike each other, and may sabotage others if doing so furthers their own welfare and / or advancement.

It's of substantial interest to Cadre leaders to shore up the collective's morale. **Cadres build trust, cohesiveness, and the capacity to engage in productive dialogue by doing real work together, such as identifying allies, enemies, and strategic partners, setting team goals, passing work between members, acquiring needed resources, and getting tasks accomplished.**

Your Cadre needs some minimal level of trust for productive dialogues to begin. If that is proving difficult, you know what to do! Work on trust, then introduce productive dialogue. Also, build a culture of nurturance and support.

Keep your expectations reasonable. Establishing high morale won't happen overnight. It takes time for members to have enough trust in each other to share their thoughts about issues. Make sure to explain this norm early and often. You've succeeded when comrades confidently point out areas where the Cadre is falling short, and when discussions stay focused on the issues rather than the shortfalls of comrades.

- - - - - - - - - - - - - - - -

There's a flip side to this. It's pretty easy to tell when comrades do not get along. Chances are pretty good your Cadre at some point will experience **conflict**. Not all conflict is bad, though. High-performing Cadres experience it, but they get conflicts on the table, focus on the issues at hand (not other comrades' faults), and develop ways to resolve disagreements. An effective Cadre isn't without conflict, but the conflict is **productive** – it's epitomized by debates, discussion of sometimes controversial topics, and occasionally competing interests or unmet expectations. It's the **nature** of these interactions that differentiate between effective and ineffective conflict.

Put another way: Cadres that are both cohesive and effective:
- Focus on solving problems, not attacking comrades.
- Identify what is and is not working, in a way that respects individuals. If comrades constructively challenge the status quo, you can find creative solutions.

The problem is, leaders often pretend conflict doesn't exist, or they deal with it by using superficial team-building activities (golf, BBQs, etc.). I get it. Conflict is anxiety-producing, uncomfortable, and can really distract from the task and mission.

But it's important to remember conflict is a normal and expected result whenever people work together for any period of time. Lean into the conflict, to get it under control, and even better, flip it into productive interactions.

You have a good sense of productive conflict. What does **destructive conflict** look like? What are some signs of a Cadre with destructive conflict?

Refusal to talk or work with comrades.	Displays of personal animosity.
Development of factions.	Chronic infighting.
Backstabbing.	Lack of trust.

Fingers crossed your group doesn't display these, but as we mentioned, it happens. When you lean into this, you're dealing with destructive conflict in a way that keeps the Cadre together, moving forward, and solving problems.

A simple way for you to manage your conflict is called **Fostering Productive Dialogue.** You can do this as part of your regular meetings or in a special gathering devoted to that purpose.[22]

Pro Tip: Don't blindside comrades with an announcement of this sort of meeting. Send out an agenda at least a few days ahead of time. Briefly explain the need to have a frank dialog about what you're seeing (or hearing about) in the collective. Give your comrades a chance to reflect on their perceptions of the situation and what they would like to see changed. Finally, post the guidelines for the meeting.

Setting Ground Rules for Productive Dialogue in meetings
- "We're here to focus on learning, not assigning blame."
- "The purpose of this meeting is:
  - To better understand what did or not happen; and
  - To learn what we need to do differently in the future."
- "We all need to be willing to ask probing questions of ourselves & each other.
  - Not to play "gotcha" but to help the cadre avoid repeating mistakes or future conflict of this sort."
- "We will redirect [with my direction if necessary] the discussion to issue at hand when the conversation gets personal."
- "When the meeting ends, we will articulate what we each have learned (round robin) to create a set of common learning for us all."

Use your judgment to add any norms you want the cadre to follow. Make sure someone takes notes, and publishes them afterwards.

---

[22] Thanks again to Curphy & Hogan for this technique.

Final thoughts on conflict:
If you want the destructive conflict to subside or flip to productive conflict, you and your comrades need to follow up on your commitments, and hold each other accountable for them. You also might want to make these conflict meetings a regular occurrence, at least for a while until you feel you've made substantial progress, and that the culture in the group is healthy and self-sustaining.

Establishing productive communication norms won't happen overnight, either. It may take time for comrades to have enough trust in each other and to share their thoughts and feelings about issues, especially if you're building a new Cadre. As leader, though, you're a major influence on the creating and enforcement of Cadre norms, so make sure to do this work. Explain the norm early and often, and show others how it is enacted (good examples) and violated. It's not unlike teaching.

We'll talk more about your teaching function right now!

Worksheet: Planning to Lead Your Cadre:

Are your cadre comrades cohesive? In a good way or bad way?

If they're cohesive but not so engaged, what will you do?

What signs of conflict do you see? Plan to address them, and consider convening a Productive Dialogue meeting.

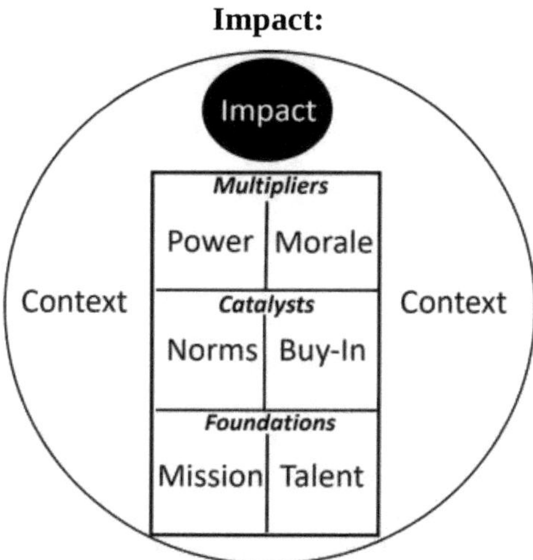

Are we winning? Are we effective? Impact is the outcome of leading well, and building a strong Cadre. What we've been talking about to this point is the "how" of Cadre leadership and functioning. Results are the "what". If we are to win (e.g., to dismantle industrial civilization in the broadest sense, to succeed in smaller campaigns, or to do our assigned work as best as possible in our resistance collective), even in the face of long odds, we need to work to shore up the model components as well as we can. Our Cadres should be relatively solid in each of those components.

We need to be clear about this Impact notion, however. Impact is not some mystical outcome that appears from the fog, the form of which surprises everyone. It's not some unexpected synergy that surpasses all expectations (that's nice and all, but let's not count on that). It's not a magical or mystical consequence that appears to result from forces beyond our ken.

Impact is **what you planned for in the first place**, the results of you achieving your goals (or not doing so). It is what you have been toiling for, and leading toward as a collective, and its form should be just what you planned and set as a goal.

What do goals have to do with results, or anything? Our **Cadres succeed when they achieve their goals.** If your Cadre has poorly defined (or worse yet, no) goals, you can't determine whether you're making progress, or are "there"!

- *"We want to strengthen the resistance!!"* Is laudable, but it's not a goal you can do much real planning around.
- *"We want to increase membership in our Save the Forest collective by 20% over the next year."* Works a lot better.

Work with your comrades to develop goals that are relevant, and therefore make it possible to measure and / or determine progress.

Choose and develop your goals carefully! They should:
- Be SMART (Specific, Measurable, Achievable, Relevant, Time-Bound)
- Not be busy work, or internally related, like "the number of Facebook posts". You should at least have a clear rationale for how these "internal" goals relate to impact.

Instead, your goals should be related to your "Theory of Method": How do you put your goals in context? What intermediate results will ultimately lead to the outcomes you want? Don't worry so much about how many posts you make. Instead reflect on whether you're making a material difference. How so?

Don't neglect relevant goals because they seem difficult to assess. There are measurement experts who can help you determine your Theory of Method, and how to assess them (I'm one of those people). Also, ask around to experienced comrades who can help. A relatively easy way to do that, though, is to compare your performance against your goals, and maybe the performance of similar Cadres. Make it easy on yourself. Don't forget, though, that the better you have developed your goals, the better you'll be able to assess your Impact. We'll talk more about goals in a later Strategy section.

- - - - - - - - - - - - - - - -

The notion to this point is that to the extent that the Cadre, led by you, is committed, has clear roles, etc., they will be effective. There's more you can do to drive your Cadre to make an impact. **You can teach your Cadre how to win.** This is a critical but often overlooked and undervalued role for the leader.

Here are the sorts of things you can do with your Cadre to make an impact (succeed or be victorious):
- Evaluate the competition (industrial civilization / local threats) and devise strategies and tactics to overcome them. Environmental scans, power maps, and other techniques we discuss later are all quite helpful.
- Use action plans to outline the steps comrades need to take to implement solutions, run campaigns, etc. Make the ethereal material.
- Believe in the power of lists!
- Define member roles and responsibilities.
- Define and cultivate healthy norms.
- Ensure you have enough talent, or react flexibly to what you have.

- Encourage comrades to develop relevant skills.
- Monitor comrade progress, **provide feedback and coaching**. To do this the best, **be a helper, not a judge**, remember? Don't make it unbearably stressful to review performance. Use setbacks as learning opportunities, a chance to ask for help, etc. Make it a habit to say, "How can I help you?"
- Create a climate of accountability.

In other words, be a disciplined Cadre leader, incorporate the best practices as best you can, and don't be afraid to try things you haven't yet.

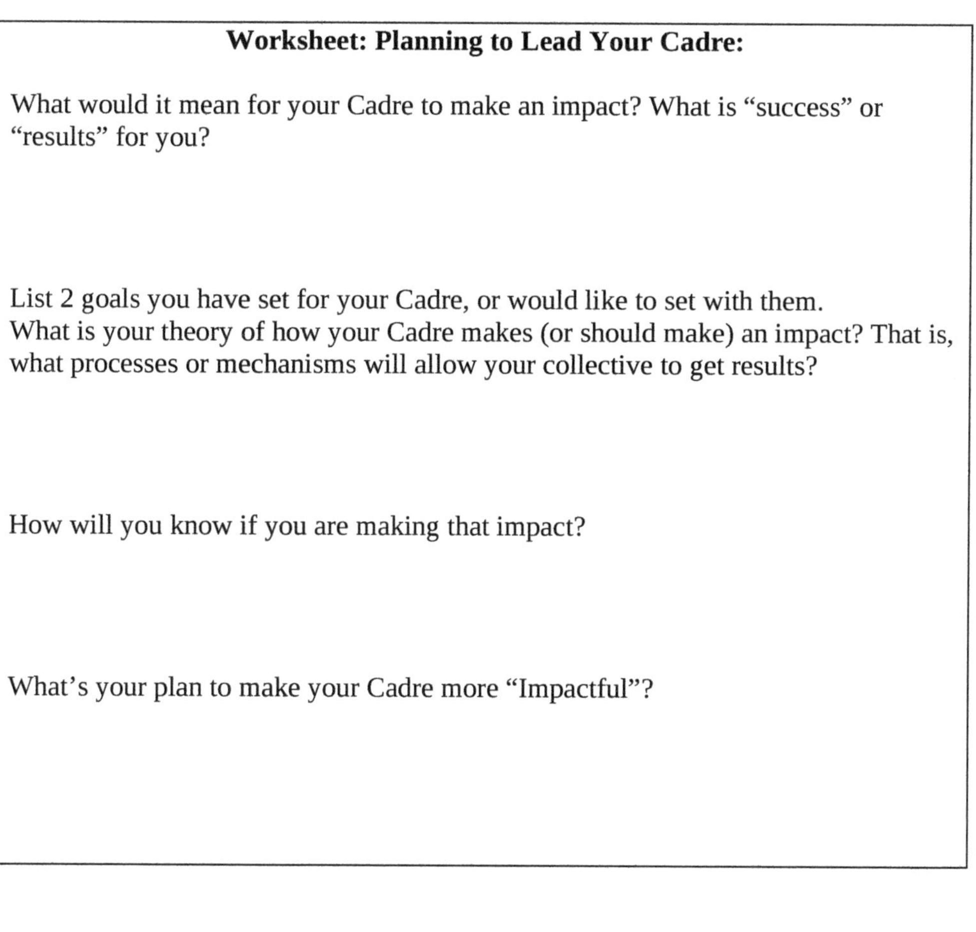

Worksheet: Planning to Lead Your Cadre:

What would it mean for your Cadre to make an impact? What is "success" or "results" for you?

List 2 goals you have set for your Cadre, or would like to set with them.
What is your theory of how your Cadre makes (or should make) an impact? That is, what processes or mechanisms will allow your collective to get results?

How will you know if you are making that impact?

What's your plan to make your Cadre more "Impactful"?

Reflections on the Impact Model

Although we may not think about the issue this way, in a sense these past two chapters have been concerned with building power – at the individual (comrade) and aggregate (Cadre) levels. We'll transition to the next level, Community, beginning with the next chapter. And again, why build power? So we can leverage it to protect and resist. It's a main theme of this book, and it occurs at every level: individual, Cadre and Community.

The Impact Model can help you **build a Cadre** from scratch. We've walked through the steps you can take to do that. We know all too well, though, that life doesn't always allow us to move in a linear way, and maybe you don't work that way either. Take the model's components and build them as you find it most reasonable, although following the model in the order I presented it will be your path of least resistance if you're building from the ground up.

The Model can also help you **recover or advance** an existing Cadre, by diagnosing your assets and problem areas and creating action plans to address the existing collective's profile. This goes a bit differently. You need to get a sense of what is **not** going well, and what **is**. How can you do that? Framing. It helps immensely if you have a schema, or frame with which to put Cadre matters in perspective. That frame, that schema, is the Impact Model.

Being able to frame a problem (put it in perspective, e.g.) is 80% of solving it. How does that happen? How can you apply the model in this way?
- Conduct an audit (survey) of the components. Using the model as a checklist of sorts, reflect on the state of affairs of your Cadre, and make a list of the pluses and minuses as you work your way through.
- Better yet, do this with your comrades. Whenever you can get multiple perspectives, you're better off. Ask comrades directly, perhaps even invoking the model components as conversation starters.
- It's a truism in the leadership development world that leaders never see themselves the same way others see them. The same principle applies here, and your comrades might see their Cadre differently than you do. Celebrate that, and use it to get the most accurate view of where you stand now. A group audit or discussion of your Cadre's profile relies on trust and good interpersonal communication, and this might be a good place to take stock before you begin.

- - - - - - - - - - - - - - - -

Moving forward with your Cadre

Whether you're building a new Cadre or dealing with an existing one, there are some takeaways outside the model and its components themselves. Let's reflect on these notions, and on where to go from here. (Thanks again to Curphy & Hogan for a general framework.)

Plan for Cadre-development sessions, gatherings, and similar activities. Sessions should reflect the priorities revealed in your analysis, audit, or framing of the major issues. Remember, you're a professional – your sessions, meetings, materials and such should reflect that.

It can take time and persistence to improve your Cadre's performance. It takes time for comrades to understand the situation, what they need to do to succeed, what needs to be accomplished, how they will work together, and so on. You have to go slow to go fast. Set aside time to work through model components. You can do this as part of regular meetings or as side sessions in larger gatherings – they don't have to be formal offsites. You can also call a time-out to review and craft strategies to deal with the issues at hand. It may therefore take a bit of persistence to build your Cadre. Try not to get distracted by the Crisis of the Day. Stay focused on what you're doing with respect to cadre-building.

Capitalize on your Cadre's natural rhythm whenever possible. Use your natural working rhythm for Cadre-building sessions. If you get together for weekly meetings for example, use that platform for your sessions. Take advantage of lulls in other activity cycles to help comrades stay focused on the sessions.

Be deliberate when bringing new members on board. Don't leave comrade socialization to your comrades only – it's mainly **your** role to help newcomers get up to speed and mesh with others. This is also a great opportunity for you to do your "culture work" before others, who maybe be less bought in, do so. You can use model components to structure your on-boarding process. Review your vision, mission, constituencies if any, goals, roles, resources, and strategy. It's time well spent – give new comrades enough information to be motivated, work independently, and contribute sooner rather than later.

Have a goal in mind regarding what you're trying to accomplish before you use a particular exercise / technique with your Cadre. Don't just engage in an activity because it looks fun or engaging. Use the Model strategically, to improve group functioning. Be mindful and planful. In addition to this practice serving you and your Cadre well and increasing your effectiveness, your comrades will see you as transformational, visionary, and wise. Because you will be, or you'll be getting there.

Practice makes perfect. Practice (behavioral and reflection) will help you get better several ways. It will facilitate quicker and more accurate framing on your part, which you'll recall often gets you 80% of the way in solving Cadre problems. It will also help you polish your leadership skills.

Don't rely on vague notions of self-improvement. Focus on action plans for yourself, and for your Cadre. Recall the notion of SMART goals, too. What do you feel you really need to shore up? What can you leverage to allow your Cadre to realize greater impact? What 2-3 things from this chapter stuck with you? What resources or help do you need?

- - - - - - - - - - - - - - - - -

Cadre leadership is not a mysterious process. You can build or rebuild a collective on the basis of the best practices we discussed, in a relatively simple model. Leading Cadres can therefore be a structured discipline. It also entails some art to complement the science, but you'll develop both as you gain experience and find your style.

Any leadership role you might take on is not reserved for the wise Elder or even the long-time activist. It's reserved for you. We need you to take on this role, to supply the resistance with one of those 1,000 Cadres we need to dismantle the dominant culture.

Radical Communities current and future also wait for you. The living planet needs you and your comrades to build these larger collectives, protect the land and life they entail, and grow new forms of societies to occupy the Earth after collapse. There's no need to wait until you've completely mastered Cadre Leadership in your evolution, either! You can progress as a leader (or effective follower) in both arenas at the same time. Given the state of the planet, it's probably a good idea to do just that.

Worksheet: Planning to Lead Your Cadre:

What do you see as your biggest challenge in terms of the Impact Model components? By now, you may have notes addressing all the model's components. This would be a good time for you to implement the plan(s) addressing the component you feel is most in need of improvement.

What aspects of an effective Cadre are strongest for your collective? How can you leverage those strengths to make the Cadre more effective overall?

UNDERSTANDING RADICAL COMMUNITY

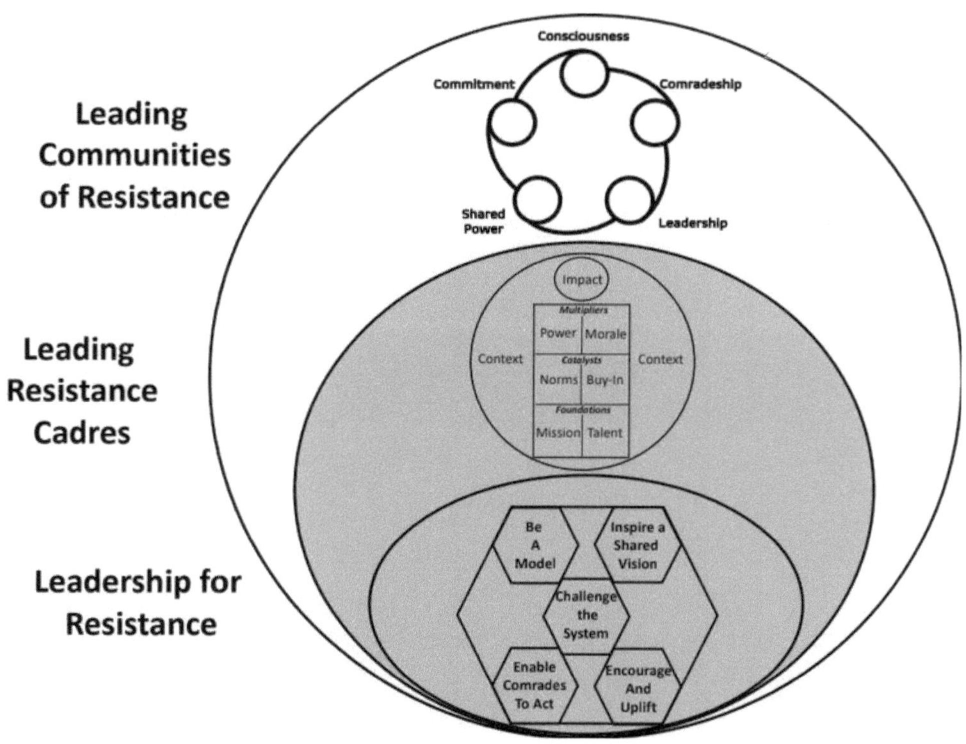

CHAPTER 3

Radical Community

"One of the most vital ways we sustain ourselves is by building communities of resistance, places where we know we are not alone."

bell hooks[23]

One day when I was about 12 years old, playing outside, my mother called me to tell me she didn't know where my sister Maureen was, and that we needed to find her. This was the early 1960s, so the first thing we thought of was not that she had been kidnapped or anything; nevertheless, we were anxious to find her. I started biking around the neighborhood calling out Maureen's name. Soon, all our neighbors were doing the same, looking high and low for my sis. No one had to be asked to do this; it was just the kind of thing one did. *We* were going to find my sis.

This is a narrow, focused example, but it exemplifies basic notions of what a Community is about. As we're committed to building Communities, it behooves us to at least explore what the concept means, so let's take the lay of the land. Was this neighborhood (Kings Park Greens) a Community? In what way(s) was it, and was it not? We'll find out, along the way, and in the process we'll discover collectives that may or may not be what we're looking for – Radical Communities.

- - - - - - - - - - - - - - - -

The Nature of Community

Why is it important to understand what Community is? Philosophers often resort to a dirty trick when debating a point – defining terms. Despite the often-maddening trips down rabbit holes this practice sometimes entails, I see the point. If we're to become effective practitioners of building Radical Community, we need to have a realistic definition and model with which to work. It's like wanting to be an effective leader without referencing a relevant, supported definition and model of leadership. The landscape of the "left" is littered with misused or appropriated constructs – "radical" and "feminist", to take some of the most popular, are so often misunderstood and abused that the left (hell, even that term has lost its meaning!) has diluted these notions as conceptual touchstones for important movements. Let's not let this happen

---

[23] https://elevatesociety.com/quotes-by-bell-hooks/ accessed October 23, 2023

to us who would build radical Community. If we want to engage in this work, we can't rely on vague or inconsistent notions of what we build.

Despite my plea for intellectual rigor, and although "Community" is often discussed in the popular media, social sciences, and elsewhere, there is not nearly as much effort spent in describing the construct in a useful way. Carolyn Shaffer and Kristin Anundsen (2005) offer that, because the term "community" can take on so many forms, it "resists being pinned down by definitions".[24] Of course, it might well be that "Community" seems to take on so many forms in practice is precisely because it has not been well defined. Be that as it may, I attempt to do just that, recognizing that we'll eventually have to rely on a discussion of Community's characteristics to flesh out our understanding of what this means. So, we'll define Community here, and incrementally via examining its components.

Community, then as a first approximation:
A collective of interrelated, interdependent entities ("members") who interact with each other in such a way as to maintain their common good. In the process, members create an entity greater than the sum of their individual contributions and relationships.[25]

Earlier conceptualizations of Community emphasize a focused geographic area. I, and many recent scholars, agree that virtual Communities are rising in prevalence and relevance, and we include them in our view. I recognize and include virtual Communities under the CPR conceptual umbrella, but my primary focus is on Communities tied to a geographic area, landbase, or waters.

- - - - - - - - - - - - - - - -

Why is [radical] Community important?

The six Premises underlying the work of Communities that Protect and Resist carry the weight here:

1. Radical Communities (aka Communities that Protect and Resist or CPR collectives) are Resistance Collectives.[26]
Communities provide a fundamental unit of opposition, based on shared interests and identity, and/or a common geographic base. The dominant culture has atomized our collectives / families and blunted joint resistance efforts by invoking the guileful,

---

[24] Shaffer, C.R., & Anundsen, K. (2005). *Creating Community Anywhere: Finding Support and Connection in a Fragmented World.* Dillon Beach, CA: CCC Press, p.10

[25] Thanks to Shaffer & Anundsen for the last element of the definition.

[26] I use these terms interchangeably, along with "Communities" with a capital C, mostly to maintain variety in the narrative.

divisive ideology of neoliberalism. We advocate for a return to Community consciousness, collective struggle and the wielding of power available only to united groups committed to each other.

Aric McBay voices a similar orientation. He argues that what we need is a culture of resistance. To counter a culture of defeat, McBay proposes, "Where we have loneliness and withdrawal, we need community engagement."[27]

"The trick is not to be isolated—if you're isolated, like Winston Smith in 1984, then sooner or later you're going to break, as he finally broke. That was the point of Orwell's story. In fact, the whole tradition of popular control has been exactly that: to keep people isolated, because if you can keep them isolated enough, you can get them to believe anything. But when people get together, all sorts of things are possible."

Noam Chomsky[28]

"Individual action is a fraught concept these days—with good reason. The individualization of responsibility for climate change may be one of corporate America's most sinister, and effective, marketing ploys..... No single person can offset the inaction of presidents or Cabinet members or the executives at Chevron and Exxon. While we do need national governments to act, individuals, when they band together as communities, have far more power than one might think."

Nick Martin[29]

2. CPR collectives are Survival Platforms

One myth of neoliberalism lionizes the strong, independent actor who survives on her own wits and strength. Rarely, though, does one survive even in the best of times without the help and support of others.

Communities are a primary mechanism of survival during Collapse and in the times beyond. As critical resources disappear, as corporate-governmental power grows as a threat to both freedoms and protections, as global climate change continues to exacerbate resource wars and social chaos, only those embedded in strong Communities will survive. Redoubts and bomb shelters provide temporary safety and a false sense of hope for the future, but are high visibility targets for desperate survivors. When hordes of starving post-collapse survivors or bands of neo-brigands descend into your valley, you'll only survive if you're part of a strong Community.

---

[27] McBay, A. (2019a). Full Spectrum Resistance, Volume One: Building Movements and Fighting to Win. New York: Seven Stories Press, p. 49

[28] Chomsky, N. (2002). Understanding Power: The Indispensable Chomsky. New York: The New Press, p.121

[29] Martin, N. (2021). When Seas Burn and Governments Do Nothing, Community Action Is the Only Way. The New Republic. https://newrepublic.com/article/162909/gulf-pemex-fire-pipeline-community-action?fbclid=IwAR0_mXN9SI9Fqvn10ZMX2pQi3TZdIxlF-STxJw5-frpwJsVDsOWIa1Xz7iHg (accessed July 7, 2021)

"The best way to prepare for [collapse] is also the best way to prepare to bring about just human societies after collapse: not by leaning even more into industry but by building communities based on self-sufficiency, biological integrity, and human rights. This is work anyone can support."[30]

3. CPR collectives are Viable Alternatives

Industrial civilization is just one form of society, and it's killing all life on this planet. As that culture dies, new forms will replace it, that reflect the needs of their members and landbases. Radical, CPR-like Communities serve as alternative social forms to help create just and sustainable cultures. We do not dictate the particular characteristics of any new Communities; we exist to facilitate their rise and flourishing.

The good news is that healthy alternative societies are numerous, perhaps unlimited in the specific forms they take. Later, I'll introduce a particular alternative, Matriarchy, from which there's a lot to learn. What's important, though, is not the specific form the Community takes, but that their orientation is life-affirming and just.

4. CPR collectives are Resistance Support

Resistance movements are difficult to instigate and even more so to maintain because many, if not most, activists later disengage in the face of financial hardship, familial responsibilities, health, or other crises they must devote energy and attention to. CPR collectives provide a liberating base of support to free front-line activists and resistance warriors for resistance work. In strong Communities, their survival and other needs are met by the collective – front-line activists can then pursue the warrior and related roles as necessary. They provide moral and material support, and serve as sanctuaries, according to McBay, where activists can rest and recuperate, and where they can strategize and organize.

Oakland farmers recently acted on the realization that protesters needed support from a larger community. A local black-owned urban farming company and a collective partnered to feed frontline protesters in the wake of George Floyd's death while in police custody. The ongoing unrest prompted Jamil Burns, founder of Raised Roots, to take action.[31]

"As part of this new wave of protests, we're seeing that the need to support each other is direr than ever," Burns said. "I think a lot of people have woken up not only to the racial injustices but the idea that in order for a community to be truly resilient,

[30] Jensen, D., Keith, L., & Wilbert, M. (2021). Bright Green Lies: How the environmental movement lost its way and what we can do about it. Monkfish publishing, p. 459

[31] Guerrero, S. (2020). Oakland farmers band together to help feed frontline protesters amid demonstrations. Sfgate.com. https://www.sfgate.com/food/slideshow/Oakland-based-farms-help-feed-frontline-203265.php?fbclid=IwAR34n3dZYFCV6ZHAxEcCvm2qIEEsWp-M6ArUjOCLs2RYZgKHh0V0Yf8g79HY (Accessed Jan 1, 2023)

Sadly, not all of us who embrace the need for resistance can take the same risks. I've cut short my presence in resistance campaigns (Standing Rock, Oak Flat) and was unable to participate in others (Thacker Pass) because of caregiving and other responsibilities at home. Were I part of a larger resistance collective instead of being isolated physically from other activists, I could have taken on larger and more protracted resistance roles in these and other actions.

5. CPR collectives are Sustenance Providers

Activism is stressful, isolating, and fraught with risk and danger. Even the most steadfast resisters can become drained, despondent, and distrustful of comrades in the resulting confusion and chaos.

Radical Communities serve as support groups for activists and warriors experiencing these symptoms and resulting burnout and PTSD, among other maladies. CPR collectives recognize the risks to comrades and the danger signs they exhibit; they are quick to provide the social support (or rest) resisters need to continue the struggle for the survival and independence of the collective. Just as providing social support is a critical function for resistance Cadre leaders to provide, so it is also at this level of resistance groups. It's an essential manifestation of the love we have for our comrades.

*"We are, none of us, our full selves without our community. Never forget:
Life as a whole is a series of relationships, not an assemblage of separate parts."*[32]

6. CPR collectives are the Natural Order

Industrial civilization doesn't only destroy the physical world; it destroys the spirit and soul of the living. CPR-type collectives, on the other hand, are the natural order of things. What indigenous cultures know is that Communities enrich and heal.

The damages of industrial civilization manifest as stress, illness, and addiction, among other sufferings. These infirmities affect all inhabitants of a collective – air, soil, rocks, water, animals, plants and fungi are stressed and weakened. Communities offer the intimacy, camaraderie, nurturance, support and the structures needed to thrive.

---

[32] Jensen, D., Keith, L., & Wilbert, M. (2021). Bright Green Lies: How the environmental movement lost its way and what we can do about it. Monkfish publishing, p. 452-453

*"...when resources become scarce, people push and shove their way to the front of the
line. They lie and cheat and steal. They do not act communally. They in fact act
anti-communally. But slime molds act precisely the opposite...:
when the going gets tough, slime molds recognize the importance of community."*
Derrick Jensen [33]

Yes, even slime molds.

CPR-type collectives (radical Communities) offer our best hope to resist the
destruction of the planet, to survive collapse in whatever form it takes, and to
replenish the world with societies that ensure just and sustainable relationships with
the land and waters. Let's find out how best to build these collectives.

- - - - - - - - - - - - - - - -

Dimensions of Community

The Premises give us a sense of the "why" of Community. To be able to build and
lead effective Communities, we need to figure out a bit more – we need to talk about
the "what". Let's slice the construct several ways to give us the best perspectives, and
to think critically about what we're building.

"Community" is not a simple, monolithic, all-or-none notion. One way to examine
your collective as a potential Community is to see how it stacks up along three
dimensions described by Shaffer & Anundsen:

> **LENGTH**: How long the collective has shared experience, and how
> committed the group is to continue that sharing.
> **BREADTH**: How many facets of life are shared, and how wide a range of
> [people] and experiences the collective includes.
> **DEPTH**: How deeply, thoroughly or intimately collective comrades share.

Were you a participant in the No DAPL protest at Standing Rock in North Dakota,
USA? If so, you may have experienced a profound sense of community with your
comrade protestors. But while there may have been a wide range of people at
Standing Rock, the depth at which you shared your feelings, for example, other than
with respect to environmental and social justice issues, likely was lacking. Even
dedicated Standing Rock protestors were present for just a few days, or rarely, weeks,
and then moved on, even if they were to continue good work. Sadly, although many
Standing Rock participants claim to have been part of a community, our analysis begs

---

[33]   Jensen, D (2016). The Myth of Human Supremacy. Seven Stories Press, p.118

to differ. Perhaps the magic they felt was being part of a group gathered for a similar focus, but that didn't last in any material way.

On the other hand, maybe you're a member of Wild Cooperative, a self-proclaimed Community:

> *We are a community that cultivates cooperative and facilitating relationship with nature and each other and that shares the knowledge of our regenerative and responsible living experiences. We are focusing on changing our life's perspective from human-centric to bio-centric where all life is part of our family and relatives. We are creating a natural and regenerative ecosystem that energizes all life, allows for individual growth, and shares and returns the surplus of energy and knowledge. This healthy village with resilient social, cultural, economic, educational, and ecological guilds is a building block of a biotic culture.*[34]

Given Wild Cooperative's mission at least, it's fair to say they share a wide range of facets of life. What we don't know is the diversity of people involved, although they are clear that Community members do not include just people, and in that regard are diverse. Conversations with members of this group indicate they also participate in deep conversation and sharing with each other. While Wild Cooperative is a recent development (less than five years), they stack up impressively in the other dimensions.

I mentioned Kings Park Greens above, the neighborhood in which I spent most of my childhood. Since that took place in the 1950s and 1960s, there was a lot less isolation between neighbors than we generally experience today. Members of various households, children and adults, hung out together indoors, on the stoops, and in the woods. Moms and dads went to each other's houses for parties and to have coffee, or to get a cup of sugar. In the process, it was standard practice to talk about relationships, illnesses, successes and failures, triumphs and disasters. Many of the neighbors had spent a decade or more in that place, and the relationships spanned more than one generation. Although we didn't address each other as "comrade", our neighborhood stacked up pretty well against the dimensions we listed. In terms of *these* dimension at least, we were a Community.

Tell the truth, though – weren't you expecting a little more? We've examined three collectives which in various degrees exemplify the dimensions of Community. And while these collectives are pleasant to talk about, my guess is that you're looking for stronger exemplars of the notion of radical Community. We'll circle back around in a

---

[34]   https://wildcooperative.wordpress.com/mission-statement/

bit, with consideration of collectives that might be more familiar to you in the resistance world.

The Shaffer & Anundsen dimensions (Length, Breadth, Depth) are one perspective through which we can examine the notion of Community. However, it's clear that this model describes little more than demographics. While they allow us to gain insight as to the background of a collective, there's also not a lot we can do to change them if needed. This model allows us to form a baseline, low-level analysis of our collectives, which is fine, but we need to make use of a model or frame that's a bit more incisive.

We would benefit from a frame that provides more profound insights to our respective collectives. To that end, let's take a moment to reflect, and then introduce a frame that moves us forward in our ability to think critically about resistance collectives.

- - - - - - - - - - - - - - - - -

Why is it important to engage in this inventory of Community dimensions? Because your collective may **not** be a Community at all, at least not in the sense we're considering. A collective only together for a short time that does not exemplify the dimensions of breadth or depth to a significant degree is more likely a **Proto-Community**. Recall the Standing Rock protest collective.

While groups like these "provide great opportunities for experiencing mutual support and connection" if they remain together, and while they might serve as platforms to practice Community-building skills, they do not serve a wide range of functions, and in general do not last as long as true Communities. Think of a group of people who band together to help after a flood, or a support group. Without a compelling vision, sense of purpose or feeling of uniqueness, such collectives often disband or collapse after their initial rescue, relief or protest. And that assumes the collective is even able to remain connected long enough to complete that initial initiative.

Don't overestimate the potential of disasters or crises to catalyze collectives into strong Communities. It doesn't happen, for the most part. In the immediate aftermath of the attacks on the Twin Towers in New York, I recall national leaders and local organizations swore mutual allegiance and unity. However, within three days (three days!) New York City Firefighters and Police were at each other's throats about whose jurisdiction the disaster site belonged to, and who was allowed to engage in what work. So much for unity, allegiance, and Community.

Collectives need more than Length, Breadth, and Depth to evolve beyond the "Proto" characterization in order to be a Community, particularly one capable of Protecting and Resisting. We'll discuss these additional requirements later in this chapter. Community builders seek to move beyond the temporary, less durable form of the Proto-Community. What do these more durable forms look like?

Functional vs. Conscious vs. Deep Community
In the collectives we're generally most familiar with and maybe grew up in, survival and well-being were primary. Members mutually looked after the physical and social welfare of the members. In the example at the top, our neighbors looked for Maureen to attempt to assure her (and our family's) safety. We were a Functional Community, in Shaffer & Anundsen's taxonomy. Most neighborhoods fall into this category.

Functional Communities traditionally ensure members are afforded the essentials (food, shelter, education, etc.) so they can "be productive and maintain the social order."[35] My neighbors sometimes did not know a lot about each other's private lives, and we didn't do much emotional labor concerned with our internal dynamics. We were a Functional Community perhaps, but no more.

More recently conceptualized, and less popularized as yet, is the **Conscious Community**. This collective form maintains the survival and social control aspects of the Functional Community, but seems influenced by the neoliberalism rampant in the dominant culture. In that regard, Conscious Community emphasizes "members' needs for personal expression, growth, and transformation."[36] Despite the individualistic, identity orientation, Conscious Community exhibits a redeeming feature or two. For one, members reflect on their common purpose, internal processes, and group dynamics. In this sense Conscious Community evokes qualities of an effective Cadre. Shaffer & Anundsen point out, promisingly, that Conscious Communities incorporate a "systems understanding of reality."[37]

While the systems that Conscious Communities emphasize are mostly internal (likening members to components of a living body), there is some recognition of the importance of avoiding isolation from the human and natural systems the collective is part of. This interdependent focus, weak as it might be, keeps Conscious Communities flexible and willing to embrace new people and ideas. Despite a nod to the external world, this external orientation is clearly not a dominant focus of this model of Community building. (We'll examine the critical role of taking the external environment into account when we discuss strategy.) The Foundation for Intentional Community fits the profile of this sort of collective, and serves to facilitate the formation of other such collectives.

---

[35]   Shaffer, C.R., & Anundsen, K. (2005). Creating Community Anywhere: Finding Support and Connection in a Fragmented World. Dillon Beach, CA: CCC Press, p.10
[36]   Ibid. p.11
[37]   Ibid.

*"At a time when too many of us feel isolated and alone,
intentional communities offer more sustainable and just ways of living together."*[38]

As a Conscious Community matures, its members might aspire to becoming a **Deep Community**, in which the attitudes and behaviors associated with maintaining and improving their internal processes "have become so internalized they are second nature."[39] Shaffer & Anundsen declare, "members easily and naturally attune to what is best for themselves and the group."[40] Deep Community doubles down on the internal focus and on the individual, but leaves a bit of space for the group as a collective.

Achieving Deep Community is a laudable goal. Community members absolutely should know "how to lead, follow, listen, speak from the heart, and mediate conflicts, and perform these functions spontaneously whenever a situation calls for them."[41] The maturation regarding internal processes is absolutely worthy of our engagement and commitment. Still, the emphasis on internal process to the detriment of a focus on environmental factors limits the potential of this organizing form for resistance purposes.

We'll explore how to guide your Community toward a "deeper" collective. But our comrades and friends understand more is needed from Communities, as articulated in the CPR Premises. The forces of the dominant culture are too powerful, and the dangers to life on this planet, clear and present, necessitate more of us. As a preview, let's posit this as the sort of journey Community Builders might help their collectives undergo.

The larger challenge for Community builders / leaders is to move their collectives toward the Deep Community form, while driving toward, or cultivating, a radical orientation, which we describe in the next section.

---

[38] FIC website front page: https://www.ic.org, accessed Nov 19, 2022
[39] Shaffer, C.R., & Anundsen, K. (2005). Creating Community Anywhere: Finding Support and Connection in a Fragmented World. Dillon Beach, CA: CCC Press, p.13
[40] Ibid.
[41] Ibid.

Hypothetical Journey of a Community Toward a Deep, Radical Orientation

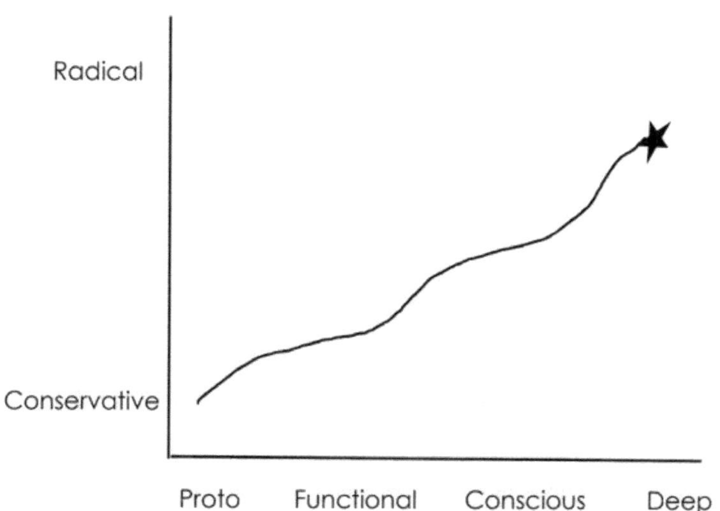

Deep Community is a necessary but insufficient form for our collectives to be of use in a resistance context, as I mentioned above. I hope you'll commit to a charter of leading your collective not just to greater "deepness", but also of a sounder radical orientation. In the next several chapters we'll describe the components of a CPR collective – a Radical Community. **If you're able to build a collective that is strong in the components, you'll by necessity be guiding your collective to achieve both Deep Community and a radical state.**

The specific arc of your Community's journey can look any number of ways. If you're already Radical and Deep, congratulations! You're either lucky, a brilliant Community builder, or both! Don't rest on your laurels, though. You need to maintain your collective's culture and focus. Either can fade or wander at any time.

As the graphic above suggests, we need to be aware that this is not a linear journey. Expect downturns and occasional recidivism. Your role in this non-linear journey is to maintain a constant cultural drive toward the aspirational end state.

- This is a fundamental role for leaders at any level, but particularly of Community leaders.
- In a later chapter I'll outline guidelines for dealing with the stages of maturation of your collective, and for spotting potential backward movement.

There is a journey ahead of you. How might that proceed? Let's start by exploring Community from that other orientation, its radical nature.

The Radical Community

Radical Community is the necessary, critical response, and the final lens / frame with which we can understand CPR collectives. We love our sibling Communities focused on healthy relationships with each other and the land, and want them to succeed. However, our situation is desperate enough to ask ourselves to reflect on including in our focus a more radical orientation, and/or incorporate a radical perspective into our collectives.

I reassure the weak of heart that Radical Community is distinct from a Community of radicals (not that there's necessarily anything wrong with that). What we aspire to is not merely a collection, a herd; it is Community much as has been described here.

CPR Collectives are not like others we've been exposed to in mainstream news and literature, for the most part. The collectives we aspire to are not your grandparents' communities:
> Not Community Development Corporations.
> Not the Civic League.
> Not Housing Co-ops.
> Not even ACORN.

What **are** we talking about? This is a start:
> *"In the world we currently inhabit here in america, community is often a loose concept that is devalued or destroyed altogether by the need to create and maintain material possessions and capital. People don't have time to build, nurture and grow their communities.... I add "radical" to community. Radical community is here defined as a group of people who intentionally come together and are unified toward common goals outside of acquiring property and material wealth. Those goals can be food, shelter, self-governance, public education – all of these things and more happen toward a common purpose which is betterness. Betterness is what we build and who we become out of the ashes of oppressive institutions..."*[42]

Kudos to Merin for explicitly linking the Community construct with the notion of "radical". Rejecting property and material wealth – while embracing collective Community goals of food, shelter, self-governance, public education for members –

---

[42]   Merin, M. (2019). School is a Riot. In Mink, John (Ed.). Teaching Resistance: Radicals, Revolutionaries, and Cultural Subversives in the Classroom. Oakland, CA: PM Press, p.20

offers a promising platform of sorts with which we can build out our conception of a Radical Community.

What Makes a Community Radical? What characteristics are embodied in a true radical Community? Three features set the Radical Community apart from mainstream notions of these collectives:
- Purpose
- Practices
- Indigenous Perspectives

Purpose
The Radical Community (that Protects and Resists) comes together (or exists) for a common purpose outside the capitalist norm of acquiring property, and in pursuit of our own notion of "betterness", encapsulated in our CPR Vision. We are intentional.

Our orientation is part internal, and we aspire to aspects of Deep Community. Who wouldn't want to be part of a Community that emphasizes healthy, open and honest internal processes? In a Radical Community we maintain focus on the external, too. The forces of the dominant culture infiltrate all living systems, and in the process commoditize or destroy them in part and in whole. We are morally obligated not merely to **escape** their influence, but to **oppose** them.

Radical Communities are **oppositional.** We're not content merely to rise from the ashes of oppressive institutions; we actively oppose them in all their forms. Perhaps contrary to popular notions, "Oppositional" does not rule out nurturing and supportive cultural elements. CPR collectives are all this *and* oppositional. We'll touch on Matriarchy later in the book, as an example of a social alternative to the dominant culture. I mention that here as one example of a nurturing, supportive Community that also protects and resists.

An example of a potential Oppositional Community is one I introduced earlier, **Women's Liberation Front (WoLF)**, a radical feminist organization dedicated to the total liberation of women. WoLF fights to end male violence, regain reproductive sovereignty, and ultimately dismantle the gender-caste system. Their Mission: To restore, protect, and advance the rights of women and girls using legal argument, policy advocacy, and public education.[43] WoLF is also an example of a virtual community, focused on protecting women regardless of physical location.

We can also point to the **Black Panther Party**. Formed in the U.S. in the late 1960s in response to chronic discrimination and police brutality against blacks, the Panthers

---

[43] https://womensliberationfront.org/our-work

"rejected the legitimacy of the U.S. government. The Panthers saw black communities in the United States as a colony and the police as an occupying army."[44] Among the arguments articulated by Huey Newton validating the formation of the Party are assertions that American police are agents of an oppressive imperial power – an occupying force with no legitimate power. In response to this occupation, Newton proposed that by arming and organizing the ghetto, blacks could obtain power (Bloom & Martin). It's important to note, and we'll explore this later, that a fundamental aspect of the Panther's revolutionary response was Community organizing.

In the Alto Turiaçu Indigenous Territory in Brazil's Maranhão state, the **Ka'apor people** have taken the defense of their land into their own hands following years of neglect and corruption by the state.[45] They have created a self-defense force to retake logging sites and access roads from illegal loggers, and established a network of settlements at each site to make their gains permanent.

- As with so many indigenous peoples, the Ka'apor and their land are threatened by outsiders who are attempting to exploit their natural resources.
- Since their government has chosen not to intervene in this extraction campaign, the Ka'apor took measures to resist and protect their community. Among other responses, they created an autonomous Indigenous territory that doesn't require the presence of the state.
- They did away with the one-chief system imposed by the federal agency for Indigenous affairs, and revived the traditional council of chiefs. By the way, this aspect of their collective exemplifies the Practices aspect of the radical Community (considered next).

The **Zapatistas** are an indigenous movement based in the southern state of Chiapas, Mexico. The name derives from Emiliano Zapata, who led the Liberation Army of the South during the Mexican Revolution, which lasted approximately from 1910-1920. Zapata's main rallying cry was "land and liberty", echoing the sentiments of the many indigenous populations who supported and formed his army. Modern-day Zapatistas declare themselves the ideological heirs to these struggles, again representing many indigenous struggles in southern Mexico. While the Zapatistas became public in 1994, as their name implies, their struggle is the culmination of decades of struggle.[46]

Oppositional Communities exist. Collectives that resist are not unique or bizarre. Any doubts or second thoughts you might have about steering your collective toward an oppositional stance, or encouraging its continued future in that

[44] Bloom, J. & Martin, W. (2013). Black Against Empire: The History and Politics of the Black Panther Party. Berkeley: University of California Press, p.2

[45] Johnson, Andrew. In Brazil, Indigenous Ka'apor take their territory's defense into their own hands. March 14, 2022. Mongabay. https://news.mongabay.com/2022/03/in-brazil-indigenous-kaapor-take-their-territorys-defense-into-their-own-hands/ [Accessed Nov 21 2022]

[46] Coughlin, Frank (2014). The Humility of Love: A Lesson from Chiapas. In Deep Green Resistance News Service Nov 6, 2014. https://dgrnewsservice.org/resistance-culture/indigenous/humility-love-lesson-chiapas/

orientation, should be assuaged by noting these collectives are not limited to geographic area, culture, form, or target. Your collective can oppose, too.

It's also true that a Radical Community **need not have been formed with radical or oppositional intent**; many traditional, geographic-based Communities might shift to a radical focus as they recognize the threats to their existence and that of other Communities for whom they care. Alternately, it may be that a traditional Community finds it necessary to maintain their original focus and to incorporate a (possibly covert) radical feature to their organizing. This work is dedicated to them, too.

As we're thinking critically about Radical Community, we should note that the notion of "oppositional" isn't monolithic. DeFilippis, Fisher, & Shragge (2010) describe "five types of community mobilization":[47]
1. **Reactionary**: tries to turn back the clock to a prior, real or imagined, time and state of affairs.
2. **Conservative**: attempts to maintain a status quo that resists the advancement of social, economic, and political justice.
3. **Adaptive/Reformist**: accepts the basic premise of the status quo but tries to tweak it a bit around the edges. Tries to reform gross inequities to improve and maintain society.
4. **Radical/Revolutionary**: uses the language and realm of Community as a basis to try to fundamentally transform the social relations of their time.
5. **Opt-out:** uses the context of Community to try to withdraw from the larger-scale social relations of their time.

It's important to understand where your collective stands in terms of Purpose, and this taxonomy can help with that appreciation. On the other hand, if you discover or realize your collective doesn't fit the "Radical / Revolutionary" category, this taxonomy might be the catalyst you need to create movement toward that end. The taxonomy also provides clues as to what you might do to generate that movement.
- Convening a collective reflection on what the past was really like might provide a more realistic appraisal of what the collective really should aspire to.
- Similarly, critically appraising the status quo and the realities it embodies for your Community and the planet could change the attitudes of comrades toward resistance.
- For Adaptive / Reformist comrades, that appraisal of the status quo might help, as well as a realistic view of the time we have left to save the planet (not much) and how much things need to change to do that (a lot) could be what you need.

47   DeFilippis, J., Fisher, R., & Shragge, E. (2010). Contesting Community: The Limits and Potential of Local Organizing. New Brunswick: Rutgers University Press.

- If you find your Community is in danger of opting out, you can talk about the false security such a perspective holds. If you're comfortable with it, invoke the moral imperative we all face to use whatever skills and resources we have to save the living.

A Two-Minute History.

Why History? Because knowing the history of resistance and of your collective makes you a better leader and Elder. It does so because this knowledge provides you a broader perspective regarding your collective's place in the larger world, strategy and tactics that may or may not have helped protect and resist, and a deeper connection to the collective itself resulting from that knowledge and sense of history.

History helps in another way, too. It's the Janus Effect, as explained by Kouzes & Posner. Essentially the Janus Effect states that leaders who look backward while imagining future opportunities often find more meaningful outcomes.

- Often common and enduring threads emerge, such as clarity of purpose and values. Looking backward to answer, "How did we get here?" can uncover critical paths along the journey, as well as provide direction for continuing or even altering that journey into the future.
- A valuable way to mark your path forward, then, is to look at its past (or the past of similar collectives, if yours is relatively new).
- We'll see later that this practice allows you to craft more realistic and effective strategic plans for your collective.

To repeat: CPR collectives (Radical Communities) are oppositional, not "appositional". This oppositional stance, while "radical", is not new *per se*. In fact, the rules or texts considered to be authoritative regarding Community organizing follow the conflict model, as opposed to the consensus model. **A theme we will come back to from time to time is "collaboration internally, conflict externally".**

The oppositional Community began as we know it in the "Progressive Era" (early 20th century) in the settlement houses, and included:

- Rejection of individual causes of poverty;
- Cross-class solidarity; and
- Willingness to organize and advocate for justice.

This approach carried through the organizing of Saul Alinsky, to the 1960s work and up to today, although neoliberalism has surely dampened its effects. From DeFilippis et al.: The inherently oppositional nature of local community was part of the theoretical grounding of some organizing in the 1960s. "Community was used as both a site [of resistance] and an alternative."

Resistance Communities have a history. My purpose is not to detail that history more than I have, in part because the details vary from country to country, collective to collective, and culture to culture. You'd be well served to learn the history of resistance in your collective or close to it, conceptually or geographically. You'll be a wiser and more strategic Community leader in the process, and your collective will benefit from the greater sense of grounding, values and way forward.

- - - - - - - - - - - - - - - -

Practices

A Radical Community is not necessarily an effective one, though we'd be better off if that were the case. I distinguish between the (radical) **orientation** of a community, and its **effectiveness** in either managing relationships internally or pursuing its radical orientation externally. Maybe your Community emphasizes an internal (process) focus over external, or vice versa. Or perhaps it's just not coming together well, or is ineffective in realizing its intent, whether stated or implied, of protecting and resisting. In either case, we're not living up to our moral imperative, so we need to address effectiveness as well as simply purpose.

What the planet needs are Communities not only committed to internal process as well as radical orientation, but striving for effectiveness in **both** aspirations. One "radical" practice for CPR collectives is to **reject patriarchy,** as a root cause of much of the toxicity in our dominant culture. Instead, we work to practice a more matriarchal orientation, or at least an "a-patriarchal" one. I allude to this orientation in the Shared Power chapter.

Another way in which CPR collectives are radical is in **the set of features** of the collectives themselves. The following paragraphs briefly introduce the components. I'll discuss each on a separate chapter. As you read through the introductory paragraphs and the expanded chapters devoted to each component, you might feel overwhelmed. Don't be. I provide examples of each component from Communities that exemplify one or more of these aspects of CPR collectives. In other words, resistance comrades have already built these components in various Communities around the world. You can, too.

---

[48]   DeFilippis, J., Fisher, R., &Shragge, E. (2010). Contesting Community: The Limits and Potential of Local Organizing. New Brunswick: Rutgers University Press, p.32

Think of this model of Radical Community as aspirational. Work, struggle and plan to build these components into your collective as well as you can. Even if you don't realize these aspirational components to the fullest, you're probably much farther along the way than you'd be otherwise. Celebrate your progress, and your enhanced Community Power.

- - - - - - - - - - - - - - - -

CPR collectives exemplify the following characteristics:

The CPR Model of Community

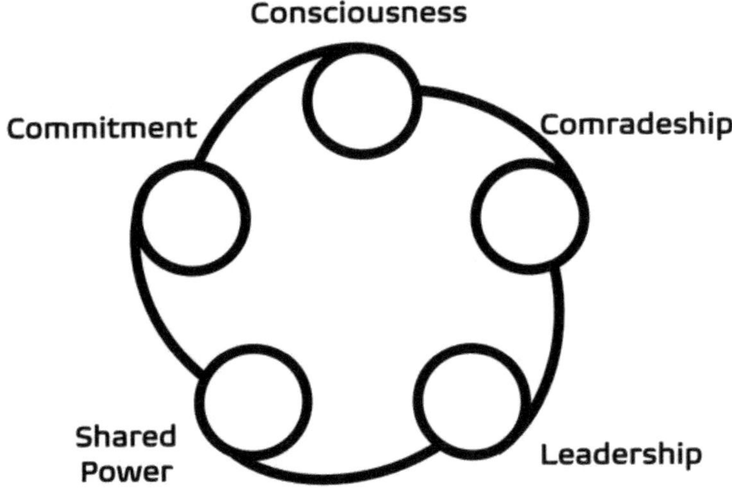

[Community] Consciousness. Community Builders and Leaders develop awareness, not just of the problems facing the collective, but of the power we can wield when we recapture our Community belongingness and selves.
Effective CPR collectives explore and cultivate their Consciousness, possibly the aspect that most clearly enables resistance and that impels a Community toward becoming radical.

Community Consciousness is best thought of as a scaling down of class consciousness. A conscious Community is fully aware of and knowledgeable about its current social, economic and environmental conditions. Moreover, the Community understands the history of its people, economy and environment, and it has a well-defined vision for the future.

Comradeship. The set of collective bonds among members - the connective tissue of Community. Without social cohesion, there are no Community members – merely acquaintances. Comradeship consists of two components:
- **Social ties**. Interactions based on kinships, friendships, familiarity and mutual recognition with others in a geographic area, ideological or class focus.
- **Psychological ties**. Feelings of attachment, identity, mutual respect and sense of belonging to that place or focus. These ties manifest also in a sense of camaraderie with fellow inhabitants.

Comradeship generates a Community's **Social Capacity**: the ability of members of a Community to work together effectively.

Commitment. It's challenging enough for a CPR collective to function as an intentional Community. The challenge is greater when we struggle to achieve Deep Community. To then progress to a radical, oppositional Community and continue to exist and thrive, while beset by isolation, oppression, and repression, takes something special. We need commitment. Commitment takes several forms:
- Commitment to coexist.
- Commitment to exercise discipline.
- Commitment to the long-term well-being of all.
- Commitment to the development of young people.

Shared Power. Communities offer an essential source of power to protect and resist. They may be our only real, robust source of power. We need to leverage their potential more than we have. However, for CPR collectives to be effective as sources of power for resistance **externally**, they first need to be strong (powerful) **internally**. CPR collectives are strong because they share power among themselves. The features of Shared Power:
- Shared Power is Shared Decision Making.
- Shared Power is Justice.
- Shared Power is the Absence of Class.

Leadership. Our resistance struggles aren't as effective as they need to be to save the planet. And the barriers don't spring just from the enormity of the problem (industrial civilization), but also issues very much in our control, such as recruitment, activist turnover, and commitment. Effective leadership among Resistance members can go a long way to overcoming these barriers. What does effective leadership do for us, that makes it such a valuable asset for activists and Community builders? In part, Leadership Inspires. And it's needed in your respective groups and cadres, as you know.

But more is required of Leadership in a Community context. To some extent, Community Leadership accomplishes these functions via core practices:
- Facilitating a shared vision for the Community.
- Cultivating a strong and healthy culture.
- Encouraging comradeship.
- Involving and **encouraging** comrades to do well.

For the well-being of CPR collectives, leadership must transcend the mainstream "inspirational" forms we emphasize in Western leadership literature and practice. Centering and sustaining are critical. There is more. That "more" comes from Community Leadership Perspectives from Indigenous Groups.

- - - - - - - - - - - - - - - -

(Indigenous) Perspectives
Yet another way in which CPR collectives can be thought of as radical is in our acknowledgment of Community leadership perspectives from Indigenous Groups.
Much of what we know about leading just and sustainable collectives derives from indigenous people around the world. The "progressive" or post-industrial school of leadership literature that focuses more on mutual purpose, inspiration, and de-emphasis of hierarchical relationships is already known to and deeply embedded in indigenous Communities.

It only makes sense to look to indigenous collectives for guidance about protecting, resisting and thriving. How can we ignore the practices of Communities that have lived in balance with their natural worlds for thousands of years, and who have in innumerable ways resisted the incursion and violence of industrial civilization?
Community Leaders who are wise enough to emulate the practices of Indigenous Communities among the other disciplines I explore in this book may find the guidepost to a path that leads to becoming more than "just" a Leader – they may be well on their path to finding their cloak of Eldership. We'll discuss this in more detail in our section on Community Leadership.

Finally, while not a feature per se: We'd do well to **consider the long game:**
> *"It is clear that the kind of social change we are discussing goes beyond local communities and cannot be achieved solely through the work of organizations tied to them [because they are too limited and fragmented to*

achieve much on their own] …. But we still believe in community because of the importance of local work in reaching people who can organize for power and critically understand the underlying causes of social and economic problems" "…without a conscious wider vision, community organizations will remain focused on the local.
The challenge is to build an agenda that transcends local work and to find ways to connect with broader organizations, and build
alliances to work for fundamental social change."[49]

As we discuss what the critical building blocks of a CPR collective, keep in mind the complementary imperative to build bridges with other collectives and like-minded groups. Even the Black Panther Party, as militant as some see them, were amenable to allying with others who shared goals, such as the New Left. We'll talk about alliances and coalitions toward the end of the book.

Before we address the Community components and how to build them, we'd do well to do two things:
- Reflect on ourselves as acting or potential Community Leaders and Land Protectors (next chapter). Understanding ourselves and our values and motivations allows us to be more authentic and committed leaders of our collectives.
- Prepare ourselves to think strategically about our Community. Incorporating a strategic mindset allows us to understand how the Community components can be used to build power in the short and long term, and how we can leverage our collective clout to protect and resist.

- - - - - - - - - - - - - - - - -

Maureen Redux
Did you make it this far, and are you the slightest bit curious? Maureen was up in her bedroom the whole time. She got sleepy and went for a nap. Thanks for staying with me this far!

---

[49] DeFilippis, J., Fisher, R., & Shragge, E. (2010). Contesting Community: The Limits and Potential of Local Organizing. New Brunswick: Rutgers University Press, p.32

Worksheet: Planning to Lead Your Community

Reflect on the nature of the Community you belong to:

Does your collective have a name or title? Would having one help you create a sense of identity?

Where are you located? Is your Community a landbase (or water-base), a group of people, or flora and / or fauna?

How "Deep" do you consider your collective to be?

Would you consider your Community to be a radical one, in the ways I described?

If not, is that something you would like to advocate for in your collective? How might you go about doing that?

CHAPTER 4

On Being/Becoming a
Community Builder, Leader, Defender

A few years ago, some comrades and I were touring western Nevada to bear witness to the eradication of the Pinyon Juniper forests there. I had met an indigenous Elder who had joined us a day or two earlier. We shared a quiet moment that afternoon, and I asked him about something I had heard from others. I said, "I heard you were Chief of your tribe. Is that true?" He paused a few moments before answering, "That's a big word."

Yes it is. Building or leading a Community is a considerable responsibility and challenge. We need more comrades willing to take on that mantle, whether it be framed as Chieftain, Matriarch, Community Builder, Elder or whatever title you choose.

This challenge is why I wrote this book – to serve as a resource and motivation for you to develop yourself and your Community in the face of the challenges we're all faced with. Let's explore and reflect on this role.

- - - - - - - - - - - - - - - - -

I honor Community leaders and those who aspire to that role. I praise your devotion to the land, waters, life, and the spaces you and your Community need to live in justice and flourish. Unless you're experienced and reflective, though, the Protector notion might seem theoretical or vague. I offer my perspective on what being a Protector might entail, in hope that clarity concerning the role will lead to commitment to it. Realizing our potential and calling as Builders for a CPR collective begins with reflecting on the meaning and responsibilities associated with such a trust.

As context, I recognize the separation that exists, cultivated by industrial civilization, between "civilized" humanity and the natural world. This estrangement results in humans treating the land as a shopping mall, a factory, a playground, and a dump, which in turn leads to abuse, destruction, and depletion. This estrangement and subsequent abuse work exactly the same when we substitute "women" or "oppressed class" members for "the natural world". Take a moment to do that substitution and see for yourself the truth in this, and the associated horror. Industrial civilization destroys everything in its path, as it commodifies the living world. It will not stop on its own. Our radical Communities are the front lines in fighting for a living world.

For us in the deadly-serious business of defending the natural world, women and oppressed classes, and of replacing the dominant culture's psychopathy, it's critical to explore our adopted role. When I engage in this exploration with fellow Protectors, I'm struck by the mutual discovery that the role is comprised not only of a motivational component, but emotional and spiritual aspects too. Building and protecting our Communities emerges as the highest imperative we can respond to. You likely agree, given that you're invested in this work. Let's see if we can articulate that imperative and determine what we need to navigate its path.

The Calling

Here's an eloquent description of the radical activist. It serves as a firm foundation for our work as resistance leaders, too, and as a point of departure for exploring the role of Community Protector.

"The role of smart, radical activists is to encourage, protract, organize, and multiply the chipping away not only at the mythology of presumed supremacy, but at power and its social and physical infrastructure. To find weak points within scriptures and structures of the system, as one might examine an old block wall before demolition, seeking out crumbling mortar lines and cracked blocks.
Then, to strike, and recruit more help - more and more –
and strike, and strike, and bring it down."

Michael Carter[50]

Let's start a conversation about what a commitment to protecting a Community means conceptually, and then in practice, and the implications for your respective personal development.

In gatherings with resistance comrades, when we in CPR introduce ourselves we take pains to point out the indigenous land or waters we inhabit. No matter where we are, chances are we are on stolen land. We acknowledge this legacy because the long, brutal history of colonization sometimes causes us to forget about whose land this is, and the true nature of our relationship with it. Most of us are settlers or visitors in some sense. And yet, our sense is that comrades, certainly those who work in environmental justice work and resistance organizing, feel the land or water is "home".

---

[50] Carter, M. (2012). Kingfisher's Song: Memories Against Civilization. Shelbyville, Kentucky: Wasteland Press.

Similarly, colonization and civilization induce a great forgetting concerning egalitarian relationships between men and women, and concerning times when there were no classes in Communities.

What does "home" or "Community" mean to you? Do you identify with the land, water or collective? Is this area or collective part of your identity? This is what all this means to me: In conversations I've had with other activists, a common theme is that the Land/Water/Community is:
- Where Protectors are most themselves.
- Where we're able to make meaning of the world and our place in it.
- Where our relationships are clear and nurturing.
- Where we partake, without struggle or competition, of the elements that allow us to live and flourish.

No wonder our comrades are committed to protecting these places. Yet those of us who would Protect and Resist are often labeled "eco-terrorists," "feminazis," "tree-huggers" and "race traitors" among other slurs to dismiss what we feel compelled to do, in order to demonize and marginalize our work. Clearly, we're doing something right!

Of course we're painted with these brushes – as Protectors we stand by nature (in both senses of that phrase) in opposition to the dominant culture destroying the planet, and that labels us that way. Unfortunately insults, hurled often and long enough, can create stress among us, and more damaging, create doubt about our calling, and/or an urge to escape resistance work to end the onslaughts. Is there anything we can do about this?

One safeguard we can take proactively is a practice I borrow from the Organizational Behavior literature – the Realistic Job Preview, or RJP.[51] An RJP communicates both the good and bad aspects of a job. It gives a candidate (or budding Community Builder) a realistic view of what the role entails. RJPs provide a fuller description of the role or calling which we can use to help us decide if we are a good match for that calling.

A critical aspect of RJPs is that they can reduce turnover and enhance commitment. Comrades who have been inoculated against the unpleasant, stressful, or even dangerous aspects of Community Building or resistance in general and who still accept the responsibility are more likely to persevere and commit to the challenges. Given the trials we face as resistance leaders regarding our own turnover and commitment from comrades, the RJP or related practice is one we should pay

---

[51] Dugoni, B. & Ilgen, D. (1981). "Realistic Job Previews and the Adjustment of New Employees". The Academy of Management Journal. 24 (3): 579–591.

attention to. By reflecting on the meaning of "Protector" now, we'll be steeled against doubts and strengthened with greater clarity about and commitment toward our Protector calling. To counter doubts or insecurities brought about by slurs, labels and other verbal abuse, we are obliged to explore and validate our authentic role with respect to our Community. An unintended positive consequence of the reflection and clarification process we embark on is that it facilitates a greater sense of comradeship and belonging. When we have articulated our roles as Community Builders or Elders, and identified and accepted the consequences of the role we take on, we become part of a meta-Community of Sisters and Brothers who have taken the same journey, sworn the same oaths. To my mind, there are few bonds as strong as this.

Let's get to it then, and reflect on what our Elder/Builder role entails, and in the process experience a self-administered RJP, with all the attendant benefits.

- - - - - - - - - - - - - - - -

What does it mean to you to be a Community Builder or Protector? I'm pretty sure you **don't** think of yourself as: Visitor, Mistress, Master, Steward, Manager or Administrator, or any role of this sort. At best, these roles are disinterested, dispassionate, and indicate a disconnected relationship with a Community. At worst, they can be exploitative. No wonder the Protectors I interact with don't subscribe to them. **Instead**, the roles our comrades advocate without exception point to an entirely different dynamic, such as:

Protector	Defender	Warrior	Culture Builder
Nourisher	Storyteller	Catalyst	Family Member
	Organizer	Follower	

Ideally, Protectors enact these roles based on their status of belonging, of "being within" the Community. These roles assume and define a Community member's status as an integral part of the collective, who willingly behaves in accordance with the associated expectations the collective holds for each role. How do you define these roles for yourself? These are roles – multiple faces of one role, actually – that I view as essential to build and maintain sustainable, just Communities in the face of omnipresent threats. What would you add? More importantly, how do we achieve authenticity in them?

The Path

When you explore and clarify your role as Community Builder or Land Defender, or whatever title you assign to the role, you provide a context and foundation for your personal evolution – your Calling. It's one thing to aspire to this role and its facets, and I hope you do. It's another thing, though, to reflect about how to **realize** your Calling – this is your Path. How can we prepare ourselves for bearing this mantle?

We might begin by considering the **Chain of Values** as a means of discovering your personal context. The corporate world talks about the Value Chain, a business model that describes the range of activities needed to create a product or service. Let's subvert and adapt that corporate construct, and focus on what sequence of personal developments lead to one's culmination as a Builder/Protector/Elder. My take on what this chain might look like is that the components (links) of the chain are checkpoints along the way toward expressing your Community-oriented set of values. The values imply a temporal order, although life is rarely this linear. Nevertheless, as you contemplate your own Path, consider this a rough guide for how your values chain might progress through these stages, if you think of them that way.

First, there is **a deep connection** with the land, waters or collective you commit to protecting. Connection involves placing significance on discovering who you are and your relationship with the land / waters and your Community. **Connection springs from time spent in the Community, and a willingness to explore it and to learn from it.**

- *Where is this place? How is it a Community?*
- *Where did it come from?*
- *What is my Community's place in the world?*
- *How are all the elements interrelated?*
- *How do I find meaning in / from my Community?*

Our society suffers from Nature Deficit Disorder. It's time to heal our relationship with our MOTHER and see the beauty of natural life.[52]

Second, you develop an **understanding** of the Community, including its inhabitants (human and otherwise), culture, social and other structures, and issues. **Understanding springs from a deep connection.**

- *What is the history of this Community?*
- *What values and norms inform the Community?*
- *What are its needs, frustrations and problems?*

---

[52]   Ann Marie Sayers, as quoted in Mohawk Nation Facebook page, Accessed Dec 9, 2022

109

Third, you experience a **love** of place / collective. **Love also comes from that deep connection, and that understanding. We cannot love what we don't know, and love without understanding is merely infatuation.**

- *What emotional touchstones does the collective provide for me? For others?*
- *What deep part of me sings in celebration of my Community?*

"At the risk of seeming ridiculous, let me say that the true revolutionary is guided by a great feeling of love. It is impossible to think of a genuine revolutionary lacking this quality."

Ernesto "Che" Guevara

Fourth, you internalize a **commitment** to your Community and its survival and well-being. **Commitment comes from your connection to and love for the collective.**

- *Do I value the collective's well-being over my own?*
- *Do I feel ready and willing to act on that value?*
- *Amy I honest in my dealings with Community members?*

Fifth, you rejoice in a relationship of **trust** between you and your collective's elements. **Trust comes from a recognition on the part of your Community that you connect with it, understand it, love it, and are committed to it.**

- *Do I trust my comrades and inhabitants? Do they trust me?*
- *Do comrades and inhabitants see that I look out for their interests?*
- *Do I follow through on my commitments to the collective?*

Here's an alternate take on the chain that may resonate with you:

Connection begets Understanding
Understanding begets Love
Love begets Commitment
Commitment begets Trust

It's an unfolding of sorts.[53]

You may be inclined to view this unfolding as a spiral instead of a chain. I won't argue. You may find yourself revisiting various "stations" over time, with a deeper appreciation of what that station entails and how it relates to the larger actualization, much like the Spiral of Experience in the first chapter. Consider this "model" as a heuristic, then, for orienting your Path toward becoming a Community Protector.

---

[53]   Jennifer Murnan, Personal communication

- - - - - - - - - - - - - - - - -

It makes sense to assert that Protectors are connected, loving, and committed. You are too, or you would not be considering this path. A challenge in building CPR collectives begins with this sort of self-preparation journey. The Values Chain – this discovery process and unfolding - suggests ways to facilitate your movement along the Path.

One aspect of facilitating your movement along the path is ascertaining your **dedication to preparing yourself for the Protector role**, which comes from your commitment to your land, waters, or Community.

- *What experiences have you undertaken to deepen or broaden your expertise in building a collective?*
- *Do you have the discipline to stay on a path of development? How might you foster that?*

---

[54]   From Michael Asher, Facebook, Dec 31, 2022, accessed Jan 2 2023.

Another aspect of moving your path forward includes **gauging your readiness to sacrifice**, which comes from your commitment to preparing yourself for the Protector role.

- *What are you willing to sacrifice for the well-being of your Community? Your Job? Your reputation? Your comfort? Your health or safety?*
- *Have you made plans for the eventuality of your potential sacrifices?*

Speak not of revolution until you are willing to eat rats to survive.[55]

OK, perhaps that quote's a bit melodramatic, but it underscores what is sometimes a necessary condition for effective resistance. Consider it a potential RJP for whatever resistance role you might take on.

- - - - - - - - - - - - - - - - -

There is power in following this spiritual/motivational Path to becoming. But I should complement that aspect of the Path with a more material, skills-based orientation. What are the **aptitudes** of a successful Protector we can point to, to focus our development?

Community Builders should possess:
- **Building/organizing experience.** This book should help you with the basics to begin that journey if you aren't already experienced in collective building. At the same time, the concepts and models I introduce will prepare you to make the most of your experiences. You'll be better able to make sense of your experiences, put them in perspective, frame them appropriately and generate a range of options for how to proceed.
- **Flexibility and adaptability**, particularly in fluid situations, in changing climates, etc. The knowledge and training contained here will help once again, as you'll be able to borrow from the best practices I offer.
- **A de-colonized mind.**
- **Strength (fitness; emotional resilience; moral strength; steadfastness).**
- **Discipline, integrity, loyalty.**

This is a daunting list, but if you love your Community, you'll have little difficulty screwing up the strength, courage, and so on needed to protect them.

Leadership development is personal development.

- - - - - - - - - - - - - - - -

---

[55] The Last Poets: When the Revolution Comes (1970 Album)

You may find the quest involved in following this Path is a useful and fulfilling undertaking, for your growth and for the well-being of your collective. If so, you might **invite or inspire comrades to take the same journey with you.** When others join you in preparing for Community Leadership, the load is lighter, the Path clearer, and the passage never lonely. But there is a less selfish reason for bringing others along – in particular, you will be creating a deep wellspring of talent, leadership and guidance for your collective.

My comrades and I in Communities that Protect and Resist commit to establishing long-term relationships and alliances with Community Builders. It's our plan to work with Protectors everywhere to mutually develop Paths, skills and resources with which we can assume the mantle we claim for ourselves as Community Protectors. Check us out at the addresses at the end of this book.

Here's a hint about where you can focus in the meantime:
- Take stock of your developmental assets and needs as you progress through the following chapters.
- Make notes you can use in crafting a development plan.
- Brainstorm who you might work with in your development journey.

Do you identify yourself as a Protector, or do you aspire to be one? The planet depends on as many of you as possible saying, "YES".

Worksheet: Planning to Lead Your Community
This chapter is full of reflection questions as is! Here are a couple more.

You are likely reading this book because of your willingness to take responsibility for building, guiding or protecting your Community. All love and respect to you for that! Do you internalize the Values Chain that characterizes a Land Defender?

What can you do now, and later, to move along the Path I described?

Is your collective part of your identity? Does your Community help you make meaning of your world? How would you say your spiritual journey is shaping up?

Have external events, including the reactions of others, dampened your enthusiasm, motivation or confidence in serving as a land defender? Who can you turn to for help, inspiration or support?

Everything we've talked about to this point in the book is designed to give you the resources you can use to grow as a leader. Starting with the next chapter, we'll consider an expanded sphere of influence, and turn to how you can help your collective grow, strengthen, and flourish by beginning to think strategically about your collective's characteristics.

BUILDING COMMUNITY POWER

CHAPTER 5

Thinking Strategically, Part 1:
Strategic Context (Assets and Obstacles)

The Strategic Context of Leveraging Power

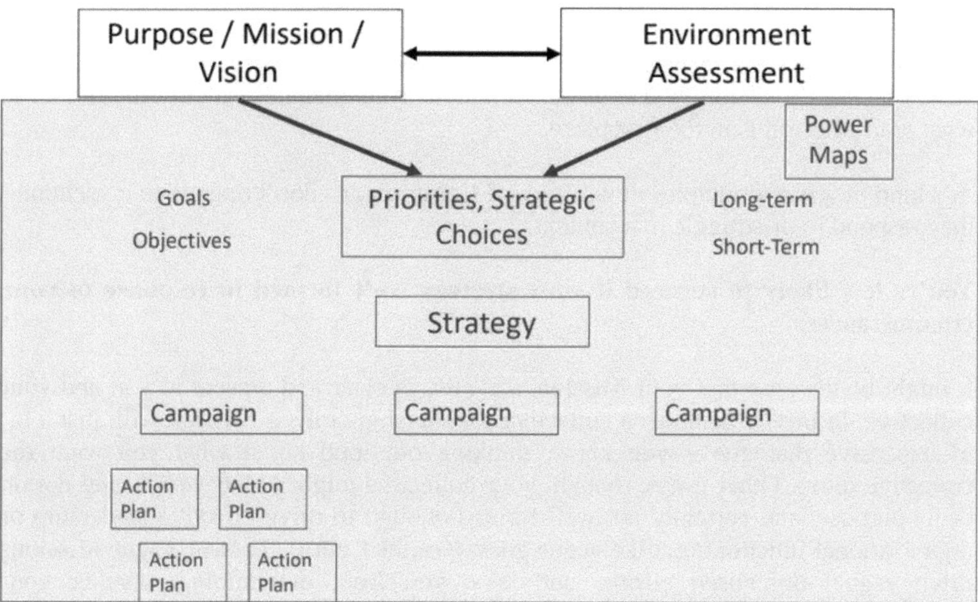

So far we've focused on your personal development as Community Builder and leader. Now we expand our concentration to developing **your collective**, building its power, and leveraging that power to protect and resist. There are two aspects of this larger challenge. First, such an expanded focus and scope requires we think beyond the tactical, person-to-person and small group (Cadre) leadership we introduced earlier. It's a priority that you **think strategically** about your collectives. Second, we need to discover **what to build and how to do so**. I'll provide examples and tools to allow you enough insight to begin to build and leverage your Community's' newfound power. I'll address the former challenge beginning in this chapter, and the second challenge in the ensuing five chapters. We'll then circle back and revisit strategy given what we discussed.

To build or improve your collective's strength and potential for success in protecting or resisting, one of the first things you need to do is to take stock of where you are now. This is exploring your **Strategic Context.** The most logical place to begin is to articulate your collective's Mission.

Mission

Mission is your purpose – it is what your collective commits to doing. It's not an exaggeration to suggest that your Mission is the reason your collective exists. You can't think strategically without the foundation your Mission provides. Later in this chapter I'll explain a technique for evaluating your larger strategic context (SWOT analysis), but the factors you consider in that analysis make sense only in relation to what your Mission is in the first place.

 It's kind of a first principles thing. Radical Communities don't operate in a vacuum – they respond to or struggle in a context.

You're less likely to succeed if your strategy isn't formed in response to your circumstances.

It might be the case that your Mission was always clear and present to you and your collective. In fact, oftentimes a collective's leadership crafts a Mission with just a bit of expansive dialogue – you know, thinking out loud about what you want the collective to do. Other times, though, your collective might just have a vague notion of its purpose, and certainly not well-formed enough to drive effective leadership or organizational functioning. Like vague goals (see the Cadres chapter), vague Missions drive vague, unfocused efforts, and keep you from determining whether your Community is succeeding. In cases like these, a bit of collective introspection and analysis can help you clarify and discover your Mission.

One technique that can help you build or discover your Mission is **Constituency Analysis** (Curphy & Hogan highlight a version of this approach).[56]

One of the first questions you should answer in exploring your Context: Who are our constituents? **Constituent**: any entity that influences or is influenced by the Community's work. You'll find that they are important factors in characterizing your strategic context, your strategy and plans.

---

[56]   Curphy, G. & Hogan, R. (2012). The Rocket Model: Practical Advice for Building High Performing Teams. Tulsa, OK: Hogan Press.

Who might fall into this notion? Here are some common Constituents in much resistance work, but of course you'll want to bring your own contributions to these lists.

External Constituencies	Internal Constituencies
Legal System / Regulatory Agencies	Boards / Steering Committees
Allies	Volunteers
Donors / Funders	Organizational culture
Media	Comrades
Possible volunteers	Allies
Religious groups	The Living World / beneficiaries

Don't assume all constituents have the same needs or present the same challenges. As you proceed with this analysis, keep track of what these challenges and needs might be, as these items may color the plans you put in place to address each party. If possible, work as a group to identify shared assumptions about these parties. You can also benefit by agreeing on how much influence they have over you, and you have over them. You might not have much influence over regulatory agencies (see Rights of Nature suits!), but you may exercise influence over board members, allies, comrades, etc.

Constituencies over whom you have greater influence should probably exert greater influence on the Mission you develop than those you have little or no control over. Constituents who exert substantial influence over your collective should be accounted for, too, if not by including them explicitly in your Mission, then by taking note of them in your larger environmental scan (which we discuss shortly).

Your analysis will help you determine, among other things, how your collective serves your identified constituents. What do you have to offer each group? It's also useful, and far-sighted, to consider an aspirational component to this. What **could** you offer to this or that constituency under better circumstances or when you evolve as a collective?

It's also important to note that key constituent lists don't remain static – your list might change over time. Periodically review your list (and the subsequent analysis), perhaps as part of your regular strategy sessions. This is a good way to stay as effective and on-target as you need to be.

The list you brainstormed serves as the input for the actual analysis you should engage in next. Below is a tool you might use in this work. The worksheet is pretty self-explanatory: Start with the list you brainstormed of all the relevant constituents. For each one, use a column to jot down agreed-on assumptions your collective has about them, the degree of influence you have on them or vice versa, and how your collective feels you should serve them.

Constituent Analysis Worksheet

Constituent				
Assumptions				
Influence (High, Moderate, Low, None)				
How we serve them				

If you find this worksheet too mechanistic, here's a way to frame this analysis and still make use of the worksheet: Ask yourself, "Who are we doing this for? And with? And how?" We tend to do a lot of this intuitively, and that element should be a part of your strategic conversations. But one of your leadership challenges, especially at this level, is to make the implicit explicit. Everyone in your Community should have a shared view of your strategic context, your Mission, and the constituents effecting what you do, or being effected by what you do.

Here's an example of the analysis, which my collective (CPR) recently undertook:

Constituent Analysis Worksheet:
Communities that Protect and Resist

Constituent	Community Builders	Donors	Social Media	The living world
Assumptions	Widely Varied knowledge, experiences, needs	Critical for us to expand our work	Powerful for presence; need for more expertise	Needs voice, protection
Influence (High, Moderate, Low, None)	High	High	High	
How we serve them	Support group, clearinghouse, resource bank, facilitator	Mutual goals re living planet, resistance communities	Positive content creation, radical analysis	Advocate

For us, the process was not complicated, and it was instructive for us to have undertaken it. We do it as part of our regular strategic planning work each year. And here's the punchline. Below is our Mission, which you can see clearly springs from our analysis:

From the CPR blog:[57]

> *Communities that Protect and Resist (CPR) is a support group, clearinghouse, resource bank, and facilitator of and for activists who want to build, then leverage strong Communities in order to pursue sustainable, just lives.*
>
> *We work to build a coalition of and for Communities (virtual and land-based) working together to actively and directly resist the forces destroying the planet, including:*
> - o *Patriarchy and misogyny*
> - o *Capitalism and consumerism*
> - o *Racism*
> - o *Militarism*
> - o *Environmental destruction*

---

[57] https://ctpr.home.blog/

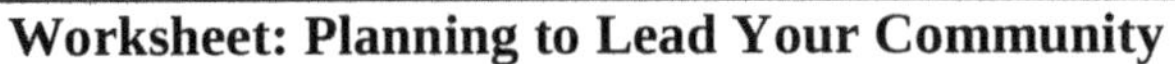

Worksheet: Planning to Lead Your Community

What is your collective's Mission?

If you don't have one, or if you think it should be adapted or revised, how will you go about doing so – Constituency Analysis, or brainstorming? Whom can you ask to help with this undertaking?

- - - - - - - - - - - - - - - -

Your Mission now can be used to conduct an environmental scan. Once your Mission is clear, you can take stock of the **Assets** that will help enable your collective in pursuit of its Mission, and the **Obstacles** that stand in your way.

- Maybe think of things this way: **Constituent Analysis** is a technique to help you figure out what your collective is **supposed to be doing**:
- **SWOT Analysis**, which we discuss next, helps you articulate the **assets and obstacles** that effect what you're supposed to be doing.

- - - - - - - - - - - - - - - -

SWOT Analysis

Eneiza Hernandez, writing of a community organizing training program in Venezuela, indicated three changes in participants were necessary for the organizing process:

- Recognition of <u>their own capacities</u>.
- Identification with <u>their environment</u>.
- Identification with their <u>human group</u>.[58]

These necessary changes suggest the importance of thinking strategically, particularly the first one. Effective Community Builders and leaders understand themselves, their environment, and their collective members. Let's then deepen our ability to think

---

[58] Hernandez, E. (1998). Assets and Obstacles in Community Leadership. Journal of Community Psychology, Vol. 26, No. 3.

strategically by mastering a technique to scan our environment for relevant factors that impinge on our ability to realize our collective's Mission.

That technique is commonly called a **SWOT analysis**: Identifying Strengths, Weaknesses, Opportunities and Threats. SWOT is an easy-to-use tool to quickly develop an overview of your Community in a larger context. It also reminds us that whatever plans you create to build your Community or to leverage its power, must provide a **strong fit or response** to the situation, especially Opportunities and Threats.

Great planning starts with an understanding of where you are today: confronting the facts.

SWOT is often done as part of the strategic planning process, but it can and should be used any time you need to find or refresh your understanding of your Community's Mission-relevant environment. It's also a way to reveal changes which can usefully be made to adapt your collective to your strategic circumstances.

Of course, to engage fruitfully in a SWOT analysis, you need to be able to scan for factors that are relevant, instead of merely looking at every possible issue, item, development or group, for example. Clarifying your Mission will help you determine what is relevant and what is not. Where do you get the data for your analysis, then? Here are some possibilities:
- Brainstorming with comrades in your collective.
- Experience.
- Your understanding of the news, geopolitical scene, history, etc.
- Our model of effective radical Communities. The next several chapters lay out the components of such collectives. Your understanding of these components can serve as fodder for fleshing out your SWOT analysis.

As you work your way through this analysis, be **realistic**, not overly pessimistic or rose-colored. Your strategic planning will be hamstrung if you're not.

SWOT Components

Components <u>internal</u> to your collective.

STRENGTHS: Areas in which your Community holds advantages, superiority, or simply resources and skills you can draw on to exploit opportunities and respond to threats.

> What are your advantages?
> What do you do well?
> What makes you resilient, adaptive?

> <u>Examples:</u> *Isolated from civilization. Dedication to saving the planet. Writing and speaking skills*

How to respond to Strengths:
- Leverage them. Use them to realize your Mission. Be creative in finding ways to do so. Use your writing skills, for example, to persuade others to join your campaign, or to influence environmental legislation.
- Build them. Make them stronger, not only because you don't know when you'll need to be stronger in an area, but attempt to become a force to be reckoned with.

WEAKNESSES: Areas that inhibit your ability to protect and resist. They must be overcome to avoid failure. Again, **be realistic!** Face unpleasant truths as soon as possible. And don't be discouraged if the list is long or daunting. You're finding your path forward and addressing pitfalls, and your plans will be all the better for ensuring your analysis is as accurate as possible.

> What talents or resources do we lack?
> What do we do badly as a collective?
> What do we need to avoid?

> <u>Examples:</u> *Lack of strategic direction, lack of leadership, apathy, paternalism, tradition (inertia), fatalism, resources.*

How to respond to Weaknesses:
- Shore them up. If you don't have many comrades, recruit. If you don't have the skills to move toward your Mission, get training, consulting, or recruit comrades who have the skills.

124

Components <u>external</u> to your collective.

OPPORTUNITIES: Taking a scan beyond your Community *per se,* what in the environment can you capitalize on to make your collective more likely to succeed, or to become stronger and more resilient?

What are the beneficial forces or changes facing your collective?

What are interesting trends you need to know about?

Examples: *Peak oil. Public sentiment. Changes in social patterns. Increased awareness of social injustice or climate change.*

How to respond to Opportunities:
- Capitalize on them and/or invest in them. If public opinion is becoming less favorable to mining in your area, lean into that. Spread the word about the shift in attitudes (through a Social Norms Marketing campaign, e.g.), make your analysis known to more and more people, etc.

THREATS: Trends or factors which can threaten your survival or ability to thrive, or to realize your strategic purpose.

What do we fear as a collective?

What obstacles keep us from realizing our potential or threaten our existence as a collective?

<u>Examples</u>: *Industrial civilization, militarization, prejudice against our people or land, government policies, population growth, disease, etc.*

How to respond to Threats:
- Monitor them. This is an area in which you're likely to have less control, but you want to make sure you're abreast of any changes to these factors, so you can respond with changes to your strategy quickly and appropriately.

You may want to engage in the SWOT process with comrades, to maximize the collective wisdom, experience, and knowledge you need to do this work effectively. A group of core members of your collective, Elders, or the like can serve as a great resource for this analysis.

The following figure can be used as a tool to help visualize the SWOT process. You could make a handout of this for planning meetings or draw a likeness of it on a blackboard in a group setting to focus the discussion.

The SWOT Matrix

Strengths (Positive, Internal Factors) Ex: Strong culture LEVERAGE/BUILD	**Weaknesses** (Negative, Internal Factors) Ex: Paternalism, apathy SHORE UP
Opportunities (Positive, External Factors) Ex: Peak oil, public sentiment INVEST/CAPITALIZE ON	**Threats** (Negative, External Factors) Ex: Militarism, climate change MONITOR

SWOT Reflections

Do you get the idea that, in the process of engaging in this analysis, you'll have a better grasp of your Community? This is an example of a mutually influential process – getting to know your Community better allows you to prepare a more accurate SWOT analysis, and doing the work to prepare an effective SWOT analysis helps you learn more about your collective.

Factors you include in your analysis may be "relative". For example, a small collective may be good (it allows you to be nimble) or bad (it can keep you from engaging in larger campaigns or actions). We'll talk about this again when we revisit Strategy.

Your analysis depends on your vision, purpose, and mission. The factors you consider in your analysis are only relevant as they might effect what you are trying to do in the first place. If your Mission is to disrupt deep sea mining, you may not care about fracking policies inasmuch as they do not impact your main focus.
Don't just rely on your own insights – ask others! Leverage the collective wisdom of comrades whenever and wherever possible. Get out of your own head.

You might need to prioritize the factors after the analysis is completed. If your analysis ends up with multiple entries in any of the S, W, O or T categories, you may not be able to address them all. Figure out which are most critical to your work, and prepare your plans with that in mind. The extent to which your collective can control situational factors varies greatly, so you need to be able to distinguish between those you can control and those you need to cope with / adapt to.

Processing your SWOT:
Since we in resistance always seem to have limited resources and time, the smart move should be for you to determine the order in which you respond to your results. For example, you may focus on Strengths or Weaknesses first, since these components are internal to your collective, and are more likely to be in your control.

Opportunities might be next, as your ability to capitalize on them is not generally constrained by others. As for Threats, you generally can't do much other than monitor them, so keep them in mind, but you won't reap much from making extensive plans in response to them.

> *"What any movement needs is an effective strategy. That means identifying*
> *two things: where is power weak and where are you strong?*
> *The overlap is where you strike."*

Lierre Keith

Interesting perspective on strategic planning. What activity helps you determine the factors Lierre mentions? Hint: Its initials are S.W.O.T.

Worksheet: Planning to Lead Your Community

As practice before you engage in this with a larger group, conduct your own SWOT analysis for your collective. What patterns or insights do you notice?

What's your plan to incorporate the results into your collective's strategy?

SWOT is a way you can get a bearing on your Strategic Context. It is a useful way to scan your environment in order to take stock of the factors that impinge on your collective's ability to realize its Mission. To ensure whatever strategies or plans you make in response to your environmental scan are most effective, you'll want to populate the matrix with relevant factors – to fill in each of the quadrants with your lists of appropriate factors. We already discussed ways you can do this – brainstorming, experience, your understanding of the news, geopolitical scene, history, etc.

It also really helps to have a **frame or model** we can use to filter in or out all the potential environmental factors for your strategic planning. The model I suggest is the CPR model of effective radical Communities. The next five chapters lay out these components. As we shift our focus, we're doing two things:

- We're **describing what makes a strong, just and sustainable Community**. The components can help you populate the SWOT Matrix – i.e., they are facets that may be applicable to your strategic context and therefore usable to create a strategic plan for your Community.
- However, the CPR components in this model are internal. Opportunities and Threats must be discovered by other means, like your awareness of your environment, history, etc.
- We're also **listing actions you can take to build each CPR-collective component**. This "audit" of sorts not only helps you discover your Assets and Obstacles, it should also result in a detailed action plan you can use to build, rebuild, fix, or strengthen your Community.

Don't be overwhelmed by the thought that you need to perfect all these components. The more of them you can build the better, but begin by taking stock. This model is **aspirational**. Work with your comrades to build it, but realize you'll likely never be done.

This is not a complete blueprint. It's more likely a set of specs. You have to fill in the local details. Again, be realistic.

- - - - - - - - - - - - - - - - -

I'll share best practices and guidelines for building each component as we proceed through the next chapters. I tried to sort the action items into the components they are most suited to, but keep in mind these practices (a celebration, say) can be used to shore up more than one component (I'll try to point them out as we go). That's good news, by the way! A well-designed celebration can build Consciousness, Comradeship, and so on. As you plan for your Community building, one strategy you can take is to make use of the initiatives that get you the most bang for your buck.

Remember too that the five components in the model above are conceptually different but not unrelated – they are related to each other in ways, but deserving of separate treatment as a way for us to maintain clarity of thought.
A caution and a reminder: You can't do all this yourself. It takes a Community to build a Community. That's where leadership comes in!

CHAPTER 6

Building Community:
Community Consciousness

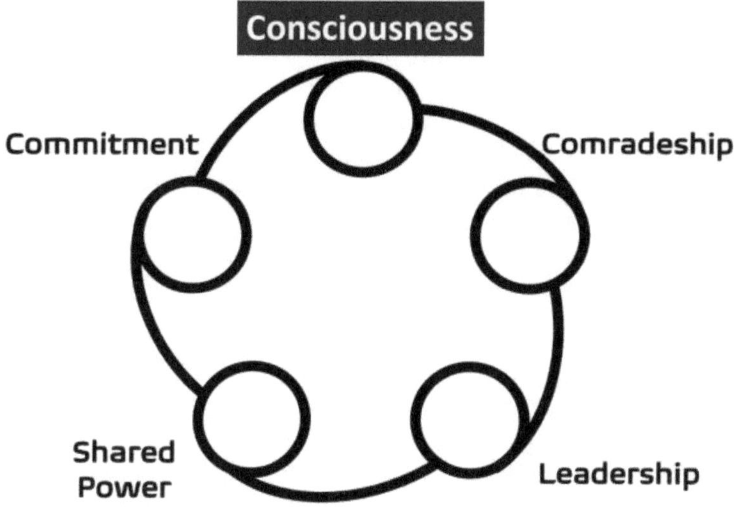

"Revolutionary consciousness leads to the struggle for one's own freedom in unity with others who share the burden of oppression."

Greg Calvert[59]

We've been exploring the notion of Community writ large as a way of understanding it as a critical component of resistance to the dominant culture. An important outcome of these explorations is that Community builders can determine whether there is a gap between where their collective is now and where they aspire to be, and to then craft a plan to move forward. **Hence, we continue to follow up with the Assets and Obstacles theme.**

The dominant culture and the ruling class are at war with the natural world, and those of us who do not resist are fodder, ammunition or collateral damage. We are enslaved by toxic systems, isolated from our tribes and landbases, and in the process weakened, confused, and distracted from what is critical. Before we can fight back, we need to develop awareness, not just of the problem, but of the

---

59   Calvert, G., "In White America," speech, reprinted in Guardian, March 25, 1967.

power we can wield when we recapture our Community belongingness and selves. This is one aspect of the notion of Community Consciousness.

Effective Communities that Protect and Resist explore and cultivate their Consciousness. Of the characteristics in this series, Consciousness is possibly the one that most clearly enables resistance, and that impels a Community toward becoming radical. At the risk of hyperbole, I assert that Community Consciousness is the fundamental component of a CPR collective. Without a sense of collective self, without a clear shared notion of identity and intrinsic meaning, no collective can resist in any meaningful or protracted way.

> *"There are four things you should know," says David Fuertes to the youths he mentors. "You should know your **origins**, because your ancestors have paved the way. You should know your **values** and connect in those values, because that's going to drive you to make decisions. You should know your **purpose**, because that will show the 'why' of what you're doing. And you should **envision** the ultimate for yourself and your lāhui [or 'people']."[60]* (Emphasis added.)

In the absence of collective Consciousness, resistance becomes atomized railings against a toxic world, and material actions are isolated, spastic and fleeting.

- - - - - - - - - - - - - - - -

Consciousness and "Politics"

If you're familiar with Marxist theory, you know about class consciousness. It is the set of beliefs a person holds regarding their social class or economic rank in society, the structure of their class, and their class interests. Put another way, it is awareness of one's place in a system of social classes, especially (in Marxist terms) as it relates to the class struggle. According to Marx, it is an awareness that is key to sparking a revolution that would "create a dictatorship of the proletariat, transforming it from a wage-earning, property-less mass into the ruling class". Class consciousness is a necessary precursor to resistance to the ruling class.

Why aren't social classes necessarily conscious? In Marxist theory, class consciousness is not an origin, but an achievement (i.e., it must be "earned" or won). Only when consciousness is achieved will the underclasses understand the necessity of class struggle and use that as a touchstone and catalyst for material resistance. For a radical Community to be able to Protect and Resist, it must embody a certain level

---

[60]   Leonard, L. (Feb 4, 2021). Returning to the Roots of Community Resilience in Hawai'i. yesmagazine.org. https://www.yesmagazine.org/environment/2021/02/04/hawaii-local-agriculture-food-security Accessed Jan 1, 2023.

of consciousness much as Marxism's conscious classes do. **But a radical Community must work to achieve Community Consciousness.**

Can a Community form precisely *because* of a shared consciousness among its members? Maybe, but let's set aside this chicken or egg discussion for now, and worry more about whether and how much your Community possesses this critical asset.

Community Consciousness is perhaps best thought of as a scaling down of class consciousness.

Gene Theodori:
When a community is truly conscious, it is fully aware of and knowledgeable about its current social, economic and environmental conditions.
Moreover, the community understands the history of its people, economy and environment, and it has a well-defined vision for the future.[61]

McBay lists "memory" as one of the characteristics of effective cultures of resistance, inasmuch as people know their history and remember their struggles. The challenge for Community builders is to help their collective achieve awareness of these contextual forces and how they shape the current circumstances of its individual members and the whole. Based in part on this awareness, the Community must assess its purpose, inspire a shared vision, and chart its future. Effective CPR collectives, then, explore and cultivate their Consciousness.

Theodori's definition expertly, almost offhandedly, lists the features of a Conscious Community, and for the attentive reader serves as a strategic list of initiatives for Builders to address: Awareness of the collective's past, its internal issues and conditions, environmental circumstances, and vision should be on everyone's list of Community assets to audit and maintain.

> *"Always, leaders drew on their own distinctive political histories and*
> *deep local knowledge to rally broad support in their societies."*
>
> Engler & Engler (2016) discussing successful
> non-violent campaigns of the past couple of decades.[62]

I introduced the Black Panther Party (BPP) in an earlier chapter. As a CPR-type collective, the BPP took pains to cultivate Consciousness in several forms, most notably through education. So central to that Community's commitment to education

---

[61] Theodori, G.(und.). The Community Activeness/Consciousness Matrix: A Tool for Community Development. Webpage downloaded Feb 28, 2020. https://www.shsu.edu/~glt002/Outreach%20articles/Theodori%202004%20community%20activeness%20consciousness%20matrix.pdf

[62] Engler, M., & Engler, P. This is an Uprising: How Nonviolent Revolt is Shaping the Twenty-First Century. New York: Nation Books.

is that it is mentioned in the BPP Platform, which called for education "that exposes the true nature of this decadent American society" and that "teaches us our true history and our role in the present-day society" (quotes from Bloom & Martin)[63]. Political education classes were also offered by comrades in the Party. Here then are two best practices the radical Community builder can adopt in their Consciousness-building plans.

Consciousness and Identity

Indigenous populations understand the criticality of a communal identity in strong resistance collectives. I recently took note of a post on Facebook devoted exclusively to the theme that indigenous cultural identity is a core resiliency.[64]

Awareness alone constitutes only part of Consciousness. While it's important that Community members appreciate **where** they collectively stand, it's equally important they know what they stand **for**. "Identity" serves both as a way to define the often-slippery notion of Community as well as another characteristic of an effective collective. One component of Shaffer & Anundsen's definition of a community is that a group of people "identify themselves as part of something larger than the sum of their individual relationships."[65] David Ulrich (1998) poses "Forge a strong and distinct identity" as a fundamental practice for building a strong Community. In Ulrich's view, clear, strong and distinct identities give **meaning** to members and distinctness to nonmembers.[66] John Gardner (1990) laments the disintegration of Communities and the widespread loss of a sense of community, since "it is in communities that individuals develop identity and a **sense of belonging.**"[67]

For us, identity describes how the Community is viewed, and how members view themselves in that Community, how they fit in the larger collective, and how this relates to the larger world and worldview. In my childhood neighborhood, 9th Avenue (a 1-block-long suburban tract) said a lot about who we were: lower-middle to middle class and working-class families. (A neighbor around the corner won the big prize on Queen for a Day, a tv show in which the "contestant" with the most daunting recent financial and emotional hard times as voted on by the audience, received a new washing machine or some such.)

---

[63] Bloom, J. & Martin, W.E. (2013). Black Against Empire: The History and Politics of the Black Panther Party. Berkeley: University of California Press.

[64] Digital Smoke Signals, October 26, 2022

[65] Shaffer, C., & Anundsen, K. (2005). Creating Community Anywhere: Finding Support and Connection in a Fragmented World. Dillon Beach, CA: CCC Press, p.10

[66] Ulrich, D. (1998). Six Practices for Creating Communities of Value, Not Proximity. In F. Hesselbein et al. (Eds). Communities of the Future. San Francisco: Jossey-Bass

[67] Gardner, J. On Leadership. Highlighted summary of the book, published by Free Press. Accessed August 2020. p.113

In recent conceptualizations of Community, geography/location doesn't always play a major role in determining identity. Members of Deep Green Resistance (DGR), for example, are likely to view themselves as "radical" as part of their identity. "Radical" in this sense not only describes DGR as an organization, but the worldview of the individual members and provides a context for how they distinguish themselves from the larger world. This identity also functions to provide a non-geographical boundary between DGR and the "outside world".

I was struck again by the importance placed on education as a device for growing identity-spawning Consciousness in resistance collectives. Education in service of collective identity, in whatever form, is a theme across several Communities.

- Brazil's indigenous Ka'apor have resisted government and corporate incursions into their lands for years. Realizing the importance of education as a catalyst for growing Consciousness, the tribe set up their own education program prioritizing the Ka'apor language over Portuguese. They also created the Ka'apor Training and Knowledge Center (Jumu'e ha renda Keruhu), an Indigenous-run program to train and educate future leaders while preserving the ways of their ancestors.[68]
- Don't forget the programs set up by the Black Panthers. To complement the work of the education initiative, the BPP published their own newspaper, *The Black Panther*, a "Black Community News Service". The paper published news about BPP programs, attacks on the Community by the police and others, and in general functioned as a key component of the revolutionary agenda by emphasizing relevant stories, interpreting them through the BPP lens, and accentuating the identity of the Community and its place in American society at that point in time.
- The Zapatista education system is Community-rooted. Autonomous schools are administered by "education promoters"- primarily local youth who teach in their own Communities under supervision of an education committee elected by a local assembly. The curriculum is integrated in daily life and tailored to prepare a new generation for tasks of governance and self-sufficiency, including topics like autonomy, history, agroecology and veterinary medicine. Classes are taught in both Spanish and indigenous languages, with the emphasis on the preservation of local traditions and knowledge.[69]
- We're familiar with the geopolitical region known as the areas controlled by the Syrian Democratic Forces in northern and eastern Syria, known as Rojava. A document titled "The Internal System of the Communes in Rojava"

---

[68] Johnson, A. In Brazil, Indigenous Ka'apor take their territory's defense into their own hands. March 14, 2022. Mongabay. https://news.-mongabay.com/2022/03/in-brazil-indigenous-kaapor-take-their-territorys-defense-into-their-own-hands/ [Accessed Nov 21, 2022]

[69] Rebrii, A. (2020). Zapatistas: Lessons in community self-organisation in Mexico. In opendemocracy.net, 25 June 2020. https://www.opendemocracy.net/en/democraciaabierta/zapatistas-lecciones-de-auto-organización-comunitaria-en

outlines the internal structure and functioning of the communes, the "most basic unit of political organization and governance" for Rojava. An excerpt from Article Eighteen indicates the clear understanding the Rojavan Community has for Consciousness as it relates to collective identity, and a hint of their appreciation for how to cultivate that (spoiler: it's the education system):

Means of Making the Commune Active
So that the commune may be active in society, the following steps must be taken:

> *1. Every commune must have a clear name, preferably naming the communes after the names of martyrs, with a defined address like the centre of address of the komingeh, so that all institutions and members can deal with it officially.*
>
> *2. Every commune must have its own training program. If there is no training system, the democratic societal mindset and freedom cannot be understood and implemented.*[70]

Consciousness and Values

What is the basis for a collective identity? For Ulrich, an (organizational) identity "may be centered around purpose, values, or some other distinguishing feature…" It represents the collective's image, as perceived by those inside and out. A common identity is forged based on values, not proximity, in Ulrich's distinction. In fact, Ulrich describes the "fundamental shift" in how Community is conceptualized. He goes to some lengths to note how traditional Communities were defined by geography and how that notion has evolved:

> *"Today, boundaries based on values may be more common than boundaries based on geographic proximity…. Communities of the future may be less defined by where we live than by what we believe."*[71]

A member of Alcoholics Anonymous, in his example, can join a meeting anywhere and know she is surrounded by others who share similar values. We would hope a member of Women's Liberation Front could do the same. Shared core values do indeed draw comrades together who don't share land or water. For those who would build virtual Communities of resistance or geographically-oriented collectives, leveraging this aspect of commonality should be a priority.

---

[70] Jawad Al-Tamimi, A. 2018. The Internal System of the Communes in Rojava. Cooperation in Mesopotamia. https://www.aymenn-jawad.org/2018/04/the-internal-system-of-the-communes-in-rojava

[71] Ulrich, D. (1998). Six Practices for Creating Communities of Value, Not Proximity. In F. Hesselbein et al. (Eds). Communities of the Future. San Francisco: Jossey-Bass, p. 157

For John Gardner, the disintegration of communities brings with it disintegration of shared values. To counteract this trend, Gardner suggests Communities **teach** – that they impart a coherent value system.

"It is community and culture that hold the individual in a framework of values; when the framework disintegrates, individual value systems disintegrate."[72]

- - - - - - - - - - - - - - - -

To identify as part of a Community, then, means to:
- Share the **geographical space** of a collective;
- Subscribe to a common **awareness of "place"** relative to larger systems; or
- Hold **similar values** as an identified collective.

Identity provides meaning, shared purpose, and a motivation to protect those who share the identity. Let's agree that Community identity is influenced by **each focus.** If any one of the "Theodorian awareness", geographic awareness, or shared values aspects is strong, a Community's Consciousness might be considered solid, but wanting. The more factors a Community can count as robust, the stronger is its Consciousness. That Community is more apt to successfully protect its members from destructive forces.

The Sandinistas again teach us about building Consciousness. Besides their practices aimed at Consciousness-raising via the validation and celebration of identity, Sandinistans clarify and reinforce the values they share and that strengthen their sense of communality. In 2020, for example, they participated in a month-long program called "Celebration of Life," culminating in the celebration of the 1994 Zapatista uprising, when indigenous peasants of Chiapas rose up to defend their rights and land against the state and big landowners. A part of the celebration was a dance festival in which participants enacted life after 1994. Signs say "Education," "Health," and "Collective Work."

Consciousness and Uniqueness

A Conscious Community isn't necessarily unique, but it possesses a **sense** of uniqueness. How does one reinforce such a sense of distinctiveness? Let's praise once again the flexible power of celebrations. Celebrating the **collective history** and distinctive experiences and characteristics of Community members, **collective roles** played intra- and extramurally, **shared core values**, and **idiosyncratic vision** reinforces what is unique about a Community.

---

[72] Gardner, J. On Leadership. Highlighted summary of the book, published by Free Press. Accessed August 2020, p. 113

When you look at the list as such, it becomes clear that every radical Community is unique to some extent. **Capitalize on that because it reaps valuable results**. The felt uniqueness of the Community (not individuals in it) in turn fosters a **sense of worth** regarding the collective - that the land or water and world would be lesser in its absence. In turn, members are apt to appreciate the value of that Community thriving and persisting, and are motivated to struggle for its well-being.

- - - - - - - - - - - - - - - -

Taking this information forward: Education programs such as the Sandinistas and other Communities commit to, preservation of local languages and traditions, and celebrations emphasizing distinctiveness are simple (although not always easy) tactics you might investigate as part of your Community-building efforts.

Sometimes these efforts are as simple as they are powerful. Keep them in mind as you build your plans for strengthening your Community. From Dadsen, (2020):

> *A Park Ranger in Tasmania wants to ensure his children and future generations know about their ancestors. He is helping re-build traditional Aboriginal huts at Preminghana on Tasmania's west coast to educate the public about the region's Indigenous history.*
>
> *The aim of the project was to keep the area's history going.*
>
> *"To try and get it strong and get it back for myself and my children and the other children of the community." "People will learn to respect through knowledge."*
>
> *"It's just bringing culture back into the community and it's good for the kids, they can keep building off what we're going off."*
>
> *"They are critical in telling the story of Aboriginal occupation in this place, this occupation goes back thousands of years, it's the story of how the people are connected with the land to survive."[73]*

Consciousness and Intent

Let's reassert and recast our basic notion of a radical Community. We'd do well to maintain in our Community-building work that **Community Consciousness includes awareness and acceptance of radical intent**. There are lots of Community-building organizations in existence that might help you create some sense of purpose, but they rarely help us create and maintain radical intent.

---

[73] Dadsen, M. Building huts the old way to get Aboriginal culture 'strong' for future generations. https://www.abc.net.au/news/2020-06-14/traditional-aboriginal-huts-being-rebuilt-along-tasmanian-coast/12353032 Accessed Dec 30, 2022.

Let's not forget, nor allow comrades to forget, what we're in a collective to accomplish, what makes us unique, what serves to bolster our identity, and what we value. And fundamental to all these notions is that of resistance and dismantling the culture that is destroying this planet.

- - - - - - - - - - - - - - -

Building Community Consciousness

We've gotten clear direction from other CPR collectives regarding not just the importance of building Community Consciousness, but **how to do so**. The main theme of these examples centers around the imperative to **explore, and teach:** the **history** of your Community, its **place** in the natural community, its shared **values**, its **vision** for the future, its **uniqueness**, and its **intent**.

Every member should have a deep knowledge and appreciation of where their Community came from, what it is now, and where it is going. Here's a simple place to start:
- Learn the indigenous name for your landbase, and what it means.
- Try to keep that knowledge active in conversations, celebrations, meetings, etc.
- "Build a hut".

In addition, Community Builders need to facilitate important tasks: in this context this takes three forms:

Values Work. Explore, identify, discuss, choose and articulate the values your Community holds most important to acknowledge its past and guarantee its future. Many writers on Community or leadership development point to the importance of this endeavor, including Monica Sharma (2017),[74] Kouzes and Posner (2012),[75] Rushworth Kidder (1994)[76] and others. Lots of "seed lists" of values are available for members to use as a pool from which to choose or to facilitate a conversation about core values.

Values are a basic aspect of Community Consciousness. Have you reflected on or talked about your values? Why not convene an event or gathering where values can be on the table and frankly explored? Be willing to listen to the collective's

[74]   Sharma, M. (2017). Radical Transformational Leadership: Strategic Action for Change Agents. Berkeley, CA: North Atlantic Books.
[75]   Kouzes, J., & Posner, B. (2012). The Leadership Challenge: How to Make Extraordinary Things Happen in Organizations (Fifth Ed.). San Francisco: Wiley.
[76]   Kidder, R. (1994). Shared Values for a Troubled World: Conversations With Men and Women of Conscience. Jossey-Bass.

perspectives and be flexible enough to incorporate their inputs into your core values list if necessary.

How is your Community unique? Have you told anyone? How can you publicize this in your interactions and programs?

Vision Work. Incorporate your collective's values into an ideal and unique image of the future for the common good. A communal vision can be a powerful component of your Community Consciousness. It can, for example, attract commitment and energize members, who will commit voluntarily and completely to something worthwhile, something that will make life better for others, or that represents a significant improvement for their Community or locale.

Visions create meaning in members' lives, too. Lots of resources exist for engaging in your vision work, including Matusak, Kouzes & Posner, and others.

Culture Work. Culture is the deep-set, long-term collection of ways members feel, act and relate. It is both a cause and result of the shared Consciousness. Culture encompasses the collective values and behaviors that contribute to the uniqueness of a Community, as well as beliefs and principles of members. Culture also includes the collective's norms, symbols, and specific language. An effective resistance enjoys a "living culture", according to McBay, in which resistance is celebrated and enacted via a wide range of cultural undertakings.

Community builders can create and sustain a strong culture in several ways.
- Elders and other influential members **use stories and myths** to illustrate how core values play a role in the Community's formation, history and survival.
- Exemplar members (**"heroes"**) are held up for praise because they embody the cultural characteristics of the Community.
- **Rites and rituals** communicate the way things are done,[77] giving the culture a tangible form. Rites and rituals also mark passages Community members enter into or emerge from.
- Finally, **stories** serve as the oral history of the Community, spread important news, and reinforce in various ways all the aspects of a healthy, strong Community Culture and Consciousness. We'll talk later about storytelling as a core function of Community Leadership.

---

[77]   Deal, T.. & Kennedy, A. (1982). Corporate Cultures: The Rites and Rituals of Corporate Life. Reading, MA: Addison-Wesley.

Cultural events are a great way to also recruit, build networks of allies, and promote education and critical analysis.[78] Take full advantage of these events! Make speeches. Given what we talked about here, the speeches pretty much write themselves! Do street theater, etc., and always, make sure to communicate **why you're there**, the **importance** of the day / event, your **vision or purpose**, etc. For greater effect, you can time these events with seasons or natural cycles. They might take on a life of their own, which is a wonderful example of using inertia to your Community's benefit. Be creative in designing your events. Everything from plays, gatherings, film screenings, readings and songs can be used powerfully.

The leader's role in establishing and strengthening culture is such a key function that we'll return to this again and again.

In a real sense, it's all culture work.

Worksheet: Planning to Lead Your Community

Is your collective Conscious in the sense Theodori mentions? What's missing, if anything?

Do you think there's widespread agreement concerning your collective's core values? (I bet there isn't as much as you think.) How can you find out?

What does your collective do to explore and teach to strengthen Consciousness? Is there more you can do? Go back a page or two for suggestions!

---

[78] DeFilippis, J., Fisher, R., & Shragge, E. (2010). Contesting Community: The Limits and Potential of Local Organizing. New Brunswick: Rutgers University Press.

CHAPTER 7

Building Community: Comradeship

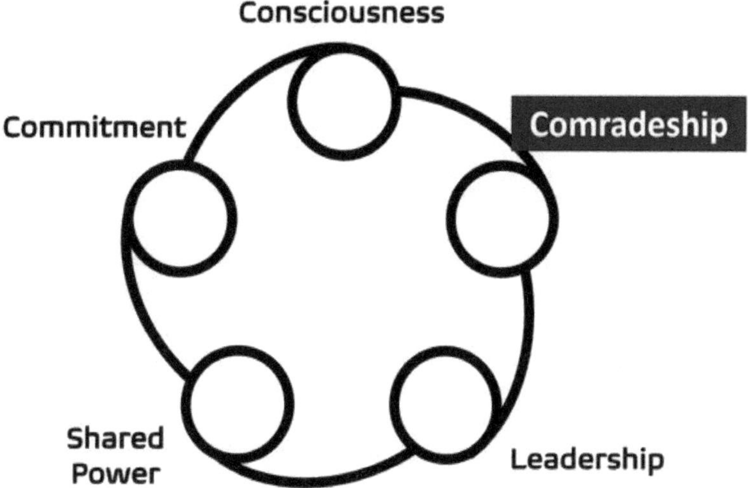

It's been said soldiers in war fight not for a cause, but for the soldiers next to them. For those of us fighting to save the planet, this is a fundamental principle we should pay attention to. Community builders should create the conditions under which we care enough for each other to struggle with them, to want them to grow and succeed, and to fight for them as much as we do for the planet.

Let's not forget, too, that Comradeship is not limited to humans, although that is the general focus of this work. A loving relationship with the land, waters, creatures and all that surround us in Community is essential if we are to build effective CPR collectives. This is what I mean by Comradeship.

Comradeship (social cohesion to some), the essence of Community, is the set of collective bonds among members – the connective tissue of Community.

Without Comradeship, there are no Community members – just acquaintances.

- - - - - - - - - - - - - - - -

That's a bold statement, and I'll stand buy it. If Comradeship is so central to a Community with a resistance orientation, the challenge is to understand the notion deeply enough that we'll know whether it exists in our collective, how strongly it is felt, and what we can do to develop it if we need to do so. Let's consider the components. Mattesich & Monsey (1997) describe two aspects of social cohesion, which resonate with our orientation.

- **Social Ties.** Interactions based on kinships, friendships, familiarity and mutual recognition with others in a geographic area, ideological or class focus.
- **Psychological Ties.** Feelings of attachment, identity, mutual respect and sense of belonging to that place or focus. These ties manifest also in a sense of camaraderie with fellow inhabitants or comrades.[79]

Comradeship in the forms described generates a Community's **Social Capacity**: the ability of members of a Community to work together effectively. According to Mattesich and Monsey:

"Communities with high social capacity can successfully identify problems and needs; achieve a workable consensus on goals and priorities; agree on how to pursue goals; and cooperate to achieve goals."[80]

A central theme of this book focuses on how to build Power in a collective. Comradeship as defined this way offers a direct connection to Power: Collectives with strong ties among comrades can get things done collectively. There's Power in that.

- - - - - - - - - - - - - - - -

You might be more familiar with Comradeship as Social Capital, a construct popularized by scholars like Robert Putnam. Similar to Social Cohesion, Social Capital refers to the stores of networks and trust members can draw on to solve Community problems. The denser these networks, the more likely members will cooperate for mutual benefit. Cooperation is more likely in this instance because networks of Community engagement foster norms of reciprocity; i.e., expectations (or trust) that favors given now will be returned later. This notion of reciprocity crops up in another context, too, as I'll address in a moment.

I talked about the importance of **trust** in a leadership context already. Trust undergirds so many of our interpersonal and collective relationships that discovering yet another context in which it exerts positive influence serves as a reminder to work

---

[79]   Mattesich, P. & Monsey, B. (1997). Community Building: What Makes it Work. Saint Paul, MN: Amherst H. Wilder Foundation.
[80]   Ibid, p.8

on your trust-building skills. The cohesive Community "nurtures its members and fosters an atmosphere of trust."[81] Caring, trust and teamwork act hand in hand to make it possible for members to work together on the tasks necessary for the Community to survive and thrive.

"[T]here is a feeling that when the [Community] wins everybody wins"[82]

Briand's Fourth Principle for a Community that works makes use of a similar construct – Cooperation.[83] For Briand, people are able and willing to talk, deliberate, and act together to solve their problems. "Cooperation" means working together for mutual benefit. Like Social Capital, Briand offers that members cooperate because they see it is in their own interest to do so, because they stand to gain personally from a pragmatic decision to heed other's interests as well as their own.

True enough, but there has to be more to it than self-interest, and there is. When we build true Comradeship, we experience a degree of love for our comrades, and for the living world. When we love someone, we're more than willing to ensure they flourish. If we've constructed the foundation for the collective based on robust Consciousness, particularly linked to a compelling vision for the collective, comrades will cooperate because they see they are part of something larger than themselves, and understand that collective power will lead them closer to success in their ability to protect and resist.

"We can trust friends to care about our well-being in addition to their own.
The odds are they'll cooperate."[84]

- - - - - - - - - - - - - - - -

Dense social networks, strong psychological ties, and feelings of trust help create the social capital that enables collectives to accomplish goals. But relationships and ties must be **bounded** for them to be healthy. Briand adds an important point in discussing Cooperation; namely, that it is based on an implied norm of **reciprocity**, that involvement in a joint undertaking depends on the expectation that members will receive a benefit in return for their contribution. Dave Ulrich (1998) includes serial reciprocity as an integral component of Communities of values:

*"**Serial reciprocity** means that community member A may serve member B and member B will repay the service, not by serving A, but by serving*

---

[81] Gardner, J. On Leadership. Highlighted summary of the book, published by Free Press. Accessed August 2020, p. 117

[82] Ibid.

[83] Briand. M. (und.). A Practical Guide to a Community that Works.

[84] Ibid. p. 54

another member (C). Serial reciprocity implies that the inevitable equity required by members to continue to participate in a community may be derived over time, not at any one point in time. "[85]

In other words, members in a healthy Community serve the collective, and not necessarily in direct bilateral transactions. As well, members build "equity" over the long haul, and the equity is generalized; fungible if you will, usable to continue membership, and to enjoy the fruits of the health of the Community being contributed to, including being repaid over time, as other members offer their service. Reciprocity in this view requires a strong Community of values, including a sense of fairness.

James Kouzes and Barry Posner take boundedness regarding reciprocity a step further. In their discussion of what it takes to foster collaboration, they point out the necessity for leaders to facilitate relationships with and among their comrades. To do so, leaders need to support "norms of reciprocity."[86] For Kouzes & Posner, reciprocity demonstrates a willingness to be cooperative, but also an unwillingness to be taken advantage of. This leads to predictability and stability in relationships. It's less stressful to work with others when you understand how they will behave in response. Members in Communities with reciprocity "understand they will be better off by cooperating...."[87]

Wow – Organizational Psychologists spend a lot of time exploring the influence of self-interest. Again, while there is credence to the notion that members need to trust that others will treat them in a reciprocal manner, and that building "credits" might allow them to be more influential, I harken back to our belief that we are motivated by more than self-interest. And we know how to reach into comrades to touch that collective- and vision-driven motivation.

Trust, reciprocity, and cooperation, yoked to the love of comrades, the collective and the living world are an unbeatable combination.
A core challenge as leaders is to struggle to tap into both.

Reciprocity then transcends mere transactional exchanges or social contracts regarding cooperation; reciprocity dovetails with and relies on a **culture** characterized by caring and trust (as does teamwork). At the risk of trying your patience, let me offer this as one more plug for the criticality of building and maintaining a healthy culture in your Community.

---

[85] Ulrich, D. (1998). Six Practices for Creating Communities of Value, Not Proximity. In F. Hesselbein et al. (Eds). Communities of the Future. San Francisco: Jossey-Bass, p. 161

[86] Kouzes, J. & Posner, B. (2012). The Leadership Challenge: How to Make Extraordinary Things Happen in Organizations (Fifth Ed.). San Francisco: Wiley, p. 232

[87] Ibid. p. 234

Portraits of Community Comradeship

The specifics of Comradeship-building efforts are limited only by the culture, creativity and traditions of the particular collective involved. Be smart in planning yours. Remember, Community-building efforts that address several components at once are going to give you a greater return for your time and resources.

How can you craft initiatives that address multiple components?
- It sounds obvious, but plan events with at least one Community component in mind.
- Where possible, frame the events to emphasize to everyone the goals you want to attain.
- Communicate the goals as part of your introduction, speeches, flyers advertising the events, etc.
- Keep in mind your ABCs: **Always Be Culture-building.**

As the following examples illustrate, you can build Comradeship and Consciousness together pretty easily.

The Native American History of Lacrosse[88]

With lacrosse surging in popularity across Minnesota, Twin Cities Native Lacrosse is reminding the Native community — and the state as a whole — how the game began. The essence of the pickup-style games centers around community, tradition — and fun. Before each game, players usually circle up and share why they came to play that day.

The traditional game is sometimes referred to as "the medicine game" for its ability to heal —physically, spiritually, and socio-emotionally.

"[A]s the larger community learns the history of the sport and develops a deeper appreciation for it, it starts to bring us together as a people of this land,"

When she's playing, she says, she feels connected to her culture, to who she is and how she wants to feel. "In the middle of the game," she says, "I just feel that this is where I'm supposed to be."

---

[88]   Eldred, S. (2022). The Native American History of Lacrosse. MplsStPl (online mag). https://mspmag.com/arts-and-culture/native-american-history-lacrosse/ Accessed Dec 30, 2022.

Snake Valley celebrates Tenth Annual Water Festival[89]

> *Aug 31 – Sept 3rd in Baker, NE: Friends and supporters of Snake Valley will gather in Baker, Nevada during Labor Day Weekend for the tenth annual Snake Valley Festival to celebrate and raise funds in support of community preservation. All are invited to join in.*
>
> *All proceeds from the festival events will benefit the Great Basin Water Network (www.greatbasinwater.net) to help protect the water and environment in eastern Nevada and the west desert of Utah.*
>
> *"The Festival helps Great Basin Water Network to keep water in Snake Valley," ….. "It's a fun way to raise awareness and money at the same time." An ice cream social at Baker Hall will kick off events Friday night. Saturday includes of a host of activities promising something for everyone. The day will begin with breakfast at Kerouac's Café in downtown Baker. The town parade, with a water theme, will start at 10 am and complete its circuit twice, lest any spectators blink and miss it.*

- - - - - - - - - - - - - - - - -

Comradeship is the center that must hold for Community to endure.

It is not enough for Community builders to rely on a mutual purpose (like social justice, for example) to keep members together. We've seen too many examples of the Left eating itself, and we need to counter that tendency in our collectives. We need to actively build Comradeship, not assume it will somehow happen by itself over time.

Comradeship-building serves another purpose, as we'll see when we discuss Leadership in a Community context. As a preview: Any group of people will over time naturally differentiate into splintering functions and factions unless Community builders invest in integrating mechanisms that keep members together and aligned. Community Leaders need to be able to provide these "centering" functions to keep the collective together and oriented toward a singular purpose. Guess what one of those mechanisms might be?

- - - - - - - - - - - - - - - - -

[89] Copelan, C. (2018). Snake Valley celebrates Tenth Annual Water Festival August 31 – September 3rd in Baker, Nevada. High Desert Advocate.
https://www.coyote-tv.com/2018/08/29/snake-valley-celebrates-tenth-annual-water-festival-august-31-september-3rd-in-baker-nevada/
Accessed Dec 30, 2022.

Building Comradeship

What can builders do to shore up this critical aspect of radical Communities?

Engage in "Relationship Work".
Make space and time for comrades to enjoy each other's company. Relationship Work is, "intentionally making the effort to reconnect themselves to each other". The best leaders take pains to balance task and relationship efforts. Take time at regular meetings, for example, to check in with each other, share stories and jokes, or offer sympathies and support.

Play! But make sure your play form is comfortable to all involved. Consider cultural differences that might make one form of play uncomfortable for some in the collective. And don't miss an opportunity to build culture in a play context. For example, you might want to ensure your games are not competitive; or if competitive, that competition is downplayed, unless there are good reasons to amp up that construct.

"Bowl together", to borrow from Putnam. Create opportunities for comrades to interact in common spaces or activities. Share meals where possible, e.g. Whenever and wherever you can, guarantee **face-to-face** interactions in place of email and other forms of time-lagged, isolating communications forms.

Engage in "Public Work".
Work together to create something of value, within your Community or with a larger collective or group of interest. Both forms have benefits. Intra-Community work helps improve the collective, while extra-Community work builds relationships, garners support, and may lead to valuable alliances. There are numerous forms either of these approaches might take, including service work, cleanup, voter registration drives, permaculture classes, and so on.

Be direct about building comradeship!
Make sure your **Community orientation** includes norms regarding cohesion, reciprocity, boundaries, and relationships. This may include social contracts new members are asked to commit to, and perhaps sign. You could, e.g., plan a rite of entry that enacts the norms of comradeship you hold comrades to. As a bonus, these rites or rituals can be fungible too – perhaps plan a rite of passage that recognizes the journey of someone from individual to Community comrade, from liberal to radical, etc.

Leverage **opportunities for dialog** among members about material issues concerning the Community. If by some chance you find yourself the hub of conversations among comrades, you may want back off from that position, intended or not. Practice being a good facilitator for meetings, gatherings, and social affairs, to make sure everyone gets to talk, and to encourage comrades to make small talk and big talk among themselves. Schedule opportunities for members to engage in conversations about the collective, so you have opportunities to practice that facilitator role or to delegate it to others.

Similarly, wherever possible, allow for **joint problem-solving, material work**. Sometimes, we find ourselves in leadership roles in the first place because we performed well in other roles. The danger that situation presents is that we might fall into the trap of micromanaging others, because we believe no one can do that job as well as we can. That management style doesn't just alienate comrades, it keeps them from working together with others and in the process strengthening their interpersonal bonds and trust. Consider delegating to others. You can ask someone to help you with that activity and / or ask two or more comrades to work together on projects. You can always monitor how things are going without getting your fingers in the pie.

Worksheet: Planning to Lead Your Community

Are your Community members more comrades-in-arms or casual acquaintances? How come?

How are you actively building comradeship in your collective? P.S. This is a process, not a one-time event.

So, **now** are you planning celebrations for your Community? This is your second warning.

CHAPTER 8

Building Community: Commitment

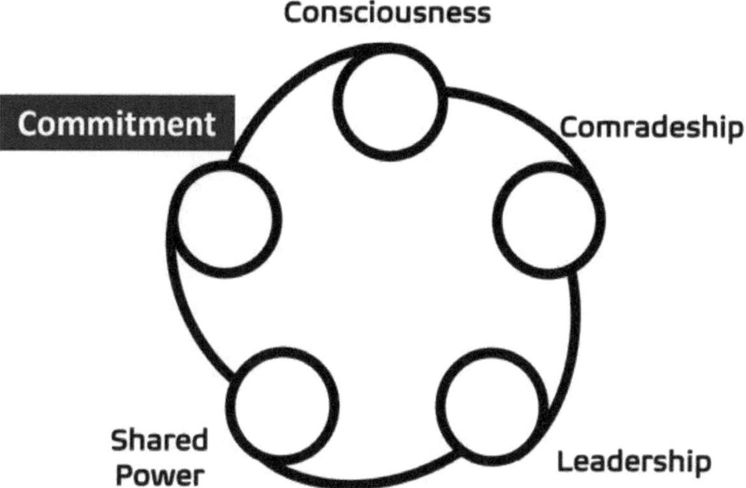

It's challenging enough for a radical Community to function as an intentional collective. The challenge is more profound when we struggle to achieve Deep Community, in which the attitudes and behaviors associated with maintaining and improving internal processes "have become so internalized they are second nature". To also progress to a radical, oppositional Community and continue to exist and thrive while beset by isolation, oppression, and repression, takes something special. We need commitment. And commitment takes several forms.

- - - - - - - - - - - - - - - - -

Commitment to Coexist.
In its most commonsense conceptualization, commitment involves a willingness to coexist; a promise, articulated or implied, to share in the development and maintenance of the collective, and to share whatever bounty it holds. Commitment is more than this, too – it is a wholehearted offering to guarantee others' safety, survival, and ability to thrive. For a radical Community, commitment involves a duty:

- To shield the collective from the invasive, destructive forces of the dominant culture and industrial civilization.
- To replenish and replace damages as they occur.

- To ensure others understand the history and context surrounding the threats as well as the values, purpose and capacities critical for the Community to protect, resist and survive (recall Community Consciousness).

This is an active commitment, not passive, as in "Live and let live". Commitment in a radical Community also means guiding or contributing to the Community's evolution beyond merely appositional to oppositional.

In the discussion of Consciousness, I offered the importance of cultivating Deep Community. Community builder Kazimierz Gozdz (1993):

"Community, in its basic form, involves a group of people who have committed themselves to a process of ever-deepening levels of communication. Such a group becomes capable of learning, self-reflective behavior, and the capacity to balance individual and group needs."[90]

A Community does not evolve, deepen, or successfully resist by dint of some collective magic: it does so because its members are committed to each other, to the Community, and to making things work.

Commitment to Exercise Discipline.

Willingness to coexist, to share in the development and maintenance of the Community, and to accept the obligation to shield others, are critical pledges and aspirations. To execute on these obligations, Community builders need more than a sense of obligation – they need the discipline to prepare and follow through on them. This is part of the role description of the Community Builder, as you'll recall. Gozdz (1993) expands:

"…community is a process rather than a state… commitment must be mustered in order to maintain it; only through purpose and discipline will the community process be maintained…."

Anyone who has been involved in building a Community or even an effective Cadre understands that success (by whatever measure) not only doesn't happen magically, it happens in the face of challenges and roadblocks – conflicts, changes to the mission or vision, external developments and sheer exhaustion all throw up roadblocks which must be overcome, and inertia itself is never enough to see Communities through. Elders, leaders, and "rank and file" members need to internalize the discipline to maintain positive movement.

In this regard, commitment means viewing Community building as a regimen, and willingness to see the process through its inevitable challenges, downturns,

---

[90] Gozdz, K. (1993). Building Community as a Leadership Discipline. In Michael Ray and Alan Rinzler (eds.) The New Paradigm in Business: Emerging Strategies for Leadership and Organizational Change. New York: J.P. Tarcher / Perigee, p. 111

frustrations, and reversals of fortune. It must be dispersed throughout the collective. We'll talk more momentarily.

"[Builders] have to hold the commitment and keep the process going, even though some in the group may become complacent."[91]

Gozdz' comments are borne from a business perspective, but they generalize beyond his intentions. He views commitment as it pertains to the organization's leadership group, but clearly to us, commitment must be dispersed throughout the Community. To emphasize an important point: Commitment is not just for the Builders/Elders. Conversely, Leaders in a Community **should have demonstrated commitment as a prerequisite to being chosen to guide the collective in the first place.**

Finally, wise Communities ensure their "leadership development system" doesn't just provide skills, but nurtures a love for the collective, maturity, and a commitment to all in its embrace. I'll expand on this in the Leadership Chapter.

Commitment to the Long-term Well-being of All.

Undertaking the hard work of creating or revitalizing a Community and dedicating efforts toward helping it evolve set the foundation for success – a Community epitomized by Capacity and Confidence, as we outline in the Communities that Protect and Resist Mission Statement. Missing to this point is the third facet, Continuity. CPR collectives must also focus on the long term.

"Lastly, the only way a community will succeed is if everyone involved is committed to the long-term wellbeing of the health of the group over an extended period of time. When I talk to individuals who are part of a healthy community they always express that preservation of the community and its continued wellbeing is their biggest commitment."[92]

In the strong view, a successful Community is by definition committed to the long term.

"Successful communities think as much about tomorrow as they do about today."[93]

Let's explore what this commitment means in practice. Commitment to the long term is especially important to the planet, not just to the Community. Radical Communities will serve as alternatives to the dominant culture, and will populate the planet with

---

[91]   Ibid. p. 114

[92]   https://www.womenlivingincommunity.com.what-is-community/

[93]   Morse, S. (1998). Five Building Blocks for Successful Communities. In F. Hesselbein et al. (Eds) Communities of the Future. San Francisco: Jossey-Bass, p. 234

just and sustainable forms of coexistence. To do that, they must outlast the dominant culture. And to do *that*, they must be oriented toward the long term.

Indigenous societies understand and appreciate the long view. The Seventh Generation notion describes just how "long-term" works.

> *The Seventh Generation takes its name from the Great Law of the Haudenosaunee, the founding document of the Iroquois Confederacy, the oldest living participatory democracy on Earth. It is based on an ancient Iroquois philosophy that: "In our every deliberation, we must consider the impact of our decisions on the next seven generations."*
>
> *… In all of your deliberations in the Confederate Council, in your efforts at law making, in all your official acts, self interest shall be cast into oblivion. Cast not over your shoulder behind you the warnings of the nephews and nieces should they chide you for any error or wrong you may do, but return to the way of the Great Law which is just and right. Look and listen for the welfare of the whole people and have always in view not only the present but also the coming generations, even those whose faces are yet beneath the surface of the ground — the unborn of the future Nation."*
>
> *This philosophy is not unique to just the Iroquois nation. Many Native American nations, tribes and other indigenous people around the world have and still live by this philosophy.*
>
> *Today, The Seventh Generation Principle usually applies to decisions about the energy we use, water and natural resources, and ensuring those decisions are sustainable for seven generations in the future.*
>
> *We should apply the Seventh Generation Principle to relationships – so that every decision we make results in sustainable relationships that last at least seven generations into the future.*[94]

This is long-term thinking and commitment. Our challenge is to put aside the short term, quarter-to-quarter orientation the dominant culture presents as strategic thinking, and consider how our actions, systems and decisions will effect our Community long into the future. You might guess, rightly, that this is easier said than done. In fact, it can't be done at all by single individuals – we have to rely on the collective wisdom and experience of Elders and respected allies to guide Communities this well and truly. What follows is an essential way to achieve and demonstrate long-term thinking.

---

[94] http://7genfoundation.org/7th-generation/

Commitment to the Development of Young People.
Effective Communities ensure young members internalize the values, history, and skills shared by all, and which are essential for the continuance of that collective.

> *"…mature members ensure that the young grow up with
> a sense of obligation to the community."*[95]

Of course. It's cliché to the point of ridicule that youth are the promise of the future, but it's true. For a Community to achieve Continuity and a capacity to endure, it must be able to revitalize and renew itself. Our Communities will never replace the dominant culture if they can't provide a continuing source of lifeblood – the renewal of a population committed to the collective and ready and willing to place collective interests over individual concerns.

The Community must be a place (material or virtual) where the young are nourished, guided, informed and bounded, by members at large and not only by the nearest relatives, acquaintances or friends. Youth must be ready and willing to take on the mantle of builders and Elders when their time comes to move the Community forward.

This is the "good pipeline". Forget generational gaps. They are overrated at best, and epiphenomenal at worst. Here's a social critic's take on generational issues:
> *"The children now love luxury; they have bad manners, contempt for authority;*
> *they show disrespect for elders and love chatter in place of exercise. Children are now*
> *tyrants, not the servants of their households. They no longer rise when*
> *elders enter the room. They contradict their parents, chatter before company,*
> *gobble up dainties at the table, cross their legs, and tyrannize their teachers."*
>
> [Guess Who][96]

The Zapatistas display their wisdom by preparing youth for leadership, as we saw. The collective has carried out training programs to prepare education promoters and develop curricula in collaboration with solidarity groups, non-governmental organizations (NGOs) and volunteers from outside, as well as in consultation with the local population.

- - - - - - - - - - - - - - - - - -

---

[95] Gardner, J. On Leadership. Highlighted summary of the book, published by Free Press, p. 118. Accessed August 2020.

[96] This quote is attributed to Socrates. Apparently, unhealthy Communities have been around for a while. More to the point, this "generation gap" issue has always been around, and never been around – while it's natural for youth to explore identities and boundaries, outright rejection of Community values results from a failure of the Elders and the Community at large to socialize and nurture their offspring.

Building Commitment

I've mentioned this approach before, but it bears repeating: Be Direct. Build Commitment Directly.

There's no need to finesse building commitment. As with building Cadres, Community builders can ask new members (in new or virtual Communities especially) to pledge to a social contract outlining roles, norms and expectations regarding how the collective operates and maintains order, justice, and sustainability. While this technique lacks romance, it can be effective. Don't ignore the obvious in building commitment.

Do Your Culture Work.

Social contracts can be an effective tool for guaranteeing commitment, but they rely on a degree of monitoring and enforcement that may be inefficient or distasteful to some. Better to rely on a more robust tack - a strong, healthy culture: From Shaffer and Anundsen:

> *"Chief among these [timeless qualities of communities] is commitment.*
> *Commitment...requires that community members embody ...*
> *timeless values as trust, honesty, compassion and respect."*[97]

Use your culture-building skills and practices to incorporate these values into your collective's culture. We've talked before about the critical role a Community's culture can play in, e.g., its Consciousness. Pay constant attention to cultivating a strong culture, centered on your core values.

Rites, rituals, heroes, myths, and stories all reinforce your values and culture. Don't relegate them to afterthoughts – use them as frontline guardians of your Community building. Culture-building activities that require work or sacrifice, for example, are particularly relevant and valuable. The Bat Mitzvah is one example of such a rite.

Do Your Vision Work.

Gozdz:

> *"A commitment to community ... has to be reflected in the framework that*
> *defines the very reason for ... existence. Some call this framework a 'purpose'.*
> *others call it ... 'mission'; still others, a 'vision'."*[98]

---

[97] Shaffer, C., & Anundsen, K. (2005). Creating Community Anywhere: Finding Support and Connection in a Fragmented World. Dillon Beach, CA: CCC Press, p. 10

[98] Gozdz, K. (1993). Building Community as a Leadership Discipline. In Michael Ray and Alan Rinzler (eds.) The New Paradigm in Business: Emerging Strategies for Leadership and Organizational Change. New York: J.P. Tarcher / Perigee, p. 115

By its very nature, an effective vision attracts commitment and energizes people (Kouzes & Posner). Comrades are eager to commit voluntarily and completely to something truly worthwhile, something that will make life better for others, or that represents a significant improvement for their Community, land or water. This commitment arises in part because an effective vision creates meaning in people's lives. Individuals see themselves as part of something unique, special, and valuable to the planet. And they are more likely to commit to helping that succeed and endure.

The vision for your Community should tap into core values shared by members. Incorporating the long view into the development of your vision is also critical. For one, it helps craft an effective, galvanizing vision. Second, this process supports the commitment to the long-term survival among Community members.

How is this done? Through utilizing the Janus effect (Kouzes and Posner):
> *"Looking into your past can reveal much about the future. … executives who were asked to think first about things that had happened to them in the past—before they thought about future possibilities—were subsequently able to extrapolate significantly further into the future than those who were asked to think first about things that might happen to them in the future.*
> *As a [Community Builder], your ability to look both to your past and your future for guidance opens up more possibilities than doing one or the other alone. When you gaze first into your past, you essentially elongate your future. You enrich your imagination about the future and give it detail as you recall the richness of your past experiences.*
> *Looking back enables you to better understand that the central, recurring themes [in your Community] didn't just materialize this morning. It's been there for a long time.*
> *Another benefit to looking back before looking ahead is that you gain a greater appreciation for how long it can take to fulfill aspirations. You also realize that there are many, many avenues to pursue."*[99]

Prepare the Next Generation(s) / Develop Your Youth.
One way to start is "unschooling" – removing youth from the toxic propaganda and obedience-oriented fire hose that passes for education. Instead, use schooling at home (even better, in the Community) to reinforce a material history of the Community, its values, and to build skills necessary for building, maintaining and protecting the collective.

---

[99]   Kouzes, J., & Posner, B. (2012). The Leadership Challenge: How to Make Extraordinary Things Happen in Organizations (Fifth Ed.). San Francisco: Wiley, adapted from p. 107-108)

Provide Community youth with real opportunities to build skills, learn leadership and teamwork, and express Community values through practical tasks, duties, and roles. You might think of these as internships, or more prosaically, chores!

Broaden the developmental experience beyond immediate family. Youth are better prepared by being exposed to (and mentored by) the Community as a collective, with its greater wisdom and experience, and greater capacity to monitor and guide.

Worksheet: Planning to Lead Your Community

Does your Community display any of the forms of commitment I discuss in this chapter? What's lacking?

Is your collective's vision compelling enough to engender commitment? How might you strengthen it?

Are young people an integral part of your Community and its future? If they are, how do you nurture commitment in them? If they are not, what measures can you take to change that? Consider recruitment, a change to your mission or vision, and other practices.

CHAPTER 9

Building Community: Shared Power

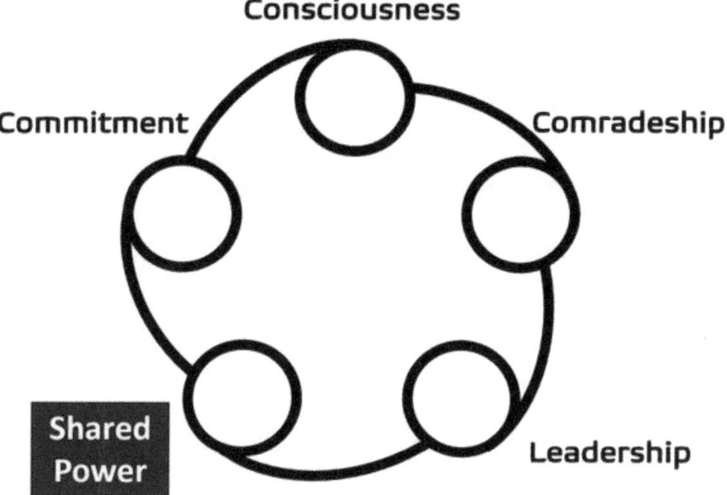

Earlier I introduced the Rojava communes and their savvy approach to building Community Consciousness. Their governing document addresses other practices for building strong CPR collectives as well:

> ***Article One:***
>
> *The commune is … established on the principle of direct democracy, woman's freedom and ecology between the people, and … it adopts the realization of democratic choices that are developed on the level of the foundation. And **all have the right to participate at all levels and all components,** individuals and organizations have the right to participate in **them and the right to ratify, discuss, offer opinions and establish communes** particular to them, **and they possess power and autonomous decisions,** aiming to build a free, democratic and ethical political society relying on itself in administering itself by itself and taking decisions and resolving problems concerned with it.*[100] *[Emphases added]*

- - - - - - - - - - - - - - - -

---

[100] Jawad Al-Tamimi, A. J., 2018. The Internal System of the Communes in Rojava. Cooperation in Mesopotamia. https://www.aymennjawad.org/2018/04/the-internal-system-of-the-communes-in-rojava

Community is sharing. This is not merely an *aspect* of a strong Community; it's more or less a definition. At the very least, Community *implies* sharing. As a starting point, consider the Merriam-Webster English Language Learners Definition of *commune* (Entry 2 of 2): a group of people who live together and share responsibilities, possessions, etc. The devil, as they say, is in the details. Here, it's in the "etc.". What more could there be to share besides responsibilities and possessions? And what aspects of sharing make a collective a CPR collective?

CPR collectives offer an aggregated level of force of and for resisters unlike any others. These collectives are a major source of strength to resist and dismantle the dominant culture. **They may be our only real source of power.** We need to leverage their potential more than we have. Let's not put the cart before the horse, however. For collectives to be effective as sources of power for resistance **externally**, they first need to be strong (powerful) **internally**. We need to talk about power within collectives. CPR collectives are strong because they share power.

The dictionary definition of Community highlights the importance of sharing, but it serves best as a conceptual foil. "Shared possessions" are immaterial in characterizing a CPR collective. I abhor the consumerist ethos that taints this toxic culture, and how and when possessions are shared make little difference in whether a Community serves to Protect and Resist. Rather than conceptualize a sharing algorithm describing who gets what stuff, let's agree that if your Community is truly committed to resisting the dominant culture, you'll minimize possessions as a rule, and share essentials like food, shelter, and social support.

Instead, mainstream writers on Community building generally focus on **practices** when discussing sharing as a critical characteristic. Rather than possessions, e.g., sharing *practices* seems a more effective avenue, and one scholars on Community agree on for the most part. Shaffer & Anundsen list "participate in common practices" as a basic building block of Community, as do Briand, and Morse. Whether and how a collective shares in the first place determines, according to Shaffer & Anundsen, whether that collective is a Full Community or merely a Proto-community. For example, "Breadth" consists of how many facets of life members share (such as personal information and aid in times of crisis), while "Depth" is how deeply and thoroughly members share.

What, then, do effective radical Communities share in the way of these ambiguous "practices"? A useful way to capture the essence and scope of these practices is under the concept of power.

Understanding Shared Power.

There's an element of common sense to this sharing notion, and it comes from the mainstream leadership literature. Kouzes & Posner, for example, explain that effective leaders continually develop comrades and cultivate their confidence and self-efficacy. They strengthen others by **sharing power and discretion**. When leaders coach, educate, enhance self-determination and otherwise share power, they demonstrate profound trust in and respect for others' abilities.

In turn, **shared power enables others to develop greater individual capacity, self-efficacy, and persistence**. They are, and feel, more powerful and able to make things happen on their own. These capacities lead to a Community in which members are committed to the joint vision, are more capable of struggling for it, and able to collaborate with others in that pursuit. This is one reason why I refer to effective leadership as a force multiplier, and a fundamental component of an effective Community.

When we share power at the individual level, we become more powerful at the Community level.

Shared Power is Shared Decision Making.

Foremost among the shared aspects of a Full Community is the decision-making process. Shaffer & Anundsen list "inclusive decision making" as a prerequisite for individuals who want to build Community. Perhaps this reflects the significance of sharing power among members of the collective. It's not unreasonable to assert that shared decision-making is shared power.

In Mattesich & Monsey's model of effective Community, success relies on the "Ability to discuss, reach consensus, and cooperate."[101] Critical activities in such collectives "offer community members the opportunity to practice open dialogue, develop trust, and increase group decision-making skills." Michael Briand's "fundamental task" for every Community is "how to make decisions that lead to actions that are effective."[102] Among the principles Briand invokes in this pursuit are **Inclusion** – "involving not just people who have a clear stake in the matter at hand, but also those 'ordinary folks', those members of the 'silent majority'."[103] Briand understands that to be effective, a Community's decision-making process must include **participation** by all [members].

Suzanne Morse lists "Mechanisms for Deciding" (dialogue and deliberation) to find the common good as an element of the framework of successful Communities of this

[101]   Mattesich, P. & Monsey, B. (1997). Community Building: What Makes it Work. Saint Paul, MN: Amherst H. Wilder Foundation, p. 24

[102]   Briand. M. (und.). A Practical Guide to a Community that Works, p. 20

[103]   Ibid. p. 23

century. Kouzes & Posner talked about trust in interpersonal leadership: Morse makes the same point for Communities:

> *"involving people in the decisions that affect their lives is not only*
> *good civic business but a critical way to build trust,*
> *relationships, and networks among citizens."*[104]

A challenge, per Morse, is to **develop a social infrastructure to ensure an accessible community life**, to connect neighborhoods and the people within them to each other and to the larger civic life. (For the attentive reader: you're already gathering action items for building shared power!) This accessibility means inclusion, and the practices that allow every Community member to participate in the direction of her or his Community.

More from the Rojava Commune:

> ***Article Two:***
> *[The commune] is considered among the most important components of the democratic society system in order to revive direct democracy, and relies on the principle of **collective, joint communal participation**. And the communes of the neighborhoods and villages are composed of the **participation of all citizens living in them** ... without discrimination between ethnicity, religion and affiliation. And they adopt their decisions publicly and **with the participation of all the citizens of the commune who are older than 16.***
> [Emphases added]

Shared decision-making is not limited to the board room or administrative rulings, or even Town Hall-type gatherings. In the Zapatista Community, there are popular banks in the form of revolving funds that make low-interest loans to members of the Community. These banks generate funds that get invested in new collective projects. Some collectives are women-only and intend to provide an opportunity for women to gain confidence and participate in the social life of their Communities.

Inclusive decision-making (which relies on active and deep listening) maximizes the opportunities for the Community's collective wisdom and collective memory to express itself and generate wider support. I can't take issue with this! I wish, though, to extend the argument a bit.

Shared Power is Justice.
In a CPR collective, when power is shared, all members, human and otherwise, exert power simply by being in the natural order. Members exercise the ability and freedom

---

[104]   Morse, S. (1998). Five Building Blocks for Successful Communities. In F. Hesselbein et al. (Eds) Communities of the Future. San Francisco: Jossey-Bass.

to interact with and among others in a way that allows each to "mutually exist, flourish, regenerate, and naturally evolve."[105]

Shared power and justice are everyone's right, but there is an obligation implied in this communal affiliation. Members do not simply bask in power and freedom - while they enjoy the fruits of this order, **they are also held to uphold** it, as responsible members and Community guardians. The assertion that each Community member is gifted with this capacity (and accountable for this responsibility) seems a form of **distributive justice,**[106] in which "resources" are allocated justly.

In our perspective on this, I borrow from Elizabeth Anderson:
> *"the positive aim of egalitarian justice is…to create a community in which [members] stand in relation of equality to others"*[107]

One more excerpt from Rojava:
Article Nine:
1. All citizens of the commune are equal before the law.
2. Every individual in the commune has a right to participate in political and societal life.
5. Every individual in the commune has the right to participate in the elections and candidacy at all levels.

What must a member do to merit power, and in the process, justice? It's not complicated; as long as one is willing to cooperate with members according to these expectations, one is entitled to their benefits. This is a tenet of the philosophy of justice outlined by John Rawls.[108] This willingness to cooperate is articulated in the Rojava Commune governing document, and their vision includes more than a willingness - it declares an **obligation** to do so:
Article Ten:
*1. Every member in the commune **must undertake obligations and missions of enlightenment** and participate in the democratic life and elections.*
2. Participating in building the ethnical, cooperative and communal society.
*3. The commune must have special training programs and it is the **responsibility of ever[y] individual** and member in the commune to take up ideological and thought training.*
4. Every individual in the commune must deal with the people and society without discriminating between ethnicity, religion and affiliation. (Emphases added)

---

[105] Falk, W. (2019). How Dams Fall: On Representing the Colorado River in the First-ever American Lawsuit Seeking Rights for a Major Ecosystem. Little Bound Books, p. 51

[106] See, e.g., Sandel, M. (2009). Justice: What's the Right Thing to Do? New York: Farrar, Straus & Giroux.

[107] Anderson, E. (1999). What is the Point of Equality?. Chicago Journals: Chicago University Press, pp. 288–289.

[108] Sandel, M. (2009). Justice: What's the Right Thing to Do? New York: Farrar, Straus & Giroux.

Here's an example of how a Community that shares power with e.g., women, benefits.

*"The Water and Development Alliance (WADA) released research findings revealing the compelling link between safe, clean water access and women's empowerment. Globally, while women remain those most deeply impacted by the lack of access to clean water, they are least likely to control or manage water infrastructure. Water is a key lever for advancing women's rights, well-being, and opportunity. **Ensuring women's participation and opportunity to design and manage water access allows them to ensure their own protection and livelihood, and leverages this simple investment for exponential ripples of impact.***

In locations in Rwanda and Uganda where water accessibility is limited, Global Grassroots helps undereducated women to design, construct, and implement their own water solutions that improve safety, health, and educational and economic opportunities for women and girls. By implementing their own non-profit enterprises, these women demonstrate their value to their communities, realize their leadership potential and, using our unique methods, build inclusive and sustainable local institutions that foster greater collective stability.

*Women who manage their own clean water access not only ensure the most vulnerable women and girls are no longer subjected to the violence and exploitation inherent in water collection, but also enable girls' access to education. **The opportunity for women to lead fosters greater confidence, self-efficacy, and engagement in their communities as change agents.** Over time, their leadership and value to their communities shift gender relations, roles, and behavior.*

*Further, women-led water infrastructure provides women with significant time savings, allows a sustainable source of income for their own livelihood, and generates revenue that they will invest in other urgent needs facing the community. Our experience has shown that **one successful experience as a change agent is quickly followed by expansion and / or an iterative problem-solving process where women take on the other challenges in their communities.** [Emphases added]*

When women lead, communities succeed."[109]

- - - - - - - - - - - - - - - - -

[109] http://www.globalwaterchallenge.org/blog/when-women-lead-communities-succeed

A more radical (fundamental) perspective on justice comes from the Rights of Nature (RoN) movement. As the Community Environmental Legal Defense Fund (CELDF) describes the construct, and the movement:

> *"Environmental degradation is advancing around the world. The United Nations has warned that we are heading toward "major planetary catastrophe." For this reason, there is a growing recognition that we must fundamentally change the relationship between humankind and nature.*
> *Making this fundamental shift means acknowledging our dependence on nature and respecting our need to live in harmony with the natural world. It means securing the highest legal protection and the highest societal value for nature through the recognition of nature's rights."*[110]

CELDF has worked with the first U.S. Communities and the first country to establish the rights of nature in law – recognizing the rights of ecosystems and natural communities to exist and thrive, and empowering people and their governments to defend and enforce these rights.[111] What the Rights of Nature movement recognizes is that Communities have the right, and obligation, to protect all life within their respective collectives. In our model, this means **ensuring that all forms of life are granted power**. What CELDF and other organizations do is take this philosophy a step further by working to instill in Communities the power to resist, from a legal orientation, the dominant culture's toxicity and extractive ideology.

Shared Power is the Absence of Class.

"Class", whether sex, race, or socioeconomic status, e.g., is a social construction used to label, demonize, extract from, and oppress others. Class is about power. In this sense, it is about denying power to oppressed groups for the benefit of oppressor classes. "Class" allows oppressors to dominate, to steal entire Communities and landbases.

This confession from a former cop (an enforcer of class domination) underscores how class serves to delineate the powerful from the oppressed:

> *"What I'm telling you is that the system we have right now is broken **beyond repair** and that it's time to consider new ways of doing community together. Those new ways need to be negotiated by members of those communities, particularly Black, indigenous, disabled, houseless, and citizens of color historically shoved into the margins of society. Instead of letting Fox News fill your head with nightmares about Hispanic gangs, ask the Hispanic community what they need to thrive. Instead of letting racist politicians scaremonger about pro-Black demonstrators, ask the Black community what they need to meet the needs of the most vulnerable. **If you truly desire safety,***

[110] https://celdf.org/advancing-community-rights/rights-of-nature/
[111] https://www.facebook.com/pg/CELDF/about/?ref=page_internal

> *ask not what your most vulnerable can do for the community, ask what the community can do for the most vulnerable.* ["112] [Emphases added]

What may be lost in this statement is that it's not a vague, New Age appeal for shared power – it's a recognition that in the real world, **Communities that share power are safer.** Mariame Kaba of Chicago Incite! complements this perspective:

> *"We believe that at its roots, violence against women is based in and relies on the maintenance of oppressions, including but not limited to colonialism, racism, sexism, … imperialism, …, and classism that cannot be separated because they work in concert to reinforce each other. Hence, we are committed to ending violence by confronting and dismantling all of these systems of oppression."*[113]

- - - - - - - - - - - - - - - -

In the event readers believe these calls for dismantling are pie-in-the-sky, childish dreams of a reality that will not work, consider that there have been uncounted Communities, over thousands of years, that thrived without patriarchal governance. A recent account, "6 Matriarchal Societies That Have Been Thriving With Women at the Helm for Centuries", provides a brief introduction to Communities in which women generally oversee everything from politics, economics, and the broader social structure.[114]

But over the course of history, societies across the globe started to bend towards a more patriarchal structure, which is pervasive in most communities in modern times. However, there are still surviving matriarchal societies to be found where women, literally, are the dominant steering factor in all matters, social, political, and economical.

The Communities: Mosuo, China; Bribri, Costa Rica; Umoja, Kenya; Minangkabau, Indonesia; Akan, Ghana; and Khasi, India. You might argue that since these Communities are generally overseen by women that there is in fact not an erasure of class. I'd respond first that a matriarchal Community is a giant first step away from the patriarchal dominant culture and worthy of pursuit on its own merits. Second, note the Akan Community is in fact not purely "matriarchal" in the sense of being dominated solely by women.

---

[112]   Cab, A. (2020). Confessions of a Former Bastard Cop.
https://medium.com/@OfcrACab/confessions-of-a-former-bastard-cop-bb14d17bc759
[113]   https://www.transformativejustice.eu/wp-content/uploads/2010/11/communities_engaged.pdf, p. 13
[114]   Madaus, S. (2019). 6 Matriarchal Societies That Have Been Thriving With Women at the Helm for Centuries. Town and Country Mag.
https://www.townandcountrymag.com/society/tradition/g28565280/matriarchal-societies-list/

"[T]he social organization of the Akan people is built around the matriclan. Within the matriclan, identity, inheritance, wealth, and politics are all decided. As the name would have it, matriclan founders are female. However, it must be noted that with in the Akan Matriclan, men do hold leadership positions."[115]

There is a stronger position to be made. As Heide Goettner-Abendroth's work (2012; und.) indicates, a Matriarchal society is not "just a reversal of patriarchy, with women ruling over men". Rather, they are gender-egalitarian societies, meaning they have **no hierarchies, classes, or domination of one gender by the other.**[116]

But equality means more than just a leveling of differences, according to Goettner-Abendroth. Instead, the natural differences between women and men and the generations are respected and honored, without using them as justifications to create hierarchies, as generally occurs in patriarchies. There seems a clear inference, particularly with regard to sex:

"Classless" Communities work.

Other Communities are working to realize this vision for a just future. We talked earlier about the Women's Liberation Front (WoLF), an intentional Community. WoLF is at the same time a form of oppositional Community; it is a radical feminist organization dedicated to the total liberation of women. WoLF fights to end male violence, regain reproductive sovereignty, and ultimately dismantle the gender-caste system.[117]

For Communities to effectively Protect and Resist, they must leverage power. That power already exists in its members, and it needs only to be identified, and freed. We can do this by sharing decision-making, sharing power, and dismantling class.

- - - - - - - - - - - - - - - -

---

[115] Ibid.
[116] Goettner-Abendroth, H. (2012). Matriarchal Societies: Studies on Indigenous Cultures across the Globe. New York: Peter Lang Publishing.
[117] http://womensliberationfront.org

Building Shared Power

Deconstruct class in your Community.
Leverage the power of education we encountered in several CPR collectives to this point. Educate yourself and all members on what class means and how it has been used to oppress and extract in the name of the dominant culture.
Actively ensure all members enjoy full membership and equal status in your collective. Building Community Consciousness will move you along this path. You may need to audit your structures, processes and systems (as a group) to uncover hidden or unintended injustices or inequities.

Drive "classlessness" deep into your Community culture.
Use effective leadership practices, establish supportive and consistent rites and rituals, stories, and heroes. Share power in the ways described here.

Construct or revise your social infrastructure.
Ensure all members have equal access to information, deliberation, and decision making. If you rely on digital social media, for example, many members will not be able to participate in these activities. Instead, wherever possible convene sessions that involve those activities in public spaces that allow for face-to-face interaction, or guarantee that disadvantaged members can participate by providing transportation, equipment, or other resources as necessary. Do not assume members will be able to access whatever mechanisms you set up.

Explore alternative cultures that share power freely.
Emulate their structures and practices consistent with your collective's circumstances.

Form your own Matriarchal Society.
This may be a bridge too far for some, but Matriarchal societies have so much to offer CPR collectives that you should at least undertake a study of their principles and practices. Should you be interested, here is a strategic step-by-step plan which is reasonable to undertake under current societal conditions. Note this is only possible with women centering the process.[118]

Review your mechanisms for deciding.
If you discover your governing bodies are primarily comprised of men, or upper socioeconomic class members, or white members, and these characteristics do not represent the vast majority of your Community members, you are doing something wrong.

---

[118] Goettner-Abendroth, H. (2007). The Way into an Egalitarian Society. https://www.hagia.de/fileadmin/user_upload/pdf/the_way.pdf

Don't stop with guaranteeing power for human members.
Understand, appreciate and materially protect the natural world in which your Community is embedded. Rights of Nature suits are a start. I'm not optimistic regarding the success rate for this approach, but in general such work does raise consciousness in a Community regarding the living world, and can lead to greater advocacy and resistance work.

Listen to what your land needs, and act to protect it.
The Rights of Nature movement will help you understand the rationale for this, but legal remedies are insufficient, and they are easily discarded by the dominant culture when it is convenient for them to do so. Be ready to defend your land with your life, because without the land, you are dead anyway.

Invest in developing "prosaic" skills.
Develop effective listening, conflict management, trust-building, effective messaging, and the like. Practice them, with all members, including non-human residents of your Community. Ensure all voices are heard.

Worksheet: Planning to Lead Your Community

To what extent do all members of your Community share in decision-making? Not every decision can or should be shared among all, but are those that effect the Community and its future, and /or the material existence of its members, available to be made by all?

If not, what adjustments might you make?

Would some members of your Community opine that there are "class distinctions" within your Community?

How do you know, if you haven't asked? And if such comrades exist, you'd better start a conversation with them!

What structures, systems or processes in your Community keep Power from being shared as widely as it should?

Again, how do you know? Who can help you figure that out, and make necessary changes?

CHAPTER 10

Building Community:
Community Leadership

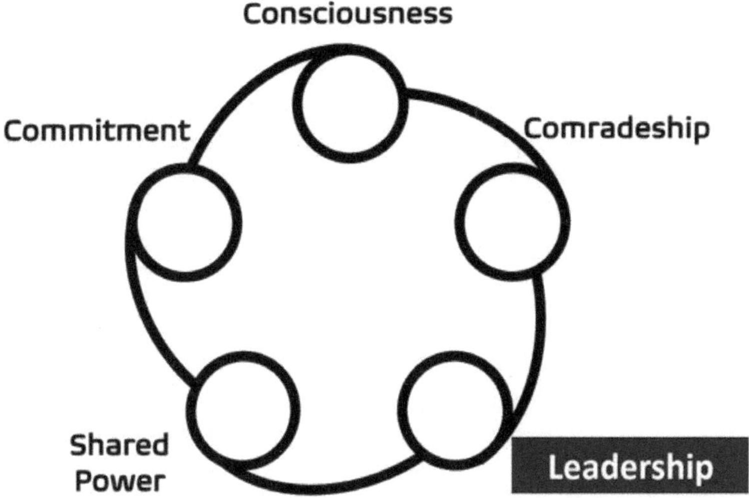

In the first chapter I introduced the practice of basic interpersonal leadership. Let's take a moment to refresh ourselves on the notion, and then transition to what leadership looks like in the Community context.

Leadership is essential for the Resistance movement to have a realistic chance to succeed. Our struggles aren't as effective as they need to be to save the planet, and the barriers are due not only the enormity of the problem (industrial civilization), but also to issues very much in our control, such as recruitment, activist turnover, and commitment.

Effective leadership in the Resistance can go a long way toward overcoming our internal barriers (in other words, we can build leadership into a strategic Strength, for its own sake and to counter our Weaknesses.)

What does effective leadership do for us, that make it such a valuable asset for activists and Community builders?

The Basics: Leadership Inspires.
John Gardner declared, "we are anxious but immobilized" by immensely threatening problems. What we need in the Resistance and CPR-type Community building is the capacity to focus our energies and a capability to build sustained commitment. This is a call for leadership, beginning with a reminder from Kouzes & Posner:

**Leadership is the art [and practice] of mobilizing others to
want to struggle for shared aspirations.**

I detailed the practices that allow Resistance members to exercise effective leadership, and outlined a process for anyone involved in this work to become a better leader. I use this model because it fits in the relatively non-hierarchical environments we often see in resistance work, where we rely on volunteers to do the work and take the risks to save the planet. In Resistance and collective-building, activists taking on leadership roles often are asked to inspire comrades who do not work for them *per se*.

Gardner:
*"… in a tumultuous, swiftly changing environment, in a world of multiple,
colliding systems, the hierarchical position of leaders within their own system is of
limited value, because some of the most critically important tasks require
lateral leadership – boundary-crossing leadership – involving groups over whom they
have no control…. They must do what they can to lead without authority"*[119]

I urge comrades working on building CPR collectives to make it a point to develop leadership skills and get in touch with your values and those of your Community. Leadership is the force multiplier that allows us to protect and resist with greater efficiency, effectiveness, and sustainability than we might otherwise bring to bear, against the dominant culture.

- - - - - - - - - - - - - - - -

This basic, mainstream model of leadership works in small groups, in Cadres, and in larger groups, including organizations and Communities. It's scalable, you could say. But a Community, especially a CPR collective, is more than just a vanilla group or organization, as we typically know these forms. This qualitative difference requires an approach to leadership that western leadership theories don't necessarily provide.

My model of the "levels" of leadership in resistance (below) indicates there is more involved in functioning as a Community Leader/Elder than the other roles I discussed to this point. In this chapter I touch on what makes one an Elder, and provide a sense for how to prepare yourself or others for that responsibility.

---

[119] Gardner, J. On Leadership. Highlighted summary of the book, published by Free Press. Accessed August 2020, p. 98

The Changing Role(s) of Resistance Leader			
Context	Role(s)		
Basic Leadership for Resistance (LFR)	Model / Modeler		
Leading Resistance Cadres (LRC)	Model / Modeler	Professional / Linchpin	
Leading Communities of Resistance (LCOR)	Model / Modeler	Professional / Linchpin	Land Defender / Protector / Elder

- - - - - - - - - - - - - - - -

Beyond Inspiration: Community Leadership

Leadership Centers, Directs, Sustains.
Harken back to my meeting with a Native American Elder in Nevada. In his humble way, he responded to my query about whether he was a Chief with, "That's a big word." As I mentioned, nothing better exemplifies the challenges of Community Leadership. In the previous chapters I outlined four of the five components of an effective CPR collective. One challenge for Community Builders, Leaders, and Elders is to craft and assemble these building blocks to construct, repair, or maintain an effective CPR collective.

The next challenge is to provide the leadership necessary to guide your collective. That is the focus of this discussion. Building Community, particularly a CPR Collective, is challenging on a good day. Nurturing Community Consciousness, Comradeship (Social Cohesion), Commitment, and Shared Power involves vision, purpose, and sustained energy, as well as large doses of wisdom and compassion.

These gains can be fleeting – they're subject to hazards, external and internal. *External* threats and obstacles might take the form of government oppression, disastrous economic or social upheaval, widespread cultural rejection, disease, or any number of other factors that either distract from the core functions of the Community, pull members away, or worse. *Internal* forces and phenomena, too, serve to fractionate collectives and blunt their progress, as we'll see in the next chapter. "Inspirational" leadership helps us leverage our energies to counter these threats. There's a more insidious threat we have to assess and respond to, however.

"Drift" and Community Leadership.
It's natural for individuals in any group or organization to drift into unique behaviors, languages, cultures and values. "Drift" in this sense merely means unregulated changing or evolution of those constructs.

I first became aware of this phenomenon when I taught Organizational Psychology. A text I used to prepare for the course described how the policy used by a supervisor to make performance ratings might evolve over time into a policy that did not reflect that of the larger organization. This generally happened without conscious effort on the rater's part, in some measure because humans actively interact behaviorally and cognitively with their environment, reframe and restructure their experiences and memories, and so on. Sometimes, too, changes just occur due to random thoughts or actions that "stick" and become the norm or habit.

The thing to consider for leadership is that in this organizational example, rating policies drift when raters are not refreshed or reminded of the larger organizational policy. Keep this in mind.

Let's continue! You've probably noticed on your own some form of drift:
- In the American Northeast and many other locations, identifiably different accents occur within just a few miles of each other.
- Isolated families develop unique language components and gestures.
- Offices within larger organizations develop unique (and sometimes counterproductive) ways of doing business, or change their direction or scope of responsibilities. This phenomenon is so prevalent it's been given a label: Mission Creep.
- Even animals of the same species have been known to develop distinct cultures when separated in some way.

Drift is just a byproduct of our constant and active interactions with our world or random fluctuations that become lasting. It occurs at all levels of organizing, from the rater/supervisor/leader to the organization and beyond.

In fact, drift influences collective as large as the nation-state. Beyond language accents, there is some evidence that in the U.S. for example, various geographic and social groups are drifting apart with respect to their collective values. Researchers suggest the United States is becoming more culturally divided across racial, gender, income, religious, geographic and political lines in some indices, and that some divisions have been rising since the early 2000s.[120] This altering of a society, with its unique traditions, morals, and behavioral trends, in time is commonly referred to as **culture drift**.[121] It's interesting that Balkanization occurs like this, even given the presence of mass media and other forces that ostensibly keep us all connected.

An important proviso: We've been treating drift like it's a monolithic threat to collectives of all sorts. It's not necessarily so:

> *"Culture drift can be positive: It's part of being an agile organization. What's vital is that leaders keep their finger on the pulse of their culture to ensure their culture evolves in a direction that supports what matters most to their organization. Perhaps most importantly, leaders need to **go beyond talking about culture. It takes intentionality and long-term dedication** to build a resilient culture that inspires people globally. No organization is immune to disruption and the consequential culture drift – and only leaders can control it."[122]* [Emphases added]
>
> *"Is your culture … succumbing to drift? If you want exceptional alignment – where employees not only understand your vision, but also align their behavior with that vision – you must make culture a long-term priority. The question isn't if your culture has drifted, but where and how.*
> *It's up to leaders to determine which shifts are beneficial and which are detrimental."*

The business world understands drift. We need to as well.

Drift really is just a form of evolution. This active interaction and adaption to the world can be healthy, as it allows us to evolve and change to shifting circumstances and to circumstances that may take on less sanguine forms. The trick for Community leaders is to recognize what's changing, determine whether the changes are healthy and adaptive or not, and to understand what to do to make changes if required. Unintended changes can be healthy for a collective, as might give rise to social, organizational or other innovations that serve the collective well. Leaders need to be vigilant regarding their emergence, as they can be a source of collective power and sustenance, but also because drift can wreak havoc.

How do you know if the drift you're observing is healthy? Here are two rules of thumb to contemplate: Is the drift consistent with your collective's core values? Is it

[120] Wacziarg, R., & Desmet, K. (2018). Are Americans Drifting Apart Culturally? https://www.promarket.org/2018/07/12/americans-drifting-apart-culturally/

[121] N., Sam M. "CULTURAL DRIFT," in *PsychologyDictionary.org*, April 7, 2013, https://psychologydictionary.org/cultural-drift/ (accessed November 15, 2023)

[122] Kar, R., Watkinson, A., & Nelson, B. (2022). How to Steer a Drifting Culture. https://www.gallup.com/workplace/397034/steer-drifting-culture.aspx

aligned with your collective's mission and vision? If the answer to one or both of these is "no", you might have to reverse or halt that drift. Be open, though, to the possibility that the drift you observe is due to something in your environment or collective that has changed and necessitated alterations to the way you interact or do business. Work with comrades to uncover the relevant issues at play and be willing to adapt your collective as necessary.

There are two forms of negative drift, each of which can be quite devastating for a Community. Collectively, the Community can drift from its initial focus or vision / mission. "Mission Creep" captures the essence of this phenomenon. If your collective's focus was on saving the living planet and/or protecting its land or waters, and somehow loses sight of that, we all lose. "Money changes everything" epitomizes a subset of this danger. I wonder how many collectives which became NGOs or pursued funding found themselves later driven to satisfy funders to the detriment or complete disregard of their initial goals.

At a lower level of aggregation, individuals or small groups within a larger collective might drift from the collective's direction. They might find themselves veering away from the vision that brought them together in the first place, or toward relationships with the land or other groups that serve to threaten the integrity and survival of the collective. While differentiation (drift)[123] is a natural and sometimes adaptive occurrence, if left alone it will fracture or diffuse focus and energy, and weaken a collective's integrity.

Resistance collectives are not immune to drift. McBay[124] lists one of the dangers to resistance movements as factionalism, in which a movement breaks into divided fragments. McBay cites the Sandinistas, who at one point in their struggles split into three "feuding tendencies". Make no mistake; although several factors may have played a role in this fragmentation, intra-collective drift seems a driving force.

- - - - - - - - - - - - - - - -

Collectives need to guard against drift. But it's not complicated to do so.
For the Collective to succeed and survive, leadership must strike a balance between naturally occurring differentiation (drift) and centering the collective, via integrating practices and structures. Integrating mechanisms bring and keep groups together in a social or cultural way. In organizational terms, integration is "the process of achieving unity of effort" toward accomplishing larger goals. Whether we talk about families, groups, organizations, or Communities, this tendency to scatter, disperse, or drift must

---

[123] Lawrence, P., and Lorsch, J. (1967). "Differentiation and Integration in Complex Organizations" Administrative Science Quarterly 12, 1-30.
[124] McBay, A. (2019a). Full Spectrum Resistance, Volume One: Building Movements and Fighting to Win. New York: Seven Stories Press.

be countered by forces that keep the collective together and moving in the same direction.

The Sandinistas, which experienced fragmentation, eventually reunited. McBay quotes a Sandinistan leader's reflection that, "we were all more or less still Sandinist. That was our common heritage and it did unite us." (p. 207) Community leaders, here's a powerful example and reminder of the importance of emphasizing common heritage as part of your culture work, particularly as part of constructing your Community Consciousness and Comradeship. In so doing, you'll not only be assembling a strong radical Community in its own right, you'll also be guarding against unhealthy internal drift / fragmentation.

Integrating systems and centering practices are the metaphorical glue that maintains a sort of corporal integrity for the collective.
Leadership applies the glue.

What do these practices look like? Very much like the practices we've already discussed. Note how some of the practices McBay recommends map onto our model:
- A shared cultural identity (Consciousness)
- Inclusive decision-making and discussion (Shared Power)
- Sharing resources to avoid conflict (the Justice aspect of Shared Power)
- Some degree of central coordination where appropriate (ok, that's just good management).

- - - - - - - - - - - - - - - - -

Not only are Communities subject to drift, they also risk experiencing **"organizational entropy"** – the winding down of energy among members of the Collective. Too many of our groups start out with enthusiasm and passion for their articulated or perceived purpose or mission, only to grind to a halt or die a slow death over months or years. CPR collectives can't afford to allow our collective energy to wane, because our obligation to resist the dominant culture and replace toxic social forms with more healthy and sustainable systems cries out for more.

We have no choice but to focus, persevere, and win. Leadership impels us to keep moving in the direction laid out by the mission and vision, on our collective Community path. Community Leadership is an essential guard against threats to Community identity, integrity (wholeness), and viability. Community Leadership centers, directs, and sustains.

Leadership holds a collective together, facilitates collective direction and purpose, and sustains collective, coordinated efforts related to survival, protection and resistance and movement toward thriving in a just and sustainable relationship with the land and waters.

For a Community to continue to exist in a recognizable form, to be able to act as a collective, the center must hold. Community Leadership is an essential source of this centering.

Don't despair. In addition to the practices that counter drift, here are some best practices Community leaders can tap into, to counter drift and entropy. You know these already!

- Effective interpersonal leadership. Facilitating a shared vision for the Community, building and cultivating a strong and healthy culture, encouraging comradeship, and involving and encouraging comrades to do well.
- Cadre leadership principles.
- The forms of leadership I discuss later in this chapter, particularly indigenous perspectives and practices.
- Adapting the techniques for leading effective campaigns (in a later chapter).

The practices we talked about in the first two chapters – the ABCs of interpersonal and cadre leadership - apply at the Community level, too, but as our theme for this chapter lays out, **more is required**. After we bring up another perspective for Community Elders, we'll stretch out and explore what "more" means.

For emphasis, let's be clear: Failure to provide these essential functions can and does generally result in catastrophic consequences for Community building and maintaining:

> *"The inability of close-knit communities to organize and develop a vision for a new society turned into another exploitative playground for the elites.…*
> *Our lack of vision creates a lack of participation. Creating truly revolutionary movements requires dedication and discipline."*[125]

We discussed commitment in an earlier chapter, but we'll address it again, and what discipline is required of leaders, in the next chapter.

---

[125] Sergio Kochergin, quoted by Vince Emmanuele in: Emmanuele, Vincent (2020).) Winning Requires Vision, Strategy and Numbers. https://www.counterpunch.org/2020/07/28/winning-requires-vision-strategy-and-numbers/

Leadership is critical for the well-being of CPR collectives, BUT it must transcend mainstream inspirational forms emphasized in Western leadership literature and practice.

The "Leaderless" Community

Because leadership is a critical component of an effective Community, and Communities vary widely in their forms, we're not surprised that leadership itself can take on various forms. The stereotypical strong, "male" leader is the least of these, in our view, given our perspective on patriarchy. One alternative is for women to share more of the power in a Community (see Shared Power), but there are other options to consider or imagine. Here are some options a Community might take. Our broader conclusion is that a CPR collective can take on many forms – this book has indicated the (five) characteristics of a CPR collective, but these can play out in innumerable ways. Builders, use the possibilities to fit your unique Community circumstance.

Leadership as a Role.

As we mentioned in the first chapter, one way to view Community Leadership as "leaderless" is to conceive of it as a role – an expectation for behaviors oriented toward a particular individual in a given circumstance. As purveyors of "shared leadership" understand, virtually any Community member can take on a leadership role in situations in which they, for example, possess relevant expertise, passion, and/or experience (see the first chapter).

The role notion is particularly important for us in Community because it's exceedingly difficult for resistance collectives or the movement to function without a broad spectrum of individual activists taking on leadership roles.

Shared Leadership.

Shared Power is an essential component of a CPR collective. But Shared Power doesn't necessarily imply shared leadership. Nevertheless, shared leadership is an often-cited characteristic of effective Communities in general. John Gardner writes that (participation and the) sharing of leadership tasks is a key ingredient of a healthy Community, although he does little to expand on that notion.

Sharing leadership tasks offers several benefits to the Community. For one, when many members of a collective are able to engage in leadership, regardless of how little or extensively, there's greater commitment to the whole. Members understand they have a say in the direction of the collective, and at least from time to time are able to make material decisions effecting the Community. Second, when leadership tasks are shared, more members are able to practice this art and science. In the process, the Community creates greater "bench strength" of leaders, and if and when a new or different leader must take the reins, candidates are available to do so.

Susan Morse expands on the "bench strength" consideration. "Successful communities, even those with long traditions of organized community leadership, will continue to broaden the circles of leadership to create a system for the community… [in which] there are many centers of leadership that interrelate."[126] In this model, "appropriate vehicles for making decisions will exist on different levels guided by a common vision held by the community." Morse points out that channels and vehicles for (Community) leadership (would be) expanded to allow (Community) work to be approached collaboratively through multiple efforts and multiple leaders.

A variation of shared leadership comes from Lorraine Matusak. She writes that (a community is) not a leaderless group, but a group of leaders who lead when appropriate. "This assumes that every member of the community is recognized and practices as a leader and a supportive follower."[127] While on its face this proposal may seem extreme, I agree leadership is a role Community members can take on as appropriate. Kazimierz Gozdz echoes this notion: "With true community, there has to be commitment, a willingness to coexist (see the Commitment chapter). It is not a leaderless group but rather a group of leaders. All capabilities in the group are utilized in a flow in which different people lead or contribute when it is appropriate."[128] Here, we close the loop in a sense. Leadership is a role, and the more a Community can disperse or rotate this role throughout the collective, the greater Capacity, Confidence and Continuity the Community will enjoy.

One Community approach to leadership which combines the "leaderless" orientation with that of leadership as a role is the Zapatistas, a leading voice of Mexico's indigenous peoples and who built a de facto autonomous system of self-governance.[129] A key principle underlying the Zapatista project, which ensures that autonomous institutions serve the people, is *mandar obedeciendo*, to lead by obeying. It implies political leaders do not make decisions on behalf of their Community as its representatives, but rather act as the Community's delegates, implementing decisions made in local assemblies – a traditional decision-making mechanism.

These exist on a village level and, in contrast to traditional assemblies of Mexico, include women, whose empowerment has been at the center of the Zapatista

[126] Morse, S. (1998). Five Building Blocks for Successful Communities. In F. Hesselbein et al. (Eds) Communities of the Future. San Francisco: Jossey-Bass, p. 234

[127] Matusak, L. (1997). Finding Your Voice: Learning to Lead…Anywhere You Want to Make a Difference. San Francisco: Jossey-Bass, p. 71

[128] Gozdz, K. (1993). Building Community as a Leadership Discipline. In Michael Ray and Alan Rinzler (eds.) The New Paradigm in Business: Emerging Strategies for Leadership and Organizational Change. New York: J.P. Tarcher / Perigee, p. 108

[129] Briy, A, 2020. Zapatistas: Lessons in community self-organisation in Mexico. In OpenDemocracy.net. https://www.opendemocracy.net/en/democraciaabierta/zapatistas-lecciones-de-auto-organización-comunitaria-en

revolution. Any ideas proposed at a higher administrative level go through the consultation process with each community, after which delegates carry their Communities' opinions back to a municipal meeting. Leaders are chosen based on the indigenous tradition of *cargo* – an obligation to serve one's Community – and commit to unremunerated posts of responsibility. Communities have the right to revoke the mandate of those officials who do not fulfill their duty of serving the people.

Sometimes, mainstream leadership teachings get it right. Shared leadership is touted by scholars in the common culture, and to the extent that aspect of a CPR collective is emphasized by indigenous Communities, shared leadership is all the more validated. There are more indigenous practices and cultural characteristics we can learn from, too. These fundamental approaches to Community and leadership provide the most valuable lessons yet for Elders who want to center, direct and sustain their Communities.

Community Leadership Perspectives from Indigenous Groups

Our understanding regarding the critical functions of leadership in Community is not new, at least to some people. Much of what we know derives from indigenous peoples around the world. What is touted in the more "progressive" or post-industrial school of leadership literature[130] i.e., those that focused more on mutual purpose, inspiration, and de-emphasis on hierarchical relationships, for example, is already known to and deeply embedded in indigenous Communities.

These observations and principles are detailed more in sources cited widely here, including Anthony De Padua and Norma Rabbitskin[131] and Carolyn Kenny and Tina Ngaroimata Fraser.[132] I offer a brief summary of these rich sources, related elsewhere in more, and more eloquent, detail. What I offer here supplements and complements the Community model I offer, and more importantly, opens a window to the wisdom other Community builders have amassed. These principles and perspectives resonate with our CPR analysis; we've already referenced the "seven generations" outlook, which informs indigenous Communities of the value of reflecting on decisions and actions in the context of seven generations in the future.

Beyond merely validating the observations of the "progressive" leadership literature most common in the West, I emphasize indigenous concepts here in great measure because these Communities show us how to live in just, sustainable collectives that

---

[130]　See e.g., Rost, J. (1993). Leadership for the Twenty-First Century. Westport, CT: Praeger.

[131]　De Padua, A., & Rabbitskin, N. Working with Indigenous Leadership and Indigenous Environments. Chapter in Leadership and Influencing Change in Nursing (Joan Wagner, Ed.) 2018. University of Regina Press. Retrieved Aug 20 from https://leadershipandinfluencingchangeinnursing.pressbooks.com/chapter/chapter-3-working-with-indigenous-leadership-and-indigenous-environments/

[132]　Kenny, C., in Carolyn Kenny and Tina Ngaroimata Fraser (Eds.). Living Indigenous Leadership: Native Narratives on Building Strong Communities. (2012). Vancouver: UBC Press

allow all members to thrive, often for tens of thousands of years. And a more indigenous orientation to Community leadership is one way in which our model can be considered "radical".

"The road to leadership is paved with land, ancestors, Elders, and story – concepts that are rarely mentioned in the mainstream leadership literature. They are embodied concepts unique to Native leadership."

Kenny

A deep and abiding sense of place.

Our CPR vision includes a planet populated by self-directed, resilient, and self-governing Communities, thriving in mutually regenerative relationships with their landbase…. These collectives recognize and guarantee the rights of all creatures and aspects of the living world (including air, rocks, bodies of water, and soil) to exist, thrive, evolve and flourish. We owe this perspective in great measure to the philosophy of our indigenous forebears. From the Kenny reference:

> *"A sense of place brings coherence to Aboriginal people and suggests an aesthetic engagement with the land – an intimate spiritual commitment to relationships with all living things….*
>
> *To maintain this sense of coherence, we can accept the earth as our first embodied concept of leadership. We follow Earth. We respond to the guidance of the processes expressed in our home place. Many say we listen and respond to our Mother. Everything begins here. We mirror the patterns, textures, colours, sounds, and processes of the earth as embodied beings."*[133]

While I acknowledge the validity and importance of virtual collectives, the connection to and foundational relationship with the land proves the strongest, most durable foundation for Community. There is no stronger love or bond than what is based on the land and water that gives us life and meaning. Our Community efforts must be informed with this basic understanding and appreciation. This connection, these relationships, are precisely what so many of us have lost in our cultural isolation, so building Community can be difficult. As I mentioned in the Values Chain discussion, a remedy for us all is to build a connection to our land, waters, and inhabitants.

The interconnection of all things.

A fundamental appreciation for the land and water as the basis of Community also recognizes the relationship among all members of that Community, as the excerpt from our vision statement testifies. I've noted this perspective elsewhere in this chapter. We (CPR) advocate for a planet where inhabitants are bonded by healthy

---

[133] Kenny, C. (1998). "The Sense of Art: A First Nations Perspective." Canadian Journal of Native Education 22, 1: 77-84.

interrelationships among other Community members, not bound by constraints, restrictions, or controls imposed by others in service to the dominant culture. Any true commitment to the land or water as a touchstone for Community inherently acknowledges that all aspects of the land are connected.

Again, from Kenny:

> *"The majority of Indigenous scholarship emphasizes the spiritual principle of the interconnectedness of all things. This principle is important in most Indigenous societies and contained in Indigenous religious and spiritual belief systems.*
>
> *'All things are related' expresses this principle in many prayers and ceremonies. Native peoples are reminded of the significance of the principle of interconnectivity throughout their lifelong learning....*
>
> *Indigenous leadership is aesthetic in nature because it has its source in coherence.*
>
> *With the flow and flux of changing circumstances, Native leaders must constantly monitor the pulse of the interconnectedness of all things and gauge how these connections challenge our communities."*

Community Leadership embedded in this worldview begins with a deep understanding of the land, and of the relationship among and between all members. Rather than scheme how to influence others, as much Western leadership literature suggests, Community Leaders need to develop this deep understanding of where they come from and where they are. Contrast this view with the belief of human supremacy, which contributes directly to the destruction of the planet.[134]

DePadua and Rabbitskin tell us:

> *"As a grandmother, and as one who has chosen a profession in nursing leadership, I appreciate how leadership decisions are made within an Indigenous community. A community foundation is shaped by the guidance provided by community knowledge keepers, healers, ceremonialists, leaders, and Elders. Through their examples I came to appreciate the full spectrum of service leadership.*
>
> *These pipe carriers, ceremonialists who dedicated their lives to maintaining medicine and cultural ways, assisted me in stepping seamlessly into a nurse leadership role. As well, my decision-making processes arose out of my Cree upbringing and this lived experience, and they are based on inclusivity, with full recognition that all life forms are sacred."*

Inclusivity in this Native view seems less oriented toward mere representation and more toward deeply diffused, meaningful participation. Community leaders worth

---

[134]   Jensen, D (2016). The Myth of Human Supremacy. Seven Stories Press.

their salt don't just ask others (including non-human members) what they want; they ensure they take part in the mutual building of the collective, and in its flourishing.

The "Burden" of Leadership.

Westerners often think of leadership as a reward for dedication to the organization, or recognition of accomplishments. A healthier view is that leaders serve the Community and the members in it, rather than impose direction or policies.

Kenny:

> *"[The] burden of Native leadership often results in decentralizing the authority of the group. In this sense, immanent or inherent value is a primary attribute of leaders who serve. Through networks of affiliation, leaders are chosen to play a role for a time. They are chosen through influence and persuasion."*

The Zapatistas call this burden *"mandar obedeciendo"*, as we learned. Leaders in this Community are chosen in the indigenous tradition of *cargo* – obligation to serve one's collective. This notion receives validation from other Communities as well.[135] Rosemary Ahtuangaruak, a community health aide in Nuiqsut, Alaska, has seen how the encroachment of fossil fuel development has harmed the Arctic's people:

> *"My elders asked me to stand up for tradition and culture. When they come and talk to you as a group waiting all day because you're busy, you listen. I knew my village needed to grow and I worked to make it better — coaching and growing the goodness."*[136]

Maria Lopez-Nuñez is the deputy director of organizing and advocacy at the Ironbound Community Corporation in Newark:

> *"Women have to be the fiercest. We're often the caretakers of our communities and with that comes a strong sense of having to defend our communities from harm, to keep them safe. That's part of what it means to nurture."*[137]

Narrative and Story: Culture.

As you know by now, I often tie effective organizational leadership to "culture work" in which rites, rituals, stories, heroes and myths, and supporting systems cultivate and maintain healthy values and expectations regarding the collective. The same is true for Community Leadership, as we've seen. But this perspective is both broadened and deepened by indigenous perspectives. Here, the stories, art, and related activities

---

[135] Surrusco, E. (2021). These Women Environmental Leaders Are Fighting For Their Communities.
https://earthjustice.org/article/these-women-environmental-leaders-are-fighting-for-their-communities Accessed Feb 12, 2023
[136] Ibid.
[137] Ibid.

enhance the connection to the land, to the view of interconnectedness, to the notion of service to others, and related aspects of the Community worldview.

From De Padua and Rabbitskin:
> *"There are a number of differences between Indigenous and other types of leadership styles. One such example is the use of traditional imagery and storytelling [...]. Lessons are taught through stories and also have a connection with the land and Indigenous identity [...]."*

From Kenny:
> *"Stories are a creative act of leadership through which we manifest our solidarity and strengthen our people to take their next steps in encouraging good and healthy lives." Our Elders often bring these teachings to us through stories. Stories provide many of the guiding lights to show us our way on Earth – to lead truly good lives....*
>
> *These stories are embodied in oral traditions, in arts, in traditional practices of all kinds. Stories, especially in the oral tradition, provide powerful bridges that connect our histories, our legends, our senses, our practices, our values, and, fundamentally, our sustainability as peoples....*
>
> *Stories presented in the oral tradition provide an opportunity for immediacy – a direct and immediate relationship with listeners. The story- teller can make immediate adjustments in the elements of the story based on relational needs and contexts.*
>
> *Last, but not least, is the ever-constant power of story [...]. Narrative is a theme throughout Indigenous scholarship. All cultures are sustained through stories that integrate past, present, and future [...].*
>
> *Stories are bridges that connect our histories, our legends, our senses, our practices, our values and, in essence, our sustainability as people."*

Storytelling as an oral medium is a powerful device for Community leaders to build a strong culture and collective. There are other ways to tell stories, however, and we'd do well to consider the wide range of artistic means of communicating within a collective.

Again, from Kenny:
> *"Miriam Jorgenson and Rachel Starks characterize Native leadership as an aesthetic engagement – one that brings us to the beauty of our lives – on the land, with each other, and in relationship to all living things. "Art and the relationships embedded in its creation provide the power to restore and transform people and communities [...].*

> *Art expressions are often how we maintain not only a sense of coherence but also our resilience and, ultimately, confidence and strength. Art expressions such as drumming, singing, dancing, carving, and painting are another way to communicate the principle of interconnectivity.*"[138]

Michael Asher:

> *"Today I have a new question - What is culture? Some will say it's art, music, literature - the intellectual achievements of a society - while some will talk about technology, artifacts, customs, behaviour, food, dress and even language. But what is it, really? While culture may include all these, it is first and foremost a story – a story we are told and that we tell our children. This story provides the answers to certain big questions humans have always asked – who are we? why are we here? how did we get here? what happens after we die? what is real? and, most of all, perhaps, how do we relate to the rest of nature? There have been millions of different cultures since humans began, but there are really only two kinds of stories.*
> *There is a story that puts us at odds with nature, and a story that puts us in harmony with it. You might call the first, the Story of Separation, and the second, the Story of Connection.*"[139]

There are fewer limits to your storytelling platforms than you might imagine. Sure, you can use a purely speaking approach, but let your imagination, talents and personality give form to how you tell your stories. A Latvian comrade of mine told me that Latvian *dainas*, for example, are short songs that help transmit the culture from generation to generation. For the more daring and coordinated of you out there, interpretive dance and blanket weaving are just a couple of other possibilities. Use what works for you and your collective!

Our neoliberal culture views storytelling as an inefficient waste of time, unrelated to what is traditionally considered task accomplishment. I dismiss most of "task accomplishment" itself as a waste of time as it is oriented toward maintenance of destructive organizations and the dominant culture. Unless the task involves nourishing and protecting the Community, task accomplishment is an artifact of the dominant culture I'd rather do without.

On the other hand, a truly Deep Community and a fundamental commitment to the land and others springs from the bone-deep knowledge of place and ourselves which only comes from the culture-building work that stories play a part in, as do other

---

[138] Kenny, C., in Carolyn Kenny and Tina Ngaroimata Fraser (Eds.). Living Indigenous Leadership: Native Narratives on Building Strong Communities. (2012). Vancouver: UBC Press

[139] https://www.facebook.com/michael.asher/posts/pfbid0dsx5hSuTmuE94KcFzuhhyrP2Mj3X2nPPmHqaQwXMyMsueVaJhCWS-GjomDzbZrA3Ql

artistic facets of indigenous collectives and Deep Community. How can you begin to ensure your stories are the ones you should share?

Listen:
- To the land and water.
- To your collective's inhabitants.
- To your heart.

Be a storyteller. That is leading, too.

Spiritual Principles.
Perhaps nothing distinguishes mainstream leadership theory from indigenous practices more than the emphasis on spirituality. Even post-industrial models of western leadership pay little or no respect to this notion. However, the deeper one understands and appreciates the land or water and the interconnectedness of all things, the more a spiritual orientation seeps into that worldview, and the more likely it is that Community Leadership will be infused with that spirituality.

From Kenny:
> *"Ancestors often guide us with deep respect for what they themselves have left behind. They communicate with us through dreams, through the teachings that have come down through the generations, through spirit. Our constant guides in our life journeys of spiritual discovery, our sense of wonder with the animation of the world, often arrive through the presence of our ancestors and Elders, who carry the knowledge that we need for continuity and integration. Traditional knowledge weaves its way into the contemporary context for our present and future endeavours.".*

From De Padua and Rabbitskin:
> *"Felicity (1999) and Nichols (2004) also reinforced the holistic view of Indigenous leadership and leaders' concerns for the community. Julien and colleagues (2010) took this notion of holistic leadership a step further by describing spirituality as a central element of Indigenous leaders' practices and beliefs:*
>
> *One respondent noted that, while his non-Aboriginal colleagues had a tendency to focus on processes and were greatly motivated by outcomes that were purely profit-driven, he felt his work was a spiritual endeavor. He expressed that 'the work we do—it's not about education, it's not about research—it's about spirituality; the other things are just part of the whole process.'"*[140]

---

[140] De Padua, A., & Rabbitskin, N. Working with Indigenous Leadership and Indigenous Environments. Chapter in Leadership and Influencing Change in Nursing (Joan Wagner, Ed.) 2018. University of Regina Press. Retrieved Aug 20 from https://leadershipandinfluenc -

Once more from Kenny:

> *"These concepts are embodied – they are premised on the idea that the parts of our being cannot be separated. We are whole. Our mental concepts are one with our bodies, hearts, spirits, and souls.*
> *Land, ancestors, Elders, stories, women, grandmothers, parents, language, education, community, performing arts, knowledge, relationships, friends, culture, collaboration, healing, and resilience – these are the concepts that unite our worlds. The notion of embodied concepts animates our leadership theories with a richness that keeps our worlds vital, integrated, and whole."*

DePadua and Rabbitskin offer a final perspective:

> *"Spiritual health [for indigenous people] refers to seeking harmony with a higher power and finding purpose in life. By adopting values, individuals can then choose activities and behaviours that are consistent with them. Individuals seek Elders for spiritual guidance and participate in sharing circles, healing circles, and talking circles."*

– – – – – – – – –

There's a reason I saved Leadership for the final discussion of the Building Community chapters. Simply put, it's because Community doesn't happen without leadership – collectives form, mature, and endure because some or all of their members take on the mantle of leading. But as we see, leadership is both simpler and more complex than many of us might have imagined.

I hope you're encouraged to engage in developing your Community's leadership capacity, and we in CPR are ready to work at your side in doing so. Together, we can bring about a network of Communities large, strong and devoted enough to bring down the dominant culture and replace it with all the forms that sustain us all.

– – – – – – – –

ingchangeinnursing.pressbooks.com/chapter/chapter-3-working-with-indigenous-leadership-and-indigenous-environments/, p. 119-120

Building Community Leadership

Revise your thinking, and the thinking of those in your Community, concerning leadership.
Dispel the common myths about leadership: that leaders are born, not made; that the only way to learn about leadership is through the school of hard knocks; and that leaders must be charismatic, among others. We may not be able to disabuse you regarding all of them, but read more on current leadership scholarship for more. Or contact me.

Read about leadership as a mutual struggle with comrades rather than an exercise in manipulating others to help individuals or small groups realize their goals.

Recognize that Community leadership is an essential function keeping a collective together, and moving forward to a sustainable future. It's also our only hope for successful Resistance, as it serves as our most valuable force multiplier.
Broaden your perspective regarding who can lead. If you've noticed that only men lead in your Community, and it's not a Friary, or that people of color or marginalized groups seem to be missing from these roles, something is wrong.

Everyone can lead, and unless everyone contributes, your Community is missing vital guidance, direction, and inspiration.
Explore the spiritual aspects of Community, and of leadership. Talk to indigenous comrades or neighbors about what leadership means to them. Ask your comrades about the spiritual nature of their relationship with the land and others. Make spirituality part of the Leadership in your collective.

Build your stories (or discover them).
- What is the story of your place? Your people? Your struggle?
- What values are embedded in your heroes, victories, defeats, accomplishments, failures?
- How do members treat each other?
- What do you look to in the future?
- Become a storyteller. Research guides on how to tell stories effectively.

Seek out leadership development opportunities for yourself and others in your collective, including hands-on opportunities to lead.
John Gardner and others suggest effective Communities develop leadership capacity in young people, as well as a sense of obligation to the Community. Incorporate youth in Community functioning and leading, rather than excusing them because of their relative lack of experience or perspective. Youth development is Community

development – do not shunt them off into activities, paths or roles that serve only to free others from having to raise them.

Ensure as many members of your Community as possible engage in some sort of leadership development. This is not a luxury; it's a critical investment in your survival and sustenance.
Provide them with an effective working model of what leadership is and how to practice it. Help them frame the world in a way that is conducive to being a leader.

Let them lead. Give them practical experience in progressively more challenging arenas under guidance of elders, and with loving support and feedback aimed at their growth. Share Leadership tasks.

Earn your stripes.
Leadership is earned by investing in Community. "In a breakout session titled "Native Women Lead: Women Innovating in Business & Beyond" held during the 2022 Reservation Economic Summit, Tsé Bii' Ndzisgai Community Center Director Shandiin Herrera said she developed leadership skills by showing up for her community during the pandemic:

> *She had to build trust with her elder community members to earn their respect. "I tell young people that they are needed here and together we can redefine what success looks like," she said. "I encourage folks to think about this and how we can foster leadership in our youth."*[141]

---

[141] https://navajotimes.com/opinion/essay/guest-column-leadership-is-earned-by-investing-in-community/

Worksheet: Planning to Lead Your Community

Have you noticed negative drift in your Community as a whole, or with parts within your collective? If so, plan for countering actions and systems you can undertake.

Is your Community "losing steam"? What are your thoughts about how to address that trend?

Does your collective have adequate bench strength? If not, plan to bring others into the leadership pipeline.

Do you feel ready to take on the roles associated with Community leadership? What aspects resonate with you?

What do you feel you need to continue to grow in?

LEVERAGING COMMUNITY POWER

CHAPTER 11

The Process of Leading Community

A (Somewhat Fictional) Story Old As Time:
Several years ago, a Cadre of seven Deep Green radicals traveled to a remote mountain town of mostly farmers and "herb gardeners". They were asked there to help the villagers protect themselves from a toxic mining operation poisoning the air and land, and probably local water sources as well.

For several days, the Cadre trained the populace on methods they might use to fight the mining threat, and armed them with the knowledge and confidence to apply the methods effectively.

By the time the Cadre left, there was a palpable feeling of newfound power and resolve among the members of the to-that-point loose collective. They spoke excitedly about the nascent campaign to dismantle the threat and reclaim the natural wonders of their mountain home.

Years later, a Cadre member got wind of a news dispatch from the village. He hurriedly read the news, eager to learn of the latest victories over the ruinous commerce the village energetically planned to resist.

He learned instead the villagers were celebrating the fact that they had banned plastic bags in their hamlet's markets. He wept (or at least felt like it).

Moral:
Not all collectives that start on the road to becoming an effective radical Community "make it". There are many reasons why, but let's investigate how we can maximize the likelihood that your collective will make progress to the desired end.

— — — — — — — — —

Our discussion of the characteristics of a CPR collective painted a somewhat static picture. You might get the impression from the profile of an effective radical Community that, once you achieve our ideal state (Community Consciousness, Comradeship, Commitment, Shared Power, and Leadership), success has been achieved. However, building a Community is not a one-time event. It is a *process*. Let's look at Community building in that light.

Communities change, evolve, and devolve. Whether due to external threats, or more organic, natural and healthy change, or even an influx of new members or loss of some, a Community's stage of evolution (maturity) can take a step or two backward. Community leaders need to adopt a dynamic view of their collective to allow them to steer it through the initial developmental stages, and to continue to provide guidance through periods of upheaval and natural variability.

The "stages" notion has been noted in other contexts, in scholarship devoted to phases of organizational growth. Each stage requires certain commitments from leadership for the collective to move forward. Commitment is a theme of sorts in this topic, in addition to serving as a critical building block in its own right. Recall the recurring theme that a Community doesn't evolve, deepen, or successfully resist via collective magic: It does so because its members are committed to each other, to the Community, and to making things work. Community builders need more than a sense of obligation – they need the discipline to prepare and follow through on their obligations.

"…community is a process rather than a state… commitment must be mustered in order to maintain it; only through purpose and discipline will the community process be maintained….
It takes great motivation and discipline to remain engaged in such cynical times."[142]

Leading the "Process" of Community:
A dynamic Orientation

One characteristic differentiating collectives is how close they approximate a Deep Community, as we discussed; as a Conscious Community matures, its members might aspire to becoming a **Deep Community** Maturation implies some sort of process, and Communities are subject to this phenomenon just as individual members might be. Moving a collective through the phases of maturity toward Deep Community or another desired end state involves a dynamic view of collectives.

For Kazimierz Gozdz, a "new kind of leadership" will be required for the Community, which needs (collectively) to:
- Function as a lifelong learner.
- Be responsive to change.
- Be receptive to challenge, and
- Become conscious of an increasingly complex array of alternatives.

---

[142] Emanuele, V. (2018). Musings on Organizing. https://dgrnewsservice.org/resistance/strategy/musings-on-organizing/, Accessed Mar 22, 2022.

This "new kind of leadership" for Gozdz maintains the "process" of Community, in great measure, via **purpose** and **discipline**. We've talked before about the critical role of culture work for leaders and Communities, as well as the importance of discipline, in the Commitment chapter. What's different here is that Community leaders aren't working toward a fixed point of the collective's maturation profile so much as adapting their respective leadership approach to the particular challenges and opportunities associated with the maturation stage in which they find their collective, and to applying the practices to move the collective forward.

I'll discuss momentarily the details characterizing maturation stages and the requirements for leadership to guide the collective in each stage and to move to the next. Note for now that collectives generally arrive at Deep Community (maturity) after a long and challenging journey. As Communities undergo maturation, the collective's leadership must effectively and wisely guide them. For Gozdz, "Leadership in community is more a context than a person. It takes strong leadership to move people to get into the process of community. But once that state is achieved, the group becomes a community of leaders."[143] We might indeed view that as a characteristic of a fully matured Community.

I've noted that Community maturation doesn't occur by magic. If only. Recall some of the obstacles: conflicts, changes to the mission or vision, external developments and sheer exhaustion all throw up roadblocks which must be overcome, and inertia itself is never enough to see Communities through. Elders, leaders, and rank and file members need to internalize the discipline to maintain movement. So, commitment means viewing Community building as a discipline, and willingness to see the process through its inevitable challenges, downturns, frustrations, and reversals of fortune, as Gozdz has alerted us.

In the enviable event that Deep Community or its equivalent is achieved, the leadership challenge becomes an obligation to counter the inevitable decay or entropy. Community leadership that works views the Community phases as the "process" of Community, and commits itself (and the collective writ large) to the process as a discipline.

Community Leadership must have the experience and wisdom to recognize threats to the Community-building process, and the expertise to address challenges and continue movement toward the desired end state of maturity. In addition, Leaders must leverage their skills, and the vision compelling the Community, to sustain commitment among the members to keeping the process moving forward. Leadership

---

[143] Gozdz, K. (1993). Building Community as a Leadership Discipline. In Michael Ray and Alan Rinzler (eds.) The New Paradigm in Business: Emerging Strategies for Leadership and Organizational Change. New York: J.P. Tarcher / Perigee, p.113

must not only maintain its discipline, but also disperse that throughout the Community in times of challenges to progress.

Says Gozdz:
> *"A leader must practice the discipline of community and nurture and maintain it in the group so everyone begins to act as a leader and takes up the discipline as a natural way of working."*[144]

Sustaining this energy and discipline is necessary because the path to a Community of real sustainability passes through "stages of frustration, grief, and instability."[145].

CAUTION: Often "Community" occurs briefly (breaks out!), due to a crisis or at least a compelling necessity. Often, however, once the collective itself or an external agent resolves the crisis or moves to another level of organizational maturity the sense of Community disappears. Community leadership needs to understand the natural ebb and flow of building a collective.

Models of thinking about Process

It's natural for a group of any sort to undergo a relatively common evolution process. If you sensed that was the case, you would not be alone. Several writers on Organizational Behavior have authored very similar models of this evolution. Below is a sampling of those models. Note how **there's a trend of unstructured or tentative forming followed by stages of upheaval and conflict, culminating (if the collective is that lucky or good) in a sort of actualizing.**

Gozdz describes a four-stage process model of Community building, which includes Pseudocommunity, Chaos, Emptiness, and Community. This sort of maturation process model is recognized elsewhere, too, and it's widely asserted that teams (Cadres) undergo a process of maturing that also consists of four stages (Forming, Storming, Norming and Performing).[146] The graphic below displays the models together for comparison. If you know me, you know I'm big on overall themes and frames. For now, use the comment above to help you determine in a general sense where your collective resides in terms of evolutionary progress.

---

[144] Ibid., p.115
[145] Gozdz, citing Bridges, W. (2003). Managing Transitions: Making the Most of Change (2nd Ed.). DaCapo Press.
[146] Tuckman, B. (1965). The Developmental Sequence in Small Groups. Psychological Bulletin 63. 384-399.

Models of thinking about "Process"

Teams (Tuckman)	Phases of Organizational Growth	[Business] Communities (Gozdz)	Radical Communities (Gibson)
Forming	Pioneering	Pseudo community	Beginning
Storming	Consolidation	Chaos	Negotiating / Exploring
Norming	Renewal	Emptiness	Becoming
Performing	Transformational	Community	Sustaining

The "Process" in Process Models.
As the models above suggest, collectives are seen to move from lower to upper stages of maturity (evolution), as if that's the most natural thing in the world. If everything works well, this is what that process looks like. I'll describe my version of each stage momentarily.

The <u>Ideal</u> Community Maturation Process

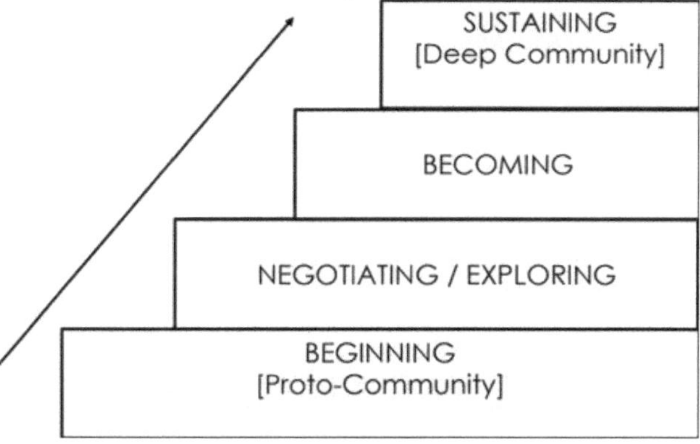

I'm sure you see where this is going. Things almost never go as exactly planned, and things don't necessarily work well, despite our best efforts. In the real world, this is what the Community evolution process looks like:

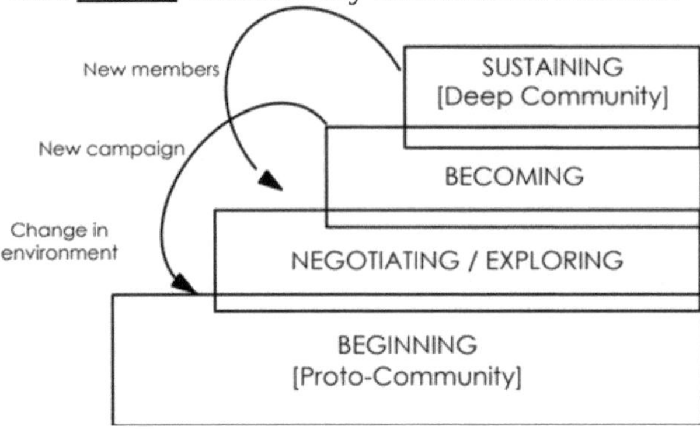

Collectives don't exist in a vacuum. External as well as internal factors can drive the group backwards one or more stages. New comrades coming aboard might cause shifts in how members interact with each other, and they might challenge norms inadvertently or otherwise. Changes to your campaign or strategy might create ripple effects throughout the collective, and alterations to the external environment might do the same. Another complicating factor of sorts is that it's not often clear what stage of evolution your collective is in, in part because the boundaries between stages are fluid and permeable.

The real-world model of Community maturation makes clear what we've talked about regarding the challenges to Elders. Leaders need to be comfortable with ambiguity and fuzziness regarding exactly where the collective is in its progress. There's also the notion that sometimes the collective moves back and forth on its own, so leaders need to take a longer view occasionally. Like following the stock market, try not to focus on short-term variability and keep your eye on the long-term progress or lack thereof. At the same time, leaders should be familiar enough with the model and the specifics associated with each stage to at least get a sense for where the collective is at any point and how to respond appropriately.

Given the variable, non-linear nature of the maturation journey, it should now be clear what we meant earlier when we mentioned that Community builders need commitment and discipline to see the collective through the process, not only to help it move from one stage to the next, but to recover when it (almost inevitably) slides back a stage or two.

What Community Builders need is enough information to determine what stage their collective currently resides in, what need to be done to lead in that stage, and what they can do to move their collective on to the next. As we proceed through these stage descriptions, keep in mind I'm trying to paint a general picture of what each of them is like. For your part, don't get bogged down in too many details – instead, work to get a **flavor** of each stage.

Exploring the Process Stages

Beginning / Acquainting

Characteristics of the stage:
The relatively new Collective pretends it's already a Deep Community and that interpersonal differences don't exist. The decision-making process and the nature of relationships go unchallenged. The collective might call itself a Community and occasionally there might be solidarity, but the experiences are fleeting.

If the collective formed in response to some crisis, emergency or disaster, the basis for the collective disappears when the catalyst wanes or ends. So does the sense of comradeship.

This stage involves a period of orientation and getting acquainted. Uncertainty is high during this stage, and comrades are often looking for leadership and direction. There is also likely indecision as members feel each other out, and wonder what the collective is going to be, or become. Leaders can provide a valuable service to collectives in this stage by reducing uncertainty, as I address below.

Lots of "false" or Proto-communities may initially look like this. The rock concert Woodstock comes to mind, as does the Standing Rock protest encampment.

Questions / Reactions for the Community builder to come to grips with.
(And be ready to answer for others who ask.)
> *What is this Collective?*
> *Who are these people? Where did we come from?*
> *Where are we going? What's the vision? Is there one?*
> *What does the collective offer me / others?*
> *What is expected of me / others? Will I, and others, fit in?*

Most interactions are social as members get to know each other. Members may be overly polite and pleasant, and interactions may not be "deep".

Most members are excited to start something new and to get to know others.
Roles and responsibilities will begin to form / evolve, but may require the leader's encouragement and direction to do so.

201

It's important for comrades to develop relationships and understand what part each person plays, although that will play out more in the next phase.

What is needed of leadership:
In a general sense, determining what's needed in each stage can be deduced by preparing to answer the basic fundamental questions that characterize that stage.
- Do your Vision Work: Encourage and conduct discussions with and among members. Be ready to answer questions about mission, purpose, and vision.
- Open and create communication channels. Listen, and talk, and make sure everyone has the chance to do so as well (e.g., about the vision, roles, etc.).
- Acknowledge the contributions of all members, with authenticity.
- Clarify the direction of the collective, and the goals to get there.
- Do your culture work. Lay the foundation for what the culture of the collective should look like. Model the expected behaviors and values, for example.
- Establish a foundation of trust.
- Help Community members get to know and appreciate each other.
- Establish some structure. Roles etc. are important, sure, but focus too on standards, decision-making methods, and so on.

Negotiating / Exploring

Characteristics of the stage:
Once individual and interpersonal differences surface (and they will), the collective almost immediately moves into chaos, even if on a small scale. Differences will come out into the open, which is natural and appropriate. The problem arises when and if Community leaders try to ignore or deny these differences. Leaders may do this because they lack confidence in their ability to manage conflict. Of course, this tendency to downplay differences comes at the cost of dialogue, and can damage the trust comrades have in the leadership function.

This stage is no fun. It is common for members to attack not only each other but also their leadership. It's the most difficult, unpleasant, but most critical stage to pass through. It is marked by conflict and competition as personalities emerge and conflicting viewpoints, values, opinions and goals come out in the open. Whatever cohesiveness and energy / effectiveness that might have already been built may decrease because energy is put into unproductive activities.

The sense of apparent control and order is disrupted when deep differences emerge. Secrets emerge and conflicts erupt.

Remember: Common cause is not enough.
An object lesson of sorts regarding the importance of cultivating Comradeship in Community building.

The reality and weight of building the collective or realizing its purpose have now hit everyone. Initial feelings of excitement and the need to be polite have likely worn off. In addition to interpersonal conflicts, members may also disagree on the collective's vision, purpose, and goals.

Subgroups may form around strong personalities or areas of agreement. The danger here is that the vision and direction of these subgroups may be at odds with the larger collective. This is one source of the dreaded Drift I discussed in the last chapter. Trust may exist only among smaller groups, not across all members.

Personalities may clash. Members might disagree over how to complete a task or voice concerns if they feel someone isn't pulling their weight. They may even question the authority and guidance of Community leaders.

Members begin to challenge each other and the norms of the Community. This is not necessarily a bad thing. It's an opportunity for growth, change and evolution, if managed well (as we discussed in the Drift section). More in a moment.

Control in all forms (such as leadership or structures) starts to be challenged.

Questions / Reactions for the Community builder to come to grips with.
(And be ready to answer for others who ask.)
>*This isn't the direction I want for this collective. Let's talk more about this vision.*
>*We aren't gonna be able to make this happen.*
>*I'm not treated well by_____.*
>*Why do you get to make all the decisions?*
>*How can we balance exploring with consensus building?*

Barriers may be broken (which could be a good thing).

Long-term silent agreements start to be broken as members believe there is another way. Relationships may be tense. There may be power struggles, depending on the issue. Not everyone participates in making decisions.

To get through this stage, members must work to overcome obstacles, to accept differences, and to work through conflicting ideas on Community tasks and goals.

Collectives can very easily get bogged down in this stage. Failure to address conflicts may result in long-term problems, so it is critical they not be allowed to fester. Recall our technique for conflict management from the Leading Cadres chapter. It's tempting to skip over this stage or to avoid conflict at whatever cost, but avoidance usually makes the problem grow until it blows up. So, recognize conflicts and resolve them early on.

As uncomfortable and threatening as the characteristics and behaviors at this stage seem, it's important to remember most groups of any sort experience conflict. Remind members that disagreements are not only normal, but healthy and necessary for the collective to mature, innovate and react to changes.

What is needed of leadership:
Trust building and maintenance.

Have you worked toward a **shared** vision?
- Relate the vision to the on-the-ground-issues and clarify line of sight.
- Reinforce the vision to build commitment.
- Remind members of the vision and mission of the collective. Don't be frustrated if others don't "get" the vision initially. You may need to repeat discussion about it 5-7 times. Sorry – it's just true.

Be honest about conflicts, difficulties. Engage in conflict management! Don't avoid it – this is the worst thing you can do.
- Often, by the way, it's simply a matter of miscommunication.
- If you do avoid this, you'll likely never get past this stage.
- Lead the development and maintenance of healthy roles and norms.
- Be an effective mediator.

Do lots of facilitating – ask questions, etc.

Becoming

Characteristics of the stage:
A crucial stage of Community maturity, in that there's now a sense of momentum or possibility among comrades. There's a feeling of, "We can make it". At the interpersonal level, "Becoming" means members shedding their individual barriers to communication. (Deep Community in part.)

After the Community matures beyond Negotiation / Exploration, much of the conflict is resolved and some degree of cohesion and unity emerges.

- Interpersonal differences begin to be resolved.
- You should find more collaboration and open communication.
- More mutual support is exhibited among comrades.
- Trust is increasing, and comrades display skill in building and maintaining trusting relationships among themselves.

Consensus begins to develop around the nature of the Community's leadership and roles. The vision, mission, values and goals are now widely understood and accepted. This stage ends in widespread acceptance of norms, goals, roles.

The strength of the Community increases as members learn to cooperate and begin to focus on direction and goals. However, the harmony is precarious, and if disagreements re-emerge the team can slide back into the Negotiating / Exploring stage.

Members start to notice and appreciate comrades' strengths. As a rule, members are contributing and working as a cohesive unit.

As new tasks or campaigns, etc. arise, subgroups may still experience a few conflicts. But if the collective has already dealt with conflict appropriately, it will be easier to address this time. In fact, members may be able to resolve them among themselves, if conflict management has been handled well by the leaders, and the values underlying that skill have been incorporated into the collective's culture.

Questions / Reactions for the Community builder to come to grips with. (And be ready to answer for others who ask.)

> *I'm beginning to see how the vision works for us, and for me. Let's work out details.*
> *We appreciate you letting us decide what we need to be and do.*
> *I can do that, if you do this.*
> *The road to accomplishing the Community vision becomes apparent with leadership help in clarifying line of sight. "Can you tell us again how our work contributes to the collective's success?"*

Greater participation in making Community decisions has been established by the Elders, and is enthusiastically embraced by most comrades.

Members feel ready and free to do what needs to be done to protect the collective without a constant leadership presence.

You may find some things have gone wrong: Some old systems no longer work, and new ones may not have had a chance to do so. Embrace this development as an opportunity to innovate, adapt, and evolve as a collective.

The collective begins the work of self-examination, giving up personal obstacles, barriers and agendas. This is the beginning of true listening, where the collective's decision-making process becomes collaborative.

What is needed of leadership:
Reinforce appropriate norms and roles, and work to change those that aren't. Identify and put in place reinforcement and/or sanctions regarding norms and roles if they aren't already there.

Help members provide effective, supportive feedback to each other.

Praise movement toward the vision, clarify further steps, continue to build commitment for the vision.

Ask what the Community needs of you – they may not need this function as much, at least for a while.

Convey admiration for exemplars (heroes) of the culture you want to build.

Build your leadership pipeline, and allow leadership to diffuse throughout the collective.

Sustaining

Characteristics of the stage:
The collective is essentially a Deep Community. Things begin to make sense; the quality of communication alters significantly. The collective is now ready for authentic communication. Differences are embraced.

The collective begins to see that the differences with which it is most frequently preoccupied are distractions. They move away from the differences when they are irrelevant and attend to true differences causing conflict.

Consensus and cooperation have been well-established, and the Community is mature, organized, and well-functioning.

There are clear and stable structures, and members are committed to the Community purpose.

Problems and conflicts still emerge, but they are dealt with constructively, often without intervention by elders or Community leaders. The Community is focused on problem solving and meeting its goals.

Members are confident, motivated and familiar enough with the direction and each other that they maintain the collective themselves to a greater extent.

Everyone is on the same page and driving full-speed ahead toward the vision and desired end state for the Community.

A word of caution, however: Even when this spirit has been achieved, it can decay with time. One more time: Community is viewed as a discipline, a process of mastery.

Questions / Reactions for the Community builder to come to grips with.
(And be ready to answer for others who ask.)
> *This is a collective I want to struggle for.*
> *This Community helps me make sense of the world, and of myself.*
> *I'm committed to this collective, this vision, this Community of members.*
> *Our vision may not work in the future, but this is the future we want and need.*
> *I may not like everyone, but I love them.*

Roles and norms are clear, appropriate, and enforced.

Participation is energized.

What is needed of leadership:
Be a facilitator, not a dictator or micromanager. By now, comrades can handle conflicts and they understand and accept the collective's direction and what each of them needs to do to contribute to it.

Celebrate! Your success in maturing as a collective, however fleeting, is a major accomplishment. Let everyone bathe in this success to maintain commitment and motivation. Keep in the back of your mind, though, the understanding that can occur, even though you're well quipped to persevere.

Institutionalize the culture, rites, rituals, heroes, myths, stories. Maintain vigilance for weaknesses and threats as they loom. Keep a balance between relationships and task work. Maintain the vision as appropriate. But be open to possible needs to revise it as circumstances warrant. Ask how you can help, although it will often not be needed. Remove obstacles to a thriving Community. Do your linchpin stuff.

Who might we look to as examples of collectives that have reached the Sustaining stage? As a start, I'd point out almost any of the examples I harken back to from time to time, from the Sandinistas to the Rojavans to the Ka'apors and beyond. These collectives might find themselves sliding back a stage from time to time, but it's clear to me their Elders and leaders have committed to the building process, and have mastered the skills they need to guide their Communities.

Reflections on the Process Model

Community-building is a practice, not an event. You are always building, rebuilding or consolidating gains. Adopt this mindset sooner rather than later, and you will be better prepared for the non-linear passage to an effective, Deep Community, which is most prepared and committed to protecting and resisting.

I can't by virtue of this book magically imbue you with the commitment and discipline to guide your collective through its maturation challenges and victories, but I humbly offer you insights to help you recognize where your collective is now, what it needs from you to survive the stage it's in, and what it needs to move on. With that in mind, here are some reflections on the model to help put the details in perspective.

Like the speed limit, these stage characterizations are a rough guide. Let your circumstances and experience guide you in assessing where you are and what you need to do in a particular circumstance. Don't forget the lessons from the Leadership for Resistance and Leading Cadres chapters; the basics are the basics for good reason. Review them occasionally, and practice them so they become second nature.

I hope the specifics make sense, but don't lose the forest for the trees. Try for a Gestalt view of "Process". Does this model make sense in a general way? It does to me! Given that there are at least four leadership practitioners who feel similarly, I think we're on to something here.

I keep coming back to themes that resonate with Community leadership and Community building, like the importance of building and maintaining trust, and nurturing Comradeship (along with raising Consciousness) as cornerstones of sustaining Communities. I also see Conflict management as a key lever in helping Communities evolve.

As to the importance of identifying stages in general and the subsequent changing role and challenge associated with the leader, given that changing context: I'm reminded of the value of the leadership skill of being able to read the situation – i.e., framing.

You can't cure what you don't diagnose. Don't just treat the *symptoms* of a collective that is struggling – frame the *issue*, and the appropriate response pretty much presents itself.

The Community Leadership Commitment

A key leadership role in Community building is to "hold the commitment" and keep the process going, even if some in the collective become complacent, as Gozdz reminds us. There is one reason in particular to attend to this wisdom; the sense of Community is repeatedly lost. Besides the insidious danger of Drift, internal and external threats to the integrity of a radical Community loom large, always. The 4-stage model explained here assumes there will occasionally be backsliding a stage or two. The good news is that since these setbacks can be expected to a degree, we can also be optimistic the sure-handed Elder will know how to keep the process alive.

Elders, maintain your sustained course of action, because to create a sustainable Community, the collective must invariably pass through stages of frustration, grief, and instability, as you know. You'll get there and regain your wins, with commitment. How do we maintain commitment to Community evolution? There are areas to focus on.

<u>For the Community at large.</u>
Continue to define the reason for the Community's existence:
- Exercise your leadership skills, and attend to your leadership roles:
    - o Model
    - o Linchpin
    - o Elder
- Allocate your energy on a continuing basis to reinforce, explain, and nurture your collective's sense of purpose: Vision and Mission
- Just knowing the maturation process exists and consists of the stages I outlined keeps comrades from losing heart in difficult times. Communicate

this knowledge to them, to enable them to gain motivation for a task they understand and commit to.

<u>For the builders themselves.</u>
Renew your pledge to the Chain of Values. Recall why you love your land or waters, and your collective's inhabitants.
- This deep, abiding love won't fade, and is impervious to external intrusions.
- Announce and rejoice in your love and commitment. This has the added benefit of helping all in the Community see that you hold the same values they do.

A key to using this model in building a sustainable Community is the understanding that it is challenging but achievable.
- The end states of effective radical, Deep Community, and of the Sustaining level of maturation, are hard-won and never guaranteed.
- We aspire to these ends. We talk about the ideal of the CPR collective, and commit to it, but we are not discouraged when we are not yet there.

The job of leadership is to keep the process alive by constantly keeping everyone's attention on the course. You are key to that. Celebrate your role, and do not despair – you are serving a critical function in the viability of your collective.

– – – – – – – – –

The trick in utilizing the process model is to be able to recognize what stage your Community is in, as we mentioned earlier. This acquired skill enables you to do what's necessary to move the Community along. In the end, you will be ready to practice a long-term "Zen" approach to Community building, in that you're never done.

There are things you can do to facilitate movement upward in maturation, but the downward process is generally going to be out of your hands. That's okay. You know what you need to do to keep movement alive.

The phases represent leverage points of a sort – differing leadership responses or approaches are often needed at different stages. How do you know what stage you're in? You know the characteristics of each, but how do you get the data you need to decide? Audit your Community to understand its stage of maturity. Working on deepening your knowledge and understanding of your collective, viewed as a continuing process, will help.

One way is to walk around – be in the Community, literally and / or virtually. Take a Community Walk. As luck would have it, the Community Walk is the subject of the next chapter! I'll provide ideas for how to conduct a Walk and how to structure the results.

- On your walk, "count" (at least note) the number of stage characteristics that apply.
- Patterns should be clear, or at least give you an idea of the ballpark you're in.

A fundamental meta-strategy for effective leadership looks something like this:
- Read (the situation).
- Frame it (using one or more of the models I laid out to this point).
- React (appropriately – relying on the models, and your growing wisdom and confidence).

Not complicated, but perhaps daunting, all this Community building stuff. Sure enough, But you don't have to think about all this in isolation! It's not all on your shoulders. Talk with elders, comrades, members, and others who can help you in this process.

Remember the story about the Little Community that Couldn't that began this chapter? What do you think happened to them? I'd guess they never made it past the Negotiating/Exploring stage. Make sure this doesn't happen to your collective.

Worksheet: Planning to Lead Your Community

Have you been in a collective that exemplified the (sad) story I started the chapter with? What do you make of your collective's experience, now?

What stage of maturity is your collective in right now? What leadership obligations associated with that stage do you view as most important?

Make a commitment to lead the way your collective needs you to, to continue to progress. Share that commitment with comrades, to demonstrate your will, and to encourage others to do the same.

Has your collective recently experienced a setback in its maturity? What do you think caused it? What do you need to do in response? Can you prioritize your actions?

CHAPTER 12

Taking Stock of Your Collective:
The Community Walk

"Being active in the Community is as high a calling as there can be."

It's time for an interlude of sorts. Although I've encouraged you to do a fair amount of reflection to this point, the emphasis has been to offer a relatively complete picture of the effective Radical Community. Now, the emphasis shifts to provide you a platform to reflect on the material *vis a vis* **your collective**. Gaining a deeper and more sophisticated knowledge of your landbase, water, people, flora, fauna, and the threats to them, is an important prerequisite for effective resistance planning and leadership.

Consider why it's important to engage in discovery-based reflection like this:

- For its **own sake,** to gain a deeper understanding of your collective, its promise and perils, and to practice a reflective, discovery-oriented approach to leadership.
- To generate **deeper Commitment** – recall our conversation on the Values Chain.
- For **context**, as we discuss resistance strategies and options in the ensuing chapters.
- To **connect** with others, build comradeship, alliances, and networks.
- To promote **greater motivation**, to keep activists going by showing us we're not alone.
- To allow you to practice **telling your story**, engaging others in your vision.
- The mere act of engaging in your Walk can aid in your **Community-building** efforts. You might find you have created or strengthened relationships, gathered others to your vision, and so on.

To do this – to become "in and of" your Community, you need to walk about. Don't ignore the obvious; the ideal form for this is to physically explore your collective: meet and interact with those who inhabit the area, the neighborhood, the union. Engage in conversations, observations, research, and activities that reveal what your Community is all about. Record important details and themes as you discover them.

An excellent place to start is to visit your local museum if there is one. Museums often display more than just artifacts from a locality – they sometimes offer displays and materials relating local history, stories of past inhabitants and the like which can be valuable in revealing issues you might focus on as part of your organizing and leadership. A recent Walk I participated in helped me discover the importance of water to the local economy and its general well-being, as well as the challenges to maintaining the river quality for the Community. The visit also alerted me to the influence of mining to the area.

If you're physically out and about, examine your surroundings. Do posters or signs tell you anything? What do trace measures, evidence of wear and tear, use, etc. tell you? The physical space itself might have a lot to say.

We talked about the Janus effect, and your Walk is a good way to gather information about the past to feed your vision for the future. Remember, the further back in time you can go, the farther into the future you can set your Community vision.

- Don't limit your journey into the past. Your first inclination might be to discover what industries or businesses your town, e.g. was based on now and in the past. However, that will likely give you little you want to incorporate into your CPR collective going forward, as that perspective exemplifies the culture we are trying to dismantle.
- You could examine what types of agriculture took place in the past, and / or how others worked with the land. Unless working with the land in your past *excluded* agriculture, there's probably little to be gained here as well, since agriculture is yet another symptom of industrial civilization. If, though, there were sustainable ways of working the land, you might have uncovered a clue as to your collective's future.
- Better yet, research how indigenous peoples and their ancestors lived on the land. You'll do your collective a service by adopting this perspective into your Community vision and plans.
- A major theme we often forget in these research expeditions is to look into what **resistance** or Community organizing has taken place in your area, or in areas with similar challenges and threats. In addition to providing you solace that you are not alone in organizing for resistance, you might discover potential tactics and strategies you can use or adapt in your Community-building and strategic plans.

You might start by assessing the Length, Breadth and Depth of the collective. Consider also whether you would characterize the collective as a Deep Community, Proto-Community, or in some other stage of maturity. If you need additional structure, use the main points describing the components of Community and/or the characteristics of the stages of collective maturation. You may want to revisit your answers to the previous worksheets based on the discoveries and insights generated by your Walk.

What other techniques or approaches could you use to conduct the Walk? If you're unable to conduct a physical Walk, you can explore your Community using digital means as well as a visit to your library. In fact, it's not a bad idea to use this research to supplement your Walk anyway. If you have a platform to do so, conduct a survey to learn about the issues facing your collective, as well as the assets you can build on.

Later chapters will give you more perspectives with which to deepen your understanding. You might even repeat the Walk when you're armed with these complementary perspectives.

You can prepare a narrative summary if that works best for your style, or create a SWOT analysis with some details and your reflections on the results, or you can do both!

In the next chapter I'll revisit the notion of strategy. What you learn in your Community Walk can be valuable input to that analysis, so don't dismiss the Walk as an academic exercise or feel-good New Age game – in addition to the outcomes I mentioned, you'll be armed with better information to assess your collective and therefore make better strategic plans to protect and resist. Later, we'll reflect on how to leverage the Power you build.

Worksheet: Planning Your Community Walk

How far back in time did you go in your research? The longer the better!

Does your Community have an identifiable identity or consciousness? What is it? Does the collective have a name or identifiable location? What is its indigenous name? How strongly would you say this is shared among inhabitants? What can you do to develop or strengthen your collective's Consciousness?

What's your take on the other characteristics of a CPR Collective? How does your Community stack up against each? What are the strengths or positive aspects? What makes you proud to be a part of it? Reference the chapters for more details on the model. Practice your framing.

Does your Community have a vision for itself? What is **your** vision for it?

What problems, weaknesses or threats do you or others see to the health, welfare, or survival of your collective? How dire are the threats? What are the implications of the threats, or problems?

Does this analysis suggest action items? Reminder: for each component, I offer suggestions for how to strengthen it. Review those suggestions and build a plan to continue building your Community.

What resistance organizing is happening, if any? What roadblocks to organizing exist?

Where is your collective in the stages of maturity? What does the collective need from you or others to progress from this point?

Did you uncover any "leverage points", or hot-button issues you can organize around, or use as a catalyst for building a collective? Awareness of damage to the water supply or the land, rise in racism experienced but not articulated, homelessness or similar indicators of collapse, can be used as a catalyst to energize a populace or help them focus on resistance where they otherwise might not. Elevator speeches, visions, and organizing documents almost write themselves when you have a deep and clear understanding of your collective.

Don't ignore the role *time* (or natural cycles) and/or *crisis* can play in facilitating building a collective. Organizing around water issues should be enhanced during times of drought or flood, for example. Wildfires or forest fires exacerbated by clearcutting or land management issues serve as clear and present dangers you can use to your advantage with regard to solidifying Consciousness and subsequent Community building work. (Remember, crises often engender the formation of Proto-Communities. Your challenge is to seize that momentum, and help steer and move that collective to a Community that is deeper and more radical.)

CHAPTER 13

Thinking Strategically, Part 2: Community Building, Organizing, Mobilizing

The Strategic Context of Leveraging Power

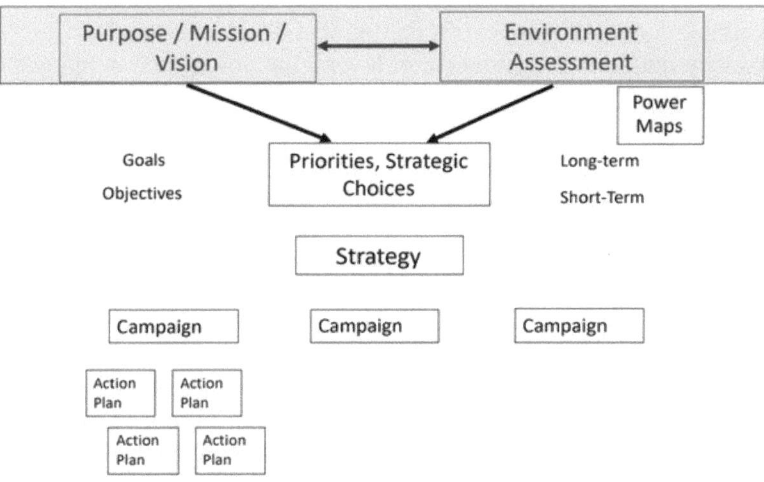

So far, we've focused on *building* Communities that Protect and Resist. We discussed the characteristics of such collectives: Consciousness, Comradeship, Commitment, Shared Power, and Leadership. We also noted action items you could accomplish to cultivate those characteristics.

This next stage is **leveraging your power**.

> *"Almost all transformative social change and social justice work historically...*
> *is the product of organizing and mobilization of local communities."*[147]

Writers who discuss organizing and mobilizing generally focus on objectives such as labor union work, political work, or similar concerns that aren't what we're committed to as a primary focus: building and leading Radical Communities.

---

[147]   DeFilippis, J., Fisher, R., & Shragge, E. (2010). Contesting Community: The Limits and Potential of Local Organizing. New Brunswick: Rutgers University Press, p.2

My model of leveraging power therefore differs somewhat, although I borrow from others as needed. I acknowledge best practices, add to them, and reframe them for Community resistance purposes. I also note that models of organizing or mobilizing often resemble lists of things to do, watch out for, and so on. While years of wisdom and experience drive the construction of these lists, I humbly offer a model that has a simple but effective rationale and conceptual structure to help you see what needs to be done to leverage Community Power most effectively. I'll do this by discussing:

- The strategic context of leveraging Community Power (mostly a review).
- The material elements of leveraging and how they interrelate.
- A simple model of campaigns, the foundation of leverage work.
- A vastly underrated component of leveraging power, action plans.

––––––––––

The graphic above reminds us of the importance of clarifying your Community's Purpose, Mission, and Vision. All strategic plans should spring from the coherent, grounded basis these factors lay out for you.

The "top line" of this strategy graphic contains elements you're already familiar with. You know how to engage in an environmental assessment, using a SWOT analysis. Our model of effective radical Communities can be used to build your collective and also as a frame to engage in your SWOT analysis with more granularity. Finally, we talked about how to process the SWOT results to make strategic choices, the results of which are the basic strategy of your Community. Let's introduce a valuable tool that serves as an adjunct to your environmental scan, the Power Map.

The Power Map.
Conscientious strategy work – articulating your vision and mission and conducting an environmental scan - results in effective Priorities and Strategic Choices. The Power Map allows you to take stock of factors not generally considered in a SWOT analysis.

Creating your Map enables you to chart your Community's key stakeholders, assess the amount of power they have (and conversely, the amount you have with respect to their success), whether each agency would be "for" or "against" you with respect to aiding in or hindering your mission accomplishment, serving as potential allies, and so forth.

Here's what a Power Map might look like, conceptually:

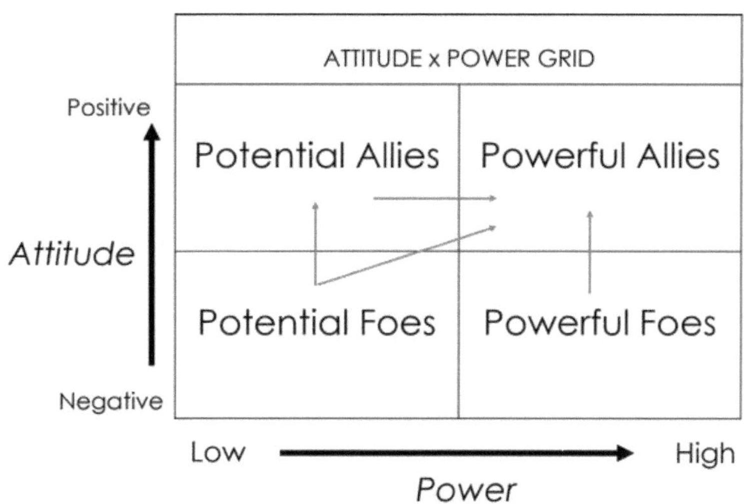

Creating the Power Map:

- Brainstorm or research the set of all relevant stakeholders (organizations, collectives or individuals) that might influence the success of your mission, or be influenced by your mission accomplishment.
- Reflect on their own power or capacity, as well as your collective's.
- Assess whether each stakeholder is supportive or potentially disruptive to your Community mission.
- Complete a 2 x 2 matrix (Powerful // Not Powerful, versus Supportive // Not Supportive) by placing each stakeholder you identify in one of the 4 cells.
- Choose the stakeholders most important for you to address initially. Limit your list to 3-5, or you'll become overwhelmed. (Pick up any remaining stakeholders when you complete your work addressing those on the initial list.)
- Develop a plan for how to address or deal with each chosen stakeholder depending on the cell they occupy in the Map.
- The arrows in the graphic indicate the type of "movement" you might aspire to bring about regarding the various stakeholders.
    - o For example, you might plan to increase the power of a relatively weak Potential Ally.
    - o You might plan to "flip" a powerful Foe so the group becomes an Ally.
    - o A weak Foe might also be flipped, and if so, you can collaborate with them to increase their power.
- Incorporate these plans into your overall strategy. You might consider the set of these plans a campaign, which we will investigate momentarily.

An example of a completed Power Map for an environmental justice collective might look like this:

A NOTIONAL POWER MAP EXAMPLE

My sense is that your Map will contain some of the same stakeholders as ours. Planners might use this map to, e.g., work with Deep Sea Defenders to increase their power, and/or ally more closely with CELDF to leverage their influence in service of your mission. What general plans might you develop if this was your Power Map?

A Bit of Power Map Philosophy:
We in the resistance lead with a purpose – to save the living world, and to replace the dominant culture with life-affirming Communities. To do that, we need to use our leadership to inspire others outside our own collectives to commit and engage – to buy in to resistance goals and missions.

The enemies of the living world are many and powerful, so to resist them we need to build our own Power, at every level – individual Comrades, Cadres, and Communities. At the same time, we need to strategically keep our eyes on others who have built their own capacity, or can influence ours, in order to make effective decisions regarding our relationships with them. It's the smart move.

This simple analysis tool can reap you a significant return. The result can be instrumental in leveraging others' (or your) influence or negating resistance. Power Maps help you get a bead on your strategic context. They have the added advantage of giving you a head start of sorts in your strategic planning. If you have completed a comprehensive Map, you will have several plans you can fold into your larger strategic plan. We'll talk about alliances more in a bit.

_ _ _ _ _ _ _ _ _

The graphic at the beginning of this chapter displayed the "big picture" or comprehensive characterization of strategic context. We talked about your Mission and Vision as the starting point of strategy – as the touchstone for addressing all the other components of a strategic plan. If you've read this far, you can create both a vision and a mission. We'll come back to these constructs again and again, but our main focus in this chapter is on the **lower portions** of the context graphic – campaigns and action plans.

Engaging in the discipline of strategic planning, though, is only useful inasmuch as it results in, well, plans! The graphic below is a way to conceptualize the various forms of plans in an overall strategy. Our focus on the lower portions of this hierarchy completes our overview of strategic planning.

Objective: A measure of progress toward achieving a goal. Milestones, for example, you need to reach to progress toward a goal.

Before we continue our journey through the Strategy landscape, though: **A Cautionary Diversion - Beware the Fractal Trap.** Have you felt uneasy differentiating between plans at the various levels in the graphic above? If this has never been a problem for you, good! Feel free to skip to the next section! However, if you have felt this unease, you're not alone – there's sometimes no clear line between where a strategy ends and a campaign begins.

It can be disconcerting trying to figure out which level you're working at – you know, "Is this a strategic plan, a campaign plan, or an action plan?" Sometimes, for example, a campaign is viewed as a strategy, and maybe vice versa. I call this phenomenon the fractal trap.

A fractal is a never-ending pattern. Fractals are infinitely complex patterns that are self-similar across different scales.[148] Many fractals possess the property of self-similarity, at least approximately, if not exactly. A self-similar object is one whose component parts resemble the whole. This reiteration of details or patterns occurs at progressively smaller scales and can, in the case of purely abstract entities, continue indefinitely, so that each part of each part, when magnified, will look basically like a fixed part of the whole object.[149] Think about snowflakes, with their unique but instantly recognizable shapes. As one zooms in on the flake, though, one notices that the overall shape appears over and over again, just at lower and lower levels of scale.

If you look too closely and too long at the plans hierarchy graphic above, you might fall into the fractal trap. You may feel there is little (surface) difference among the types of plans, since they may resemble each other, and look to be mere self-similar concepts, differentiated only by the label of level of hierarchy.

Does all this matter? Well, yes. **To be most effective in the planning context, you need to know what level of scope you're operating in.**
- If you confuse a strategic plan for a campaign plan or an action plan, you won't have enough detail to be actionable.
- If you confuse a campaign plan or an action plan for a strategy, you'll be losing sight of the larger perspective, and risk not addressing the full mission, goals and objectives.

Here's a rule of thumb that might help you determine where you are:
- If your plan directly addresses your Mission and Vision, it's likely a **Strategic Plan.**
- If your plan directly addresses goals/objectives, it's likely a **Campaign Plan.**
- If your plan directly addresses specific actions (and who performs them) it's likely an **Action Plan.**

Another helpful hint is to start with the big picture and drive down to greater levels of specificity until you've reached action plans. In other words, you should be good to go as long as you follow the general discipline of starting "global" and becoming detailed enough to take focused, repeatable action.

---

[148]   https://fractalfoundation.org/resources/what-are-fractals/
[149]   https://www.britannica.com/science/fractal_

Let's put our newfound perspective to work, and see if it helps. **Which of the following (if any) is a strategic plan?** See if you can decide by the end of each passage. I'll respond as we go along.

EXAMPLE 1: Standing Rock, AKA North Dakota Access Oil Pipeline (DAPL) Resistance.

> *"The local Standing Rock Sioux tribe and thousands of Native American supporters set up camps to try and block the oil project. Opponents of DAPL say the project threatens sacred native lands and could contaminate their water supply from the Missouri river.*
>
> *The first protest camp emerged when members of the Standing Rock Lakota and other Native American nations established a spiritual camp called Sacred Stone. Several other large camps, featuring a diverse mix of tribes and non-native supporters, later emerged nearby.*
>
> *The Standing Rock camps are all located about an hour south of Bismarck, North Dakota. Some camps are on lands controlled by the US army corps of engineers and other sites are on private land owned by Ladonna Allard, a member of the Dakota Sioux."*[150]

In the absence of a larger mission or vision I'm not aware of, the protest camp seems more like a tactic (an action planned to achieve a specific end). In my view, tactics are taken to administer an Action Plan, which I disuses shortly. I might agree the camps were established to meet the goal/objective of protecting the Missouri river waters from pollution. In that case, I'd consider this a campaign. What's your view?

EXAMPLE 2: Decisive Ecological Warfare (DEW) (Deep Green Resistance).

> *"These are the **strategies** articulated for a DGR movement, in order to achieve the goals of stopping the murder of the planet and rebuilding just, sustainable human communities."*[151] (Emphasis added.)

---

[150] https://www.theguardian.com/us-news/2016/nov/03/north-dakota-access-oil-pipeline-protests-explainer
[151] https://www.facebook.com/deepgreenresistance/photos/a.186438068081971/3839280179464390/

DGR Strategies	
STRATEGY A Engage in direct militant actions against industrial infrastructure, especially energy infrastructure.	STRATEGY B Aid and participate in ongoing social and ecological justice struggles; promote equality and undermine exploitation by those in power.
STRATEGY C Defend the land and prevent the expansion of industrial logging, mining, construction, and so on.	STRATEGY D Build and mobilize resistance organizations that will support the above activities, including decentralized training, recruitment, logistical support, and so on.
STRATEGY E Build a sustainable subsistence base for human societies (including perennial polycultures for food) and localized democratic communities that uphold human rights.	

There's more to DEW than pictured here, but if we take the introductory sentence at face value, that's a mission, right? The "strategies" A to E look like complementary campaigns designed to achieve goals and objectives in support of the larger DEW. So it might be a strategy. Maybe there could be another level of detail, like action plans, perhaps?

EXAMPLE 3: Prairie Protection Colorado (PPC)

> *"PPC advocates for prairie dogs by drawing attention to the mass exterminations of prairie dog colonies along the Front Range, and by organizing and resisting the destruction of the last remaining prairie communities. PPC organizes on the ground and works with local governments, the media and legal channels to cast a web of protection over the last remaining prairie dog colonies throughout Colorado's Front Range communities.*
> *Our overall approach consists of three core initiatives. These initiatives are not mutually exclusive – in fact, they complement and reinforce each other. "*

Habitat Protection

> *"We commit to preserving and protecting the land and its indigenous lives, both fauna and flora. Our focus centers on the prairie dogs, as they are a keystone species essential to the thriving prairie's grasslands and wildlife."*

Our Goals

"Protest, delay and/or dismantle every known effort to destroy prairie dogs and the prairie. Reverse the trend of prairie dog extermination ..."

Community Organizing

"Create supportive, genuine, robust relationships with virtual and geographic communities and individuals committed to saving the prairie and prairie dogs. Capitalize on the resources, skills, and energies of our friends and allies to create a powerful force for resistance."

Our Goals

"Identify, recruit, and engage righteous, committed allies who might focus on charges other than prairie dogs per se, and who may emphasize complementary tactics and strategies. Capture 75% of such organizations under such an umbrella..."

Education

"One reason prairie dogs ... are destroyed (and that there is so little resistance to this destruction) is that people and organizations labor under false conceptions of the value of the natural world and the imperative of resisting development, agriculture and ranching. We prepare and deliver programs to counter this deadly trend."

Our Goals

"Develop and deliver flyers and pamphlets that counter prevalent myths about prairie dogs and their place in the Front Range ecosystem..."[152]

PPC's plan seems well-fleshed out. There's a rationale up front for what the collective is trying to accomplish. The overall strategic intent statement is then supported by three campaigns. Even better, each campaign is fleshed out by several goals (not shown) that are easily translated into action plans. I give this plan a thumbs up. Couldn't have written this any better myself.

Not to pick nits, but technically, I'd make the assertion that none of these examples is a complete strategic plan since none has driven down to the action plan level. A strategy and a strategic plan are not necessarily the same thing.

----

[152] https://prairieprotectioncolorado.org/strategy

A major goal of this book is for you to be able to think critically about Community, leadership, and strategy, as these concepts are highly interrelated. Take a moment to do just that: Does your collective have a strategy? A strategic plan? Where does it fit in the hierarchy of plans we reflected on? If you have a plan but it's not complete and comprehensive, what do you have to do to strengthen it? We'll walk through what you can do to accomplish that very objective.

So much for the broader strategic thinking. Assessment of our context allows us to make strategic choices and to set expansive priorities, general goals and objectives. Let's talk now about bringing your strategy to life, by incorporating campaign plans and action plans to your strategic direction.

Campaigns: The Building Blocks of Strategy

Campaigns are how strategies get done. They complement each other, they make sense given your desired strategic direction, and they suggest the actions needed to move your strategy forward. Recall: A Campaign is work in an organized and active way toward a particular goal.

Campaigns break down Strategies into coherent, complementary initiatives that exemplify conceptual and action paths, impelled by a common strategic direction.

Campaign planning is also your best opportunity to exercise creativity, wisdom and insight in the planning process. You'd also benefit from looking at the strategic work of other resistance movements to generate a list of campaign "types" you might borrow from. You can glean some of these pearls from a well-conducted Community Walk.

You don't have to reinvent the wheel to produce a useful set of campaign types to suit your strategy, although they will of course need to be tailored to your circumstances. Here's a short list of campaign types I've gleaned from my experiences and research. For a fuller spectrum of campaigns and a description of the pros and cons of the various types, I recommend DGR's Taxonomy of Action.[153]
Public Relations / Media Outreach
Funding / Recruitment
Direct Action / Sabotage

----

[153] https://deepgreenresistance.net/nl/resistance/action-taxonomy/taxonomy-of-action/

How do you know which type(s) of campaign(s) to plan? Those decisions depend in great measure on your strategy. You know, contextual, or strategy-driven factors. We know campaign work needs to be strategic, in the sense that the campaigns materially articulate the strategy and help move resistance forward in the direction consistent with the vision.

What might a campaign look like? We've already seen several examples, like the Standing Rock protest camps, the five campaigns in support of the general DEW strategy, and the three campaigns outlined in the PPC strategy. We'll introduce a couple more in our campaign model below.

Let's look at how to construct a campaign. But first, a review of sorts. The graphic below, from Deep Green Resistance, illustrates how campaigns might fit into and support a larger strategy, and the types of support actions typically used to support campaign work.

But embedded in this larger structure should be an approach to designing campaigns we should pay attention to.

When Strategy is not enough:
The "EDS" Model of Campaigns

Resistance work is enormously difficult, fraught with the challenge of overcoming an overwhelming threat in the dominant culture. Despite the passion and commitment of activists, our work is too often not as effective as it needs to be, to save the living world. We're losing.

Resistance work has gotten smarter, though. There seems to be a greater emphasis on taking a strategic approach to our work, and we see more activist groups reflecting on their values and vision, taking stock of their strategic context, and leveraging that strategic orientation to craft campaigns to realize their strategic goals.

At the same time, Community organizing and campaign planning could use a bit of spring cleaning, and might benefit from what I believe is a more coherent approach. I acknowledge I stand on the shoulders of organizers who helped me learn about effective resistance organizing. I tip my hat to organizers who have, and do, essential work resisting the destruction of the living world. I'm looking at you, Deep Green Resistance, Deep Sea Defenders, and others.

Let's assume your collective has already come to grips with its purpose, mission, vision, environmental scan, strategic priorities and choices. This should leave you with your strategy. What needs to happen now is to make the strategy happen. That is the role of campaign work.

We would do well to also pay attention to the psychological aspects of campaign work. Activists and resistance warriors are passionate and committed, but they are also people, and the more we focus on the "people" aspects of campaigning, the more successful we are likely to be. I suggest the campaign choices you make depend on the "people" functions you need from a campaign, to complement strategy-driven factors. Let's look at how to construct a campaign using these considerations.

The EDS Model
The EDS Model asserts that an effective strategy consists of campaigns that address three intrinsic factors, not just external, strategy-drive ones. These intrinsic factors serve critical campaign functions:

Energize

Direct

Sustain

Why should we adopt a campaign design like this? Because the notional graph of the history of resistance campaigns probably looks like the one below. Would that all our resistance campaigns continue to successful fruition (*Type 1: Successful campaigns*). Sadly, though, all too many either lose steam and fade away, sometimes to be forgotten (*Type 3: Fade Away campaigns*), or suddenly stop or are canceled due to lack of interest, campaign organizers quitting, or any number of other factors (*Type 2: Sudden Death campaigns*). Too few maintain a high level of energy and commitment through the life of the campaign, resulting in successful completion of the campaign's goals and objectives.

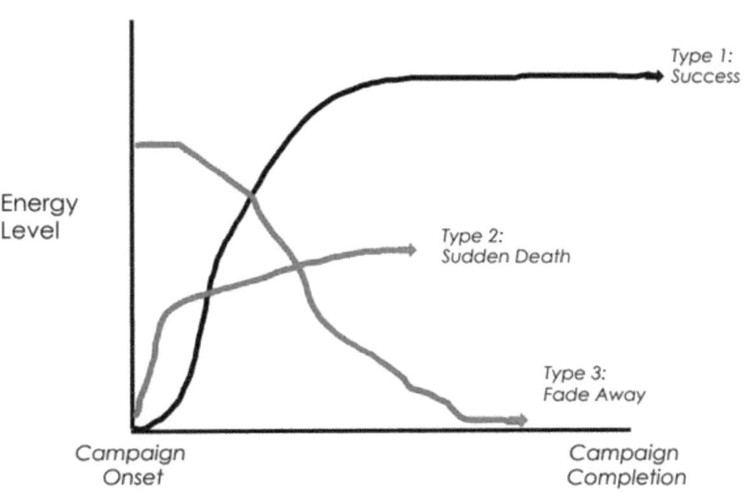

You might have noticed that Energize, Direct and Sustain collectively describe the motivation construct from psychology. Good call! Yes, we're borrowing from a common definition, but with good reason. Campaigns should collectively serve to **energize** comrades, **direct** their efforts, and **sustain** commitment over the long haul. This is what I see as missing from discussions of Community organizing in general and campaign work in particular. Let's explore each component.

Energize.
Even committed activists sometimes need to be motivated to pursue a campaign and devote substantial time and energy to it. You may find that for your campaign to be successful, you need to energize comrades **internal** to the collective as well as larger groups in the Community and/or **surrounding environs** – perhaps even regional or national audiences.

Much of the energy for campaign work springs from strong leadership on the part of the collective, whether from Elders or organizers. I urge organizers to enhance their leadership skills, as they are critical to ensuring the Community is willing to struggle for their shared aspirations. At the same time, campaign organizers can and should tap into the emotional reservoir people have regarding the living world.

"Campaigns work when people feel emotionally driven to protect someone, whether it be a natural community, river, a specific species, or a struggle against oppression. The more the issue can be refined to a particular place or individual, the more buy-in from the public and the more folks are willing to participate in the struggle."
DGR Campaign Strategy

"You can't fight for what you don't love, and you can't love what you don't know."
Deep Green Resistance

One particularly effective tactic for generating emotional attachment is to leverage **visual means**. Planners need to craft a compelling emotional appeal for comrades and the public at large to get involved. Whether it's a picture of a threatened bird species or of a massacred landscape, some kind of visual image can draw people in and give them the "hook" to want to help defend the life you are working to save. Pictures are nice, but video is even better, if you have the resources. (Thanks to the Deep Green Resistance Campaign Strategy.)

For radical environmentalists and social justice activists, it's important to focus deeper than just the imminent danger or outrage your campaign addresses. Ensure those you're communicating to understand the **root** issue at hand. Drive home (again and again if necessary) the point that the dominant culture/system must be dismantled. You want to **invoke not just rage against the forces you're resisting, but love for the living**. Help others understand, too, they are not alone in their love and rage – normalize these feelings, and focus them on where they most belong – love for the living, rage against the strategic targets and what they represent.

"The more we can highlight the broken system by illustrating what is happening to the land we love, the better equipped the … movement will be at drawing attention to the ecocidal machine bearing down on our planet."
DGR Campaign Strategy

Tell Your Story.
Complement your visuals with narratives when you can. Write an essay that tells the story of the issue and drives the emotional appeal by clarifying, "Why should I get involved?". People need to understand **why** your issue is important and just as significant, **how they can help**. Keeping people informed by telling an emotionally engaging story is essential in keeping activists involved and willing to engage in the struggle.

Get the word out.
People can't get excited about issues they aren't aware of. Get the word out. Where appropriate, petitions, fundraisers, social media, and other means help garner support for the campaign (and more generally, the issue).

Actively engage in public speaking, debates, seminars and the like to get your message across in a way that taps into the emotional component of the campaign. Attend conferences, town halls, and other meetings, too. Crash them as necessary. Host salons and educational meetings. Write (articles, posts, etc.)!

"Media power is political power."

"One can lack any of the qualities of an organizer – with one exception – and still be effective and successful. That exception is the art of communication. It does not matter what you know about anything if you cannot communicate to your people. In that event, you are not even a failure. You're just not there."[154]

Saul Alinsky

Communication is a fundamental aspect of leadership and organizing.

Are you uncomfortable with public speaking or writing? Our discomfort pales in comparison to the pain being borne by the ravaged land. So, give it a shot. And you know the only way to get better, right? Practice.

"People must make their own decisions and come to their own conclusions. All we can do is help them along. <u>Meet people where they are at</u>."[155]

Conduct educational meetings at a local library or school.
Put on your own cultural events, and emphasize the campaign goals and objectives as integral aspects. Remember Snake Valley's Annual Water Festival, discussed in the Comradeship chapter? Another example of the flexible nature of these sorts of events.

---

[154] Alinsky, S. (1971). Rules for Radicals: A Pragmatic Primer for Realistic Radicals. New York: Vintage Books.
[155] Wilbert, M. & Thompson. D. (2015). Presentation on Organizing, Deep Green Resistance Conference.

Claim the mainstream!
I'll say this metaphorically for the most part, so as not to lose my audience entirely, but: "Cut your hair and shine your shoes."
- We're recruiting, not weeding out.
- If you can come across as not "fringe'y" or extreme and keep your integrity, do it.

Communicate with confidence and conviction. You have conviction or you wouldn't be doing this work. Just practice a bit, and understand that no one understands the issue as well as you. Make others see it.

Si Kahn, Community Organizer, offers pithy tips for organizing in his book, *Creative Community Organizing*. Here are Energize-relevant offerings, followed by a comment of my own here and there:

>*"As a creative community organizer, you are always trying to figure out people's common self-interest, the glue that binds...."*
>
>Always clarify the vision, and the line of sight. You'll likely want to refer again and again to your compelling vision for your Community.

>*"It is generally useful, as a part of any creative community organizing campaign, to advocate for a positive as well as to oppose a negative."*
>
>This is what effective visions do. If you don't have one, work with comrades to develop yours.

>*"You need to believe that human beings... can somehow find some common connection. To do that, leave your stereotypes at the door."*
>
>We can do better than that! The common connection is Comradeship, and connection to the natural world. Communicate this as much as you can.

>*"... in campaigns for justice, the people are always partly united, partly divided. It's up to you to reinforce unity and to compensate for the divisions among the people with whom you work."*
>
>Again, comradeship, culture, and the unifying power of a powerful vision.

>*"Be certain [comrades] understand the risks they're taking, the things that could go wrong, losses they might suffer, before they make the decision to act."*[156]

---

[156] Kahn, S. (2010). Creative Community Organizing: A Guide for Rabble-Rousers, Activists, and Quiet Lovers of Justice. San Francisco: Berrett-Koehler.

Remember Realistic Job Previews? That can be an excellent part of your campaign communiques. RJPs will help you Sustain involvement in your campaigns, too.

Direct.
Energy without direction is chaos. When we set campaigns in motion without clear direction, we waste our comrades' time. Campaigns need to focus participants' energy to be effective. We need to make sure efforts are directed toward campaign goals and that they're consistent with the values of the Community. We also need to make sure everyone in the campaign is working toward the **same** end, although tasks might be complementary and not exactly the same.

Finally, we need to ensure participants know what to do, and how to do it. We must train comrades and build their confidence in their ability to successfully take on resistance tasks – i.e., cultivate their self-efficacy.

How can we ensure a strong sense of direction for our campaigns? A commonsense starting place is the vision – ideally, **a vision not just for the Community but also for the campaign itself**. Make it a practice to refer to your touchstone early and often, to make sure everyone is aligned with that touchstone. A benefit of this approach is that committed comrades will engage in work and generate ideas and procedures that move you toward that vision in ways you did not even anticipate. Allow comrades to use their experience and creativity to further the realization of your campaign's goals.

More than a vision, though, you need a strategy, long- and short-term. If you've been working your way through this book interactively, you already have that. Make sure the strategy is shared as widely it can be, consistent with security culture. Ensure participants in the campaign understand how their work contributes to the strategy. This "line of sight" should be made clear and revisited often.

Recruit wisely to the campaign staff (Cadre) and socialize them effectively into your collective's culture.

Where possible, share your rationale regarding target selection, if there is a target associated with your campaign. Help campaign participants understand the "why" of the target(s) selected to stimulate commitment and open the door to greater conceptual and material contributions by others to the effort. Ditto with respect to the tactics you plan to use. I'll discuss a technique for selecting targets in the next Strategy chapter.

Observe, talk to, and learn from experienced, successful organizers.

Use the information in the next section to draft effective action plans.

<u>Cultivate Community Awareness of the Issues.</u>
Successful Community efforts are more likely to occur when the process includes measuring and analyzing the needs and problems of the Community.

One effective way to do this is through Community-Based Research (CBR).[157] CBR efforts devote time and resources to understand problems and possible solutions. The next Strategy chapter explains CBR. You'd also benefit from a well-executed Community Walk. Gathering information is one way to involve members and can in itself be a way to build Community. Members gain knowledge about the Community and forge stronger relationships with other members. The results of information-gathering and analysis often provide direction for how to proceed with next steps.

<u>Stay Focused:</u>
> *"Without strategic analysis, resistance leaders will often not know what that 'next step' should be, for they have not thought carefully about the successive steps required to achieve victory…. The result of failures to plan strategically is often drastic: one's strength is dissipated, one's actions are ineffective, energy is wasted on minor issues, advantages are not utilized, and sacrifices are for naught."*
>
> *"Once a sound strategic plan is in place, the… forces should not be distracted by minor moves… that may tempt them to depart from the grand strategy [in favor of] unimportant issues.*
> *As long as the basic analysis is judged to be sound, the task of the [resistance] is to press forward stage by stage."*[158]

Gene Sharp

These quotes help explain from another vantage point the danger of the fractal trap, and give us another conceptual peek at what strategic thinking is about.

— — — — — — — — —

[157] Strand, K., Marullo, S., Cutforth, N., Stoecker, R., & Donohue, P. (2003). Community-Based Research and Higher Education. San Francisco: Jossey-Bass.

[158] Gene Sharp, quoted by Max Wilbert & Dillon Thompson in: Wilbert, M. & Thompson. D. (2015). Presentation on Organizing, Deep Green Resistance Conference.

Si Kahn again:
> *"Start the process of strategy development by imagining that instant just before victory. Then working backwards, do your best to figure out the steps that will lead to that moment."*

> *"The more complicated a strategy or tactic, the harder it is to carry out, and the less likely it will be successful. If you want 100s or 1000s to participate in a campaign, you need to ask the great majority of them to do one thing, and only one."*
A clear plan, clearly communicated, with clear roles and responsibilities, has great value. Also, Action Plans! Know how to create effective plans and how to execute them.

> *"Even in the internet age, personal relationships still count, especially when you're asking people to do something. When recruiting volunteers, give them a specific list of campaign needs from which they can choose."*
Does your collective have plans for comrades to develop and grow in resistance-relevant aspects?

You may find it difficult or distasteful to be directive, given our general rejection of the dominant culture and patriarchy. Don't worry – you're not selling out, you're providing the means for participants in your campaign to find a place, to contribute their ideas and expertise, and to find solace and confidence in the potential for the campaign, and themselves, to succeed.

Be the adult in the room, who understands the value of organizations and of being responsible to others in the pursuit of Community and resistance.
Be a good leader!

––––––––––

Sustain.
Resistance campaigns can be isolating, draining, and seemingly never-ending. Comrades need to be psychically nourished and supported to endure the rigors of campaign work and resistance in general. The best efforts to energize and direct your campaign will fade away in these circumstances unless you mindfully address the longer term.

<u>Form a Core (Cadre).</u> You need a focused, cohesive group that is collectively able to commit to on-the-ground work, planning and/or executing on important tasks. Cadre development and leadership skills are a real plus.

Build your "resistance". Beyond your Cadre, a strong group of activists, willing to put in the time and effort, is key to a successful campaign. Make sure they have meaningful work to do. Keep in constant touch with your activist base. Group emails, calls, meetings keep people connected, and help to organize and motivate them to continue to struggle. We'll talk more in the next chapter (Getting Ready to Work). Remember "Encourage and Uplift" from the first Chapter, too.

Guarantee early involvement and support from Indigenous populations and organizations. We are all on stolen land. Efforts to protect and defend the land should involve indigenous groups wherever possible. We must hear their voice before making decisions, plotting a course, etc. We should invite their leadership in our strategies, campaigns and actions.

There are practical reasons, too:
- Established contacts and pre-existing relationships with indigenous groups provide channels of communication necessary for success in leveraging power.
- Indigenous members and their leaders can legitimize attitudes toward a campaign and any other form of resistance.
- Indigenous groups may provide access to resources (people, facilities, knowledge, and ties to other organizations or Communities) necessary for the successful execution of resistance work.

Build a network of relationships inside and outside the core members of the campaign, and perhaps the Community. Build and / or join coalitions of like-minded activists.

"…without a wider vision, community organizations will remain focused on the local. The challenge is to build an agenda that transcends local work and to find ways to connect with broader organizations and build alliances to work for fundamental social change."[159]

Coalitions work because they accumulate power across organizations and other collectives. They also work when they serve to capitalize on skills, knowledge and other resources organizers need to execute on the campaign plan.

The Protect Thacker Pass Campaign vividly illustrates how this works. Campaign organizers created the campaign to protect the Nevadan landbase from harmful lithium mining. Rather than rely on a small group of activists to carry out the

---

[159] DeFilippis, J., Fisher, R., & Shragge, E. (2010). Contesting Community: The Limits and Potential of Local Organizing. New Bruns-wick: Rutgers University Press.

campaign, organizers allied themselves with local and regional organizations to build their power and exert greater leverage to protect the land.

From the Protect Thacker Pass Campaign Facebook page:
"In solidarity with the land and Paiute/Shoshone elders, we are here to stop Lithium Nevada Corporation from mining Peehee Mu'huh (aka Thacker Pass) for lithium."[160]

A recent press release reveals more allies joining the effort:
> *"Conservation and Public Accountability Groups to argue the Illegality of the proposed Thacker Pass Lithium Mine*
> *RENO, NV. —On Thursday January 5, 2023, the combined plaintiffs, a coalition of conservation and public accountability groups, Tribes, and Thacker Pass area rancher, will present oral arguments in opposition to the Thacker Pass Lithium Mine Final Environmental Impact Statement and Record of Decision in the District of Nevada, challenging the Bureau of Land Management's ("Bureau") approval of the Thacker Pass Lithium Mine."*[161]
>
> *Among the list of environmental groups joining the coalition: Great Basin Resource Watch / Basin and Range Watch / Wildlands Defense / Western Watersheds Project.*

Deep Green Resistance has a solid track record of building alliances on an *ad hoc* basis to accomplish campaign goals. (Note similarities to conducting a Power Map exercise.) Their analysis of what it takes to engage in this process effectively is summarized below.

<u>Actionable advice for coalitions (From Deep Green Resistance).</u>
Building principled alliances depends on a series of steps that must be undertaken with intelligence and great care:
1. Movement Building. You can't build an alliance as individuals. They're built between organizations. Do the work of identifying core issues, articulating core values, and bringing together a team / organization to act.
2. Objectives. Alliances depend on you clearly understanding what you're trying to achieve. Determine your objectives. Ensure they're SMART and practical. Maybe also sequence objectives along a timeline toward broader strategic goals.
3. Political Context. Conduct a "spectrum of allies" exercise [or in our case, a Power Map]. Identify Communities, individuals, and organizations involved in the situation

---

[160] https://www.facebook.com/ProtectThackerPass
[161] Protect Thacker Pass (2023). Conaservation and Public Accountability Groups to argue the Illegality of the proposed Thacker Pass Lithium Mine
https://www.protectthackerpass.org/press-release-conservation-and-public-accountability-groups-to-argue-the-illegality-of-the-proposed-thacker-pass-lithium-mine/

or who may be swayed to take part, and how sympathetic they are to your perspective.

4. Potential Allies. Determine which organizations you'll focus on. This includes "easy allies" who will work with you regardless, and pivotal allies among those who are ambivalent or opposed to you. Identify areas of overlap, shared values, and how to effectively communicate with them.

5. Relationships and Negotiation. Talk with potential allies. Build a relationship. Don't gloss over disagreements; focus on areas of mutual benefit and values. Propose specific ways to work together toward shared goals.[162]

<u>Highlight campaign successes</u>, and get media involved where possible. Celebratory emails, victory parties, and anything else that keeps the group together and builds momentum is invaluable. Show comrades that not only is success achievable, it is happening now. Use social media often to keep activists involved in the work.

<u>Remember the lesson of Realistic Job Previews (RJPs)</u>. RJPs inoculate comrades against the potential drawbacks, pitfalls and risks associated with a task or role. As a result, individuals are more likely to "stick it out" when they can prepare themselves mentally for the challenges they will face.

<u>Incorporate Humor into your Campaign.</u> No joke – the strategic use of humor can play several important roles in keeping spirits high in an otherwise stressful and demanding campaign. Gallagher and Navone (2019) provide an interesting take on how humor can be used in resistance efforts:

Humor Facilitates Outreach and Mobilization:
Humor can attract more members; it becomes more fun to be involved, and it brings energy. It especially works to attract young people and students, although the increase in membership may be an unexpected side-effect of the use of humor."

Humor Facilitates a Culture of Resistance:
"[Humor] protected people's self-respect and gave the population some sort of control in an otherwise uncontrollable situation. The jokes also served to break down isolation and create a solidarity and group identity within the population. Because so many people shared the jokes, their very existence contradicted the … propaganda that people who did not join them would stand alone…. The jokes also provided an image of nation-wide solidarity that vitally assisted the resistance effort."[163]

'Each Joke is a Tiny Revolution'[164]

---

[162] DGR News Service (2022). How to Build a Coalition. https://dgrnewsservice.org/featured/how-to-build-a-coalition/

[163] Gallagher, A., & Navone, A. Humor as a Serious Strategy of Nonviolent Resistance to Oppression
https://onlinelibrary.wiley.com/doi/full/10.1111/j.1468-0130.2008.00488.x

[164] George Orwell, quoted in Gallagher & Navone

Humor is a Healing Practice. Living under and resisting authoritarianism places immense stress on a population. Nonviolent movements can turn violent as a result. But humor can help keep the peace. Laughter can be a pressure-relief valve—releasing excess steam. Laughter relaxes individuals and shifts their tendencies away from violence.

Tension in conflict, even nonviolent conflict, can take its toll on those involved. Humor offers an effective mechanism through which nonviolent movements can assuage fears and achieve reconciliation for sustained peace.

Laughter is also a resistance tactic. Don't ignore this when you consider your strategic options. I'll discuss in a later chapter.

<u>Build Needed Organizational Structures.</u> Don't rely on emotional inertia alone to keep campaigns going. Protracted resistance efforts in particular need organizational structures to maintain momentum and to consolidate gains, material assets, and "corporate memory" from experienced activists and elders.

> *"Community organizing [sic] is premised on the assumption that building a relatively permanent [organizational] structure with clear processes of delegation of power and roles facilitates longevity and democracy."*[165]

Si Kahn one more time:
> *"Laughter really is therapeutic, and hope does heal.*
> *Be cheerful in the face of adversity, and help others feel that way."*

> *"The more sure you are of yourself, of your experiences in other communities and campaigns, the more you have to struggle to avoid the arrogance of thinking you know what's right for people."*[166]
> This is the utility of humility.

– – – – – – – – – –

Let's remind ourselves that the EDS Model or any rationalized approach to campaigns and Community organizing helps us better remember what we need to incorporate into our campaigns, since we don't have to rely on memorizing lists..

Even better, a model like this frees us to use our creativity to devise new ways and techniques of "organizing" or mobilizing. When we understand the EDS

---

[165] DeFilippis, J., Fisher, R., & Shragge, E. (2010). Contesting Community: The Limits and Potential of Local Organizing. New Brunswick: Rutgers University Press.

[166] Kahn, S. (2010). Creative Community Organizing: A Guide for Rabble-Rousers, Activists, and Quiet Lovers of Justice. San Francisco: Berrett-Koehler.

components, we can generate new and better ways of accomplishing each. And any time we can unleash the energy and creativity of organizers and comrades, our resistance work benefits.

The Hidden Lever of Strategy and Community Power:
Action Plans

There's one last bit to this discussion, and despite it occupying the bottom rung in the hierarchy of plans, it's arguably the most important, because it's where strategy becomes real. Here's a refresher if you need it.

Action Plans list all the tasks needed to finish to meet an objective; they focus on achievement of a single goal. They're useful because they give you a framework for thinking about how you'll complete a project efficiently.

Action Plans contain enough detail to achieve an objective or goal. They might include an outline of measurements, dates and responsible agents for each step. A good plan is based on clear, well-defined, easily understood objectives. General objectives like "improving morale" are ambiguous and don't lend to specific steps and plans.

Here's a way to assess whether your action plan is detailed enough: It should be **replicable** – someone else not familiar with the task should be able to use your plan and do it just like you would, with the same outcome.

As mundane as they might seem, action plans can really help successfully complete a campaign.

- Action Plans help you prepare for the obstacles ahead and keeps you on track.
- In the process, it gives you a clear direction. A good plan highlights exactly what steps to be taken and when they should be completed. The initiators of the plan will know exactly what they need to do.
- Having your goals written down and planned out in steps gives you a reason to stay motivated and committed throughout the project.
- You can track your progress toward your goal.
- Since you are listing all the steps you need to complete, it will help you prioritize your tasks based on effort and impact.

Action plans are succinct and efficient, and so will be this description! Creating an Action Plan:

> Step 1: Define your end goal / objective.
> Step 2: List down the tasks.
> Step 3: Prioritize tasks.
> Step 4: Set dates, Milestones.
> Step 5: Identify resources needed.
> Step 6: Monitor, evaluate and update.

Let's work through an example: Consider a hypothetical strategy:

Protect our landbase from the destructive effects of tourism.
Campaigns (A potential list.):

- Get local Luddite Party elected (political organizing).
- Get an anti-tourism referendum on the ballot.
- Establish a communication campaign focused on tourists.
- **Start an education campaign for residents regarding the value of protecting the landbase.** (This was chosen by me for fleshing out as an action plan, below).
- Establish a long-term blockade of the vulnerable area, and / or occupy the space with caretakers, defenders.
- Engage in outreach/alliance building with local indigenous groups.
- Dismantle roads, paths, parking lots, outhouses, water stations catering to tourists.

Example: **Education campaign** for residents re value of protecting the landbase.

TASK	TARGET DATE	AGENT	RESOURCES	MEASURES	COMMENTS
Research actual effects of tourism	May 1	R. Starkey	Library card, internet access	Report of findings	Check with local activists
Recruit education experts	May 1	C. Broadus	Roster of community members	Dr X ratings of candidates	
Create educational materials	May 20	G. Sumner	Computer, printing access	Approval of Board	Make them age-appropriate
Identify dispersal venues for handouts	May 14	R Dwight	Computer, auto	Approval of Board	Need traffic-heavy spaces
Convene "beta" event	June 5	A.M. Bullock	Venue access, rental fees	Attendees' ratings, feedback	Cheaper is better
Select speakers to serve as the face of the campaign	May 28	P. Andrejewski	Roster, interview space	Board Approval	
Schedule the talks	May 28	J. Fink	Computer, phone, rental fees	Board Approval	Try for 6-week window
Evaluate results	July 17	D. McManus	Survey software, phone, Facebook page	Post-action report	Present to Board

I hope that doesn't look complicated because it isn't. It's pretty easy stuff. If there's an art to action plan development, it's being able to generate the tasks to flesh out the plan appropriately. It can take a bit of introspection or group brainstorming to get a task list that is comprehensive and usable.

How do you know if the list is complete? As before, I invoke the notion of replicability (repeatability). The action plan should be specific enough that anyone could pick it up and to do what you envisioned, and to the level of effectiveness you want. To get a sense of this, ask someone unfamiliar with the action plan for feedback as to whether she / he could use the plan and do what's asked.

This is also an excellent opportunity for you to mentor and later delegate to others as part of their comrade and leadership development. Mentees can see how the sausage is made (in a good way) and practice deeper thinking with respect to campaign work. Use all the talents in your Community!

As a coda to this chapter, the following graphic makes the important point that strategic planning is a cyclical process. If you're good, and you are, you'll always have planning and plan revisions at the forefront of your mind. You should also always be communicating planning concepts and ideas to others, and soliciting their inputs. Internalizing this perspective allows you and your collective to be nimble and flexible, and in the process create strength for the group.

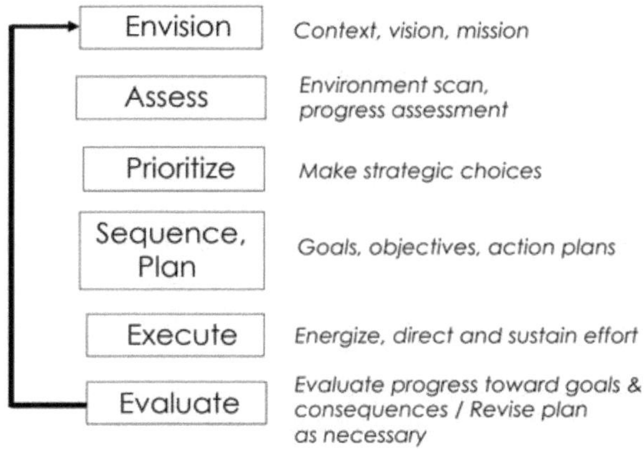

Evaluating a Strategy

As you become increasingly involved in crafting or revising a strategy for your collective, it becomes important for you to think critically about strategy, too. **We can't know for certain that a particular strategy is ideal, and neither can we guarantee it will succeed. However, we can do a disciplined job of evaluating strategies, using criteria to help determine the best option**.

Being disciplined about assessing your strategic context, developing objectives and goals, campaign plans and action plans is the wisest path you can take in your role as leader of your collective in the broad sense. Your work is likely to result in plans that serve your Community and your collective's ability to Protect and Defend, to survive and thrive.

This "front to back" approach to strategy building is really the only reasonable path. However, a "back to front" evaluation will help you adjust your Plan. As with Community Building in general, and guiding your Cadre through its inevitable stages

245

of maturation, strategy work is a process you embark on with the perspective that the work is never done – it's what you do. So, build your plan, and adjust it as necessary (using the following criteria and your reflections on the results as guides), and when you get a sense your strategic context has changed or evolved, engage in the process again. Is this all easy? No, but it's part of the burden of Community Leadership. As I've said before, though, you needn't try do this alone. Be a leader, not a loner.

<u>Strategy Evaluation Criteria (From Deep Green Resistance)</u>
Suitability:
- Is the proposed strategy consistent with foreseeable Threats and Opportunities?
- Does the strategy exploit Strengths or Opportunities?

Consistency:
- Are basic elements of the strategy consistent with each other and with the objectives being pursued?

Feasibility:
- Is the strategy appropriate given available resources?
- Are the basic elements and premises of the strategy understandable and acceptable to comrades who will implement it?

Vulnerability:
- Are the risks of failure acceptable?
- Are there contingency plans for dealing with these risks?
- Can decisions be reversed in the future? How long would it take? What are the consequences?

Potential Rewards:
- Are the projected outcomes satisfactory?

– – – – – – – – – –

Your ability to master the simple concepts discussed in this chapter will prepare you to think strategically, and to develop the same capacity in your collective. One result is that your collective will be able to navigate the strategic context and environmental changes that threaten your collective, or that provide opportunities for you to build your power and leverage it.

Armed with an effective planning discipline and the tools to bring your strategy to life, your next challenge is to set the stage for action. What's involved in getting ready to work? Let's see.

Worksheet: Planning the Implementation of Your Strategy

You may want to refer to your Community Walk results to reflect on these issues.

Were you able to assess your Strategic Context? What are your key takeaways?

What has your Power Map identified regarding stakeholders you need to plan for?

What does your Strategic Plan look like to this point? Perhaps your Plan is not completed (it never will be, by the way, as this planning work is a continual process), but do you perhaps have:

- A Vision for your Collective?
- A Mission Statement you feel good about?
- Goals? Objectives?

How does your Plan measure up against the criteria for an effective plan? What adjustments do you need to make?

Are you and your collective planning or engaging in any campaigns or campaign work? If not a campaign of your own, are you involved in a campaign led by another organization or collective? Describe!

How can you incorporate elements of the EDS Model into these campaign initiatives?

Have you contributed Action Plans related to this campaign work, or for your Strategic Plan or planning process?

CHAPTER 14

Getting Ready to Work

There are two perspectives to the challenge of "Getting Ready to Work", and if you master the concepts, you'll be more effective at the front **and** back ends of Community building and leveraging power.

The **first perspective** roughly translates to, "Now that you've crafted your strategy, how do you make it happen?" As much as you have invested in building a resistance Community and planning its continued development and/or its protection and resistance, you will still have to begin to implement the plans. I spend the rest of this chapter with this orientation guiding the discussion.

The **second perspective** is that the practices I relay in this chapter work just as well for Community builders starting from scratch! Committing to these practices will help you at the start of and throughout your Community leadership work.

A **related alternative** is that the practices I offer here could be well used as you begin the strategic planning process. These practices can and should be revisited at several points in your Community-building work. Since I view Community-building and strategic planning as unending cycles, it only makes sense that you'll touch this base over and over again as your Community unfolds.

Although the first perspective fits best here for purposes of logical flow, you might do well to revisit the early chapters after you have reflected on what's here. Like the spiral of experience I talked about in the preface, you should find that you will experience the concepts of earlier chapters with a deepened appreciation and broader viewpoint.

Fundamental Practices in Getting Ready to Work

There are four practices (areas of preparation) to consider. Mattessich & Monsey, and Murphy & Cunningham suggest a list like this in discussing the characteristics of the Community-building process. The wisdom bears discussion from our viewpoint, too.
- Form a Core (Cadre)
- Cultivate Community Awareness of the Issue(s)
- Ensure a Good System of Communication
- Guarantee early involvement and support from existing Indigenous organizations

Form a Core (Cadre)

Getting ready to build your collective, launch your plans or implement your strategy is demanding, complicated and stressful. Unless you're superpowered, you probably won't be able to tackle all this alone. Your first priority should be to convene a group to head up the effort.

You've probably noted this "Core" sounds an awful lot like the Cadre I talked about in the second chapter. For all intents and purposes, it is! Reviewing Cadre leadership concepts and reminding yourself how to build and lead a group like that is important. However, there are additional considerations to keep in mind, because the "Core" version of a Cadre is unique, and its charter more demanding than other Cadres.

<u>Why convene a Core?</u> You need a focused, cohesive group that collectively can commit to on-the-ground work, collective-building, planning, leading and/or implementing strategic and tactical initiatives. To begin, you may want your Core to serve as primary contributors to your strategic and campaign planning.

These comrades can also provide the Energize, Direct and Sustain functions for major campaigns. They can do that for more than one campaign at a time, and depending on the size of your collective, you might have several Cores involved in various campaigns.

<u>Considerations in Core Formation.</u> Make sure the Cadre is representative of the Community. Your Cadre should reflect the Shared Power you built into your CPR collective, but the diversity should complement the charter of the Cadre, and should not be for show.

How large should your Core be? If you're looking for a hard and fast rule, there isn't one, but 3-7 comrades generally is a good rule of thumb, all things being equal (which is rarely the case, but is a good starting point. Cores of this size range tend to create a balance between being wieldy enough to work well as a unit, and at the same time large enough to generate critical mass for getting things done.

If your Community is especially diverse, you may need to balance representativeness with having a workable size. When in doubt, I'd err on the side of ensuring all members' voices are represented in the Core, and if that results in a large group, you'll need to exercise your Cadre leadership skills and your centering skills to keep the group cohesive and focused. The scope of the campaign or the initiative is also a consideration. The larger or more complex the undertaking, the larger the Core may have to be.

<u>What is your Core's Charter?</u> There should be one, even if it's communicated via conversations. All members of the Core should be clear regarding what they are charged with doing, and why. If you've never written or produced this sort of "marching order", here's a boilerplate you can use:
- "Coordinate, manage and oversee the implementation of the
  - o   Community-building
  - o   Strategy
  - o   Campaign
  - o   Ad hoc efforts to protect and resist"
- Specify roles where you can (norms, too), especially those specific to the undertaking and to the members of the Core.
- Relate the Charter to the overall Strategic Plan. Keep the line of sight clear by doing the same regarding the mission and vision for the collective. Comrades in the Core should absolutely know how their Core functions contribute to the overall direction and survival of the Community.

Not everyone who works on a campaign or as part of the Community-building process is necessarily a Core member. Your Cadre are the truly trusted comrades, and/or the most experienced. This does not imply a hierarchy; Core members may be entrusted with responsibilities other Community members are not, but that is a matter of diversity regarding role, not of value.

What should you look for in a Core member if you have a choice? Here are a few desirable qualities you can use to select members. (Note: If you **can't find** a deep selection of comrades with these qualities already, don't despair: Your other option is to **develop them,** as you'll remember from the Cadres chapter.)

Here's another rule of thumb, to keep things relatively simple and thematically clear: If yours is a strong CPR Collective, many if not all comrades will already possess most or all the characteristics of a Land Defender:

- A deep connection with the land or those you protect.
- Love of place / Community coming from that deep connection.
- Commitment to Community, arising from connection to / love for it.
- Commitment to the vision and mission of the Community.
- Mutually supportive with other Core members.
- Readiness to Sacrifice.
- Trustworthiness.

These qualities are the fundamental traits you want. If you're looking for characteristics that would **really** make for a comrade who can fulfill the Core Charter, add:

- Leadership skills.
- Community organizing experience.
- Discipline, integrity, loyalty.
- Professionalism, maturity.

I hope this list doesn't look too formidable. It shouldn't – this is us! Select with care, but don't underestimate your ability to lead and develop Core members, too. Core building and maintenance is a great opportunity to practice your Cadre-building skills!

––––––––––

Cultivate Community Awareness of the Issues
Building a radical Community begins with Community Consciousness. From the Consciousness Chapter:

Community Builders / Leaders need to develop awareness, not just of the problem, but of the power we can wield when we recapture our Community belongingness and selves. Effective CPR collectives explore and cultivate their Consciousness, possibly the aspect that most clearly enables resistance and impels a Community toward becoming radical.

Getting ready to work, and relatedly, energizing action in service to the Community and its strategy, also begins with Consciousness, albeit of a slightly different sort, one which is explicit in the quote above – awareness of the problem(s) threatening a Community.

Community Consciousness and her sister, Awareness, are the twins of resistance. It's no wonder the dominant culture doesn't want us to know who we are or what's going on.

An experienced activist comrade in India knows this all too well. His message to me in a conversation about resistance Communities was essentially that **Community inhabitants, particularly in oppressed Communities, are always last to know about issues that threaten to weaken and/or destroy their collectives.**

Do you think residents of Flint, Michigan, in the US, were warned about the poisoning of their water supply? I'll give you an unneeded hint – no. In fact, as almost always occurs, government officials for a long time denied anything of the sort.[167] And it's still a problem there, years after having been exposed!

Sometimes, the headline itself is all it takes to make the case:
> *"Rail Company Claims East Palestine Water Is Safe After Funding 'Sloppy' Testing: The lab report indicates several testing errors that should have disqualified the results, one aquatic ecologist said."*[168] (Emphases added.)

And no one will be shocked to hear that indigenous populations suffer even worse water problems, although they are rarely reported.[169]

Creating and spreading awareness of Community issues can be the spark that sets a collective in motion to drive campaigns and other efforts to completion.

Expanding awareness of Community issues is a particularly relevant example of how these "Getting Ready to Work" practices can be used at several stages of Community formation and building, and also with respect to strategic planning and energizing campaigns.

Successful Community…efforts are more likely to occur when the process includes…
measuring and analyzing the needs and problems of the Community.
These efforts devote time and resources to
understand problems and possible solutions.
Mattesich & Monsey

[167] Denchak, M. (2018). Flint Water Crisis: Everything You Need to Know. https://www.nrdc.org/stories/flint-water-crisis-everything-you-need-know

[168] Conley, J. (2023). Rail Company Claims East Palestine Water Is Safe After Funding "Sloppy" Testing https://truthout.org/articles/rail-company-claims-east-palestine-water-is-safe-after-funding-sloppy-testing/ Accessed February 19, 2023

[169] Human Rights Watch (2019). Canada: Blind Eye to First Nation Water Crisis https://www.hrw.org/news/2019/10/02/canada-blind-eye-first-nation-water-crisis

Before we delve into the awareness-building practice in detail, let's remind ourselves of the flexible nature of Community-building tactics. Awareness-building is another illustration of how this phenomenon plays out: Aside from unearthing issues and threats to the Community, information gathering is one way to involve Community members and can in itself be a way to build Community. Members **gain knowledge** about the Community and **forge stronger relationships** with other members. The results of information-gathering and analysis often **provide a direction** for how to proceed with next steps in both Community building and strategic initiatives.

Cultivating Community awareness is critical for creating momentum in the collective and carries with it unintended positive consequences.

What options are available to Communities who understand the need for greater awareness? How can they proceed?

— — — — — — — — — —

COMMUNITY-BASED RESEARCH (CBR)

"Research efforts for and with [not on] community members, which challenge and transform existing social arrangements"[170]

As traditionally described, CBR is a teaching methodology, complementing service learning and similar academic programs. As such, it's often framed as a partnership between "town and gown". We'll appropriate this practice and view it as a critical function a Community can and should undertake on its own. Let's forget that "gown" stuff.

The CBR Rationale:
"We're tired of being ignored by policymakers. We have people we are trying to serve, but policies keep changing and we have to keep rethinking what we're doing…. How can we get them to listen to us?"[171]

"You [academics] don't have all the answers. Ask us sometime about our community and our problems. We've been living here and we know a lot. Respect our knowledge. We can teach you a few things."[172]

These sentiments serve as a great object lesson for those of us who would work with other Communities and/or indigenous populations. More later.

---

[170]   Strand, K., Marullo, S., Cutforth, N., Stoecker, R., & Donohue, P. (2003). Community-Based Research and Higher Education. San Francisco: Jossey-Bass, p. xiv
[171]   Ibid. p. xviii
[172]   Ibid. p. xix

"CBR is collaborative [in the service-learning paradigm] and change oriented and finds its research questions in the needs of communities, which often require information that they have neither the time nor the resources to obtain."
"CBR combines classroom learning and skills development with social action in ways that ultimately can empower community groups to address their own needs and shape their own futures."[173]

"We see CBR as a tool, a teaching technique, and an institutional change strategy for social justice..."[174]

Here's a recent example of a Community-owned CBR project. Own your own.

> WWALS Watershed Coalition (WWALS), established June 2012, is an IRS 501(c)(3) educational nonprofit charity that advocates for conservation and stewardship of the surface waters and groundwater of the Suwannee River Basin and Estuary, in south Georgia and north Florida, among them the Withlacoochee, Willacoochee, Alapaha, Little, Santa Fe, and Suwannee River watersheds, through education, awareness, **environmental monitoring**, and citizen activities.[175] (Emphasis added.) Among other activities, the WWWALS offers water quality testing.

It's unfortunate that many activists have not heard of CBR, given that it has as its goal social action and change for the purpose of achieving social justice. In fact, CBR's historical influences include:

- The popular education model, including influence from Paulo Freire.
- The Action Research Model (based on Kurt Lewin's work).[176]
- The Participatory Research Model, a conflict-oriented model begun in the 1960s and 1970s.

Again, why Community Based Research? Because we can't trust the dominant culture to warn Communities there might be problems that need to be addressed. Research, facts and data can be compelling tools for creating awareness and leveraging change.

And many more people have access to CBR research tools than they do traditional sources of power.

The CPR Mission statement views the strongest Communities as cultivating Capacity, Confidence and Continuity. Developing a facility with CBR as a tool results in a Community with greater Capacity. Knowledge of and skill in CBR bolsters the

---

[173] Ibid. p. xx
[174] Ibid. p. xx
[175] https://wwals.net
[176] See DeFilippis, J., Fisher, R., & Shragge, E. (2010). Contesting Community: The Limits and Potential of Local Organizing. New Brunswick: Rutgers University Press.

development of research, strategic planning, and evaluation tools in a collective, among other benefits. As a result, collectives enjoy greater autonomy and self-leadership. No longer do the members of a collective need to consult with academics or the government to discover the nature of their material environment. They can do so for themselves. CBR improves the ability of the Community to make more strategic decisions about their operations.

In addition, CBR can be used at several stages of Community organizing, from creating awareness of issues, to discovering and/or articulating problems to be addressed by campaigns, to motivating comrades and allies, and to identifying the success of organizing and campaign work.

<u>What forms might CBR take?</u> The basic logic of CBR is simply data gathering and interpretation in service to the Community. The good news for activists is that this approach can be used for a wide variety of aims. Here's a start:
- **Water/soil/air analysis**, to test for contamination, for example.
- **Door-to-door surveys**, to canvass a Community for potential issues, threats, solutions, etc.
- **Community meetings,** to quickly gather information on social issues, to brainstorm interpretations of data, and to generate potential solutions to Community problems.
- **Freedom of Information Act Initiatives**, to uncover what government offices and officials might be hiding from the public.
- **Police monitoring**, to assess trends in police brutality and other concerns, and to tamp down inappropriate police practices, at least to an extent.
- **Arrest rate analyses**, to ascertain whether oppressed classes are being incarcerated at inappropriate rates.
- **Toxic waste disposal examinations**, to pin down when and where such practices take place, the dangers to the environment they pose, and whether these practices are de facto racist or classist.

You no doubt have the impression there are a wide range of skills involved across all these CBR forms. True enough. You may not have all the skills to engage in all the CBR forms yourself. Another object lesson in the value of coalitions! There are lots of reasons to join or form coalitions. Besides accumulating power to protect and resist, coalition-building can help you gather relevant skills for CBR as well.

Here's another CBR example:
> **On Navajo Nation, Activists Use Citizen Science to Fight Pollution:**
> Methane pollution is poorly tracked, so Diné activists are monitoring it themselves. (Another revealing title.)

"[Kendra Pinto is] one of countless citizen scientists across the country who are tracking and reporting environmental harms committed by the oil and gas industry to regulators. And here, there are many: The Environmental Defense Fund estimates that each year, New Mexico's oil and gas companies emit more than 1.1 million metric tons of methane, a greenhouse gas around 86 times more potent in its warming potential than carbon dioxide over a 20-year period. Much of this comes from wasted natural gas—$271 million of it in this state alone, according to the EDF. It leaks out of faulty equipment and is intentionally expelled through the processes of venting and flaring, in which excess, unrefined natural gas is released or burned from oil wells and refineries to eliminate waste or reduce pressure buildups."

"…And where regulators can't (or won't) step in, residents like Pinto are. The federal government is now relying upon community monitoring, or work that citizens do to contribute to public understanding of the scope of air pollution near fossil fuel sites, a development that Eric Kills A Hundred, tribal energy program manager at EDF, believes will be 'huge'."

"Documenting these types of emissions is important because no one else is really doing it," she said. "Even the agencies that are regulating this type of thing. Because we're in a rural area, what can they actually capture when they come out here? Are they going to more than 100 sites?"

Kills A Hundred said these efforts are not only about what the Navajo Nation can contribute to government data on methane pollution, they're also about empowering the community to play a role in stopping it.

"Having been the stewards of the land for so long," he said, "it's just so important for these communities to be active and raise their voice."[177]

– – – – – – – – – –

<u>Steps in a "Social Change" CBR Project:</u> The CBR Model might look familiar to you. It's a variant of the Strategic Planning process, and I include it here to offer you an alternative to the somewhat more comprehensive process I described earlier.

- **Choose a problem or a symptom** (specifying what the range of problems might be or what the extent of a particular problem might be). For example, you may have noticed your Community's children getting sick at an alarming rate. You might feel members of your collective are arrested very often and for minor offences or seemingly trumped-up charges.

  "In many historically oppressed communities, there is no shortage of problems."[178]

- **Problem identification or articulation** might involve canvassing the Community. Sometimes, the Community is fully aware of the extent and

---

[177] https://www.yesmagazine.org/environment/2022/07/15/navajo-nation-citizen-science-pollution

[178] Strand, K., Marullo, S., Cutforth, N., Stoecker, R., & Donohue, P. (2003). Community-Based Research and Higher Education. San Francisco: Jossey-Bass, p. 85

even the cause of the problem, but needs official documentation to get funding or other support to address the problem.

- **Identify CBR-relevant resources** to document the problem, and potential solutions.
- **Develop a plan**. Your action planning skills can really help here.
- **Implement the plan.**
- **Evaluate the results.**
- **Repeat as necessary.** Stay vigilant.

ENSURE A GOOD SYSTEM OF COMMUNICATION

Successful campaigns, tactical efforts, and effective Community organizing have well-developed systems of communication among Cadre members, campaign participants, within the Community itself, and with the surrounding society.

At the **campaign level**, effective communication ensures members know the rationale for an initiative / campaign, the plan, what needs to be done and when, and what's been accomplished over time.

At the **level of Community**, effective communication sustains the momentum of the Community-building or leveraging process. Communication fosters Community members' awareness, motivation, participation, problem solving and ability to mobilize.

Effective communication also helps members in a Community assemble when necessary, particularly in response to an obstacle or crisis. Communication in this instance enables leadership and/or the Core or Cadre to quickly convey accurate information, to enlist help, to convene members, and assign tasks necessary to deal with the threat or obstacle. Maybe there's a pending ICE (US Immigration and Customs Enforcement) raid to round up foreign nationals in your Community. An effective phone tree or similar alarm system can alert everyone to the threat, and the collective can respond as needed to protect targeted individuals and families. Residents of Arivaca, Arizona, set up such a phone tree in case they needed to quickly rally aid (local law enforcement is at least an hour away) in response to incursions by threatening groups of Anti-Immigrant Extremists.[179]

Whether for alert purposes or more mundane information-sharing, don't limit yourself by relying on all-too-common new technologies for your communication system.

- Parties, meetings, festivals, celebrations and the like can all serve the communication purpose, if you subscribe to the flexibility of events for Community building, and by now you should!

---

[179] https://www.motherjones.com/politics/2019/04/immigrant-vigilantes-arizona-border-arivaca/

- Newsletters, pamphlets, flyers, and other published media are effective, too. Harken back to The Black Panther newspaper for an excellent exemplar.
- Phone trees are a relatively low-tech approach, and are relatively accessible as a result. "Non-phone" trees are even better! Using runners to spread information is secure, and depending on the size of the territory, can be quite timely.
- Firehouse alarms and similar sounds can rally a collective quickly. Another advantage of low-tech systems is that they generally offer greater security. Underserved comrades are more likely to be included when such low-tech systems are used, too, so keep them in mind when crafting your campaign and tactical plans.

GUARANTEE EARLY INVOLVEMENT AND SUPPORT FROM INDIGENOUS GROUPS

Mattessich & Monsey remind us of a critical precursor to durable Community-building efforts, and more achievable struggles to protect and resist. The great majority of us are on stolen land. Therefore, efforts to protect and defend the land should involve indigenous groups whenever and wherever possible. Community leaders must hear indigenous voices before making decisions, plotting a course, and even birthing a vision and mission for their collectives.

We should invite indigenous leadership in our strategies, campaigns, and actions. Soliciting indigenous perspectives and wisdom is the right thing to do. Their wisdom and cultural insights can also help us cultivate alternative social forms that thrive in connection with the living world. Don't try to "sell" indigenous comrades on your plans after the fact – invite them to contribute in fundamental, material ways, up front, to charting a course for the land and waters, and the living collective.

There are practical reasons for including indigenous contributions, too, as I noted in the previous chapter:
- We ignore at our peril the established contacts or pre-existing relationships they have with us, and that they have with other collectives, that provide channels of communication, people, facilities, knowledge, and ties to other organizations or Communities necessary to build and leverage collective resistance power and the successful execution of resistance work.
- Indigenous members and their leaders can legitimize attitudes toward a campaign and any other form of resistance, to aid in building acceptance for these initiatives among other collective, with allies, or in the general population.

<u>Special issues working with indigenous groups</u>. Activists who have worked with indigenous collectives and their representatives understand such relationships can be tentative and fraught, despite our sincere efforts. If you recognize and remember that we settlers are responsible for this state of affairs, you will be well on your way to an appropriate philosophy guiding your work. In my activist history, I have experienced tremendously rewarding relationships, and friction, at various times. This is to be expected. In fact, uncertainty is the only thing you can reasonably expect. Your overtures may be summarily dismissed. Deal with that. It's the fallout of centuries of oppression on our part. Persevere, and work though difficulties you might experience. You owe it to your Community and to those whose land we inhabit.

Allying with indigenous comrades must be undertaken with empathy, special vigilance and forbearance coupled with an attitude of mutual respect and understanding. There is little reason for indigenous people to trust settlers. We have to earn their trust through demonstrated actions, over time.

This general philosophy guides more specific norms governing our relationships. As you plan and make overtures toward indigenous members, you should do so after you have internalized this general philosophy as well as the more specific parameters described below.

<u>Indigenous Solidarity Guidelines.</u> (Selections adapted from Deep Green Resistance.) It's important that members of settler culture ally themselves with indigenous Communities fighting for their rights and survival, but there are right and wrong ways to express solidarity. Each Community and situation is different – but these guidelines can hopefully point you in a good direction for acting effectively and with respect.
- Recognize non-indigenous people are occupying stolen land in an ongoing genocide that has lasted for centuries. Affirm your responsibility to stand with indigenous Communities **who want support** and give everything we can to protect their land and culture from further devastation. They have been on the frontlines of biocide and genocide for centuries, and as allies, we need to step up and join them.
- We do not "help" Indigenous people: We join with, struggle with, and fight with indigenous peoples against systems of power. We must be willing to put our bodies on the line; **they do**.
- Recognize your privilege as a member of settler culture. We're not here to indulge any type of cultural, spiritual or religious needs we think we might have - we are here to engage in political action. Your political message is secondary to the cause at hand.
- Do more listening than talking. You will be surprised what you can learn.

- Recognize there will be Indigenous people who will not want you to participate in ceremonies. Humbly refrain unless asked.
- Work with integrity and respect, be trustworthy and do what you say you are going to do.

The "Getting Read to Work" practices serve as a solid foundation upon which to begin active work toward realizing your Community's creation and strategic goals. You'll be best served by incorporating them into all phases of your Community building and plan execution.

It's time, after all the planning, preparation, and building, to take resistance action. Let's talk in the next chapter about your options, how to generate your own, and how to choose well.

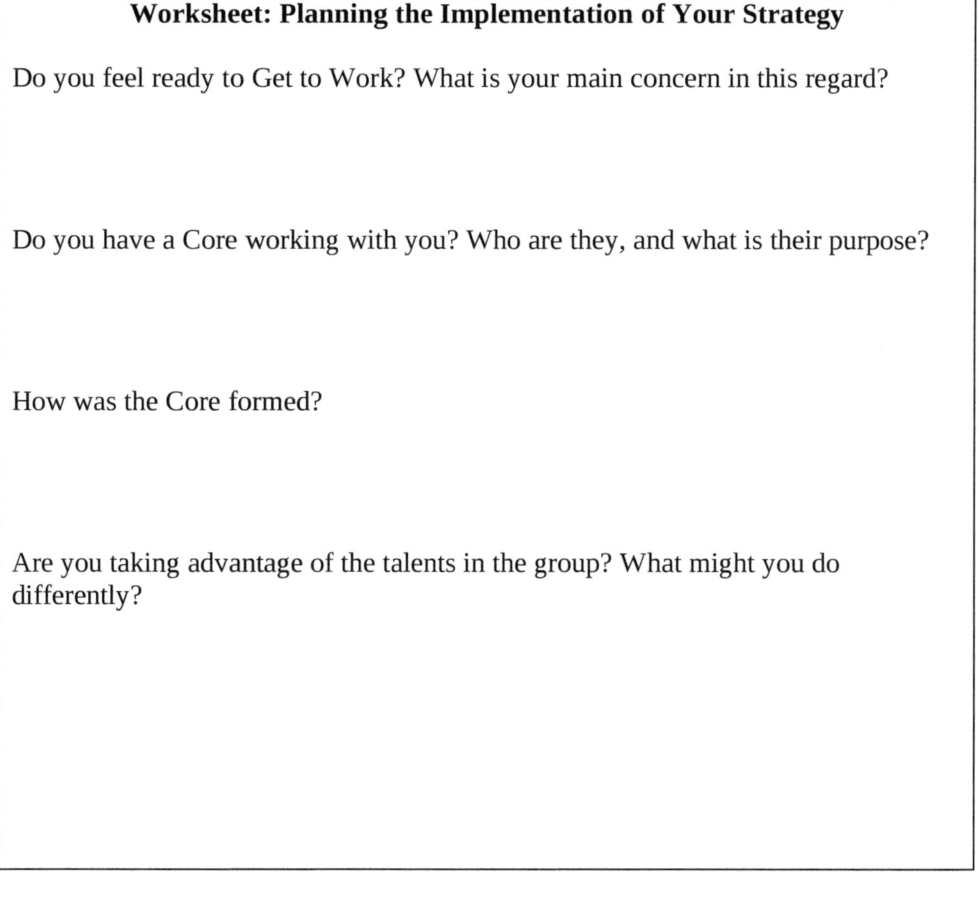

Worksheet: Planning the Implementation of Your Strategy

Do you feel ready to Get to Work? What is your main concern in this regard?

Do you have a Core working with you? Who are they, and what is their purpose?

How was the Core formed?

Are you taking advantage of the talents in the group? What might you do differently?

What aspects of the Core do you need to change? What thoughts do you have concerning how to go about that? What data can you use to discover or better articulate the challenges to the health and well-being of your collective?

What form(s) might the data or information take (e.g., water testing, surveys, etc.)?

Where can you go / who can you ally with to take advantage of the research skills you might need?

What does your Community's Communication Plan / System look like? Will everyone be "in the loop" in case of crisis or emergency? How so?

What lessons have you gained from your work with indigenous peoples?

How can you apply them to the Community work you're engaged in now?

CHAPTER 15

Thinking Strategically, Part 3:
Strategic (and Some Tactical) Options

In our final conversation exploring how to think strategically we're still concentrated on "ground-level" plans for implementing a strategy; however, we're moving beyond touching on the *structure* of the implementations *per se* (i.e., the E, D, S model).

The Strategic Context of Leveraging Power

Purpose / Mission / Vision — Environment Assessment

Goals / Objectives → Priorities, Strategic Choices ← Long-term / Short-Term / Power Maps

Strategy

Campaign | Campaign | Campaign

Action Plan | Action Plan

Action Plan | Action Plan

Our challenge now is to determine the *content* of, e.g., campaigns and action plans that flesh out our strategic resistance plan. We need to choose or develop specific, targeted campaigns and actions in support of a resistance strategy. Let's look at ways to determine how resistance might be made material by discovering what action types are generally available to us in resistance work. **I'll also comment on approaches that may not be covered in many resistance strategy writings.**

In other words, I'm going to do a couple of things by way of moving forward:
> **Give you tools with which you can choose from resistance options**, and criteria to guide your creative development efforts; and
> **Add a few strategic options** to flesh out your way forward and add to your quiver.

If we're smart, we won't try to reinvent the wheel. Instead, I refer to excellent work that organizes resistance campaigns and actions into a coherent typology, the Taxonomy of Action, published by Deep Green Resistance.

> *"We can save ourselves a lot of time and a lot of anguish with a quick and dirty resistance taxonomy. By looking over whole branches of action at once we can quickly judge which tactics are actually appropriate and effective for saving the planet (and for many specific kinds of social and ecological justice activism). A taxonomy of action can also suggest tactics we might otherwise overlook."*[180]

My focus is not on the Taxonomy of Action *per se*, although I urge resistance leaders to reference this contribution as a fundamental part of your strategic planning. As the saying goes, whatever contribution I make in this chapter is a result of standing on the shoulders of giants. Most of your campaign ideas will likely spring from your study of the Taxonomy, but we'll see if we can add a couple, or emphasize one or two I don't think get the shrift they should.

---

[180] McBay, A., Jensen, D., & Keith, L. (2011). Deep Green Resistance: Strategy to Save the Planet. 7Stories Press, p. 242

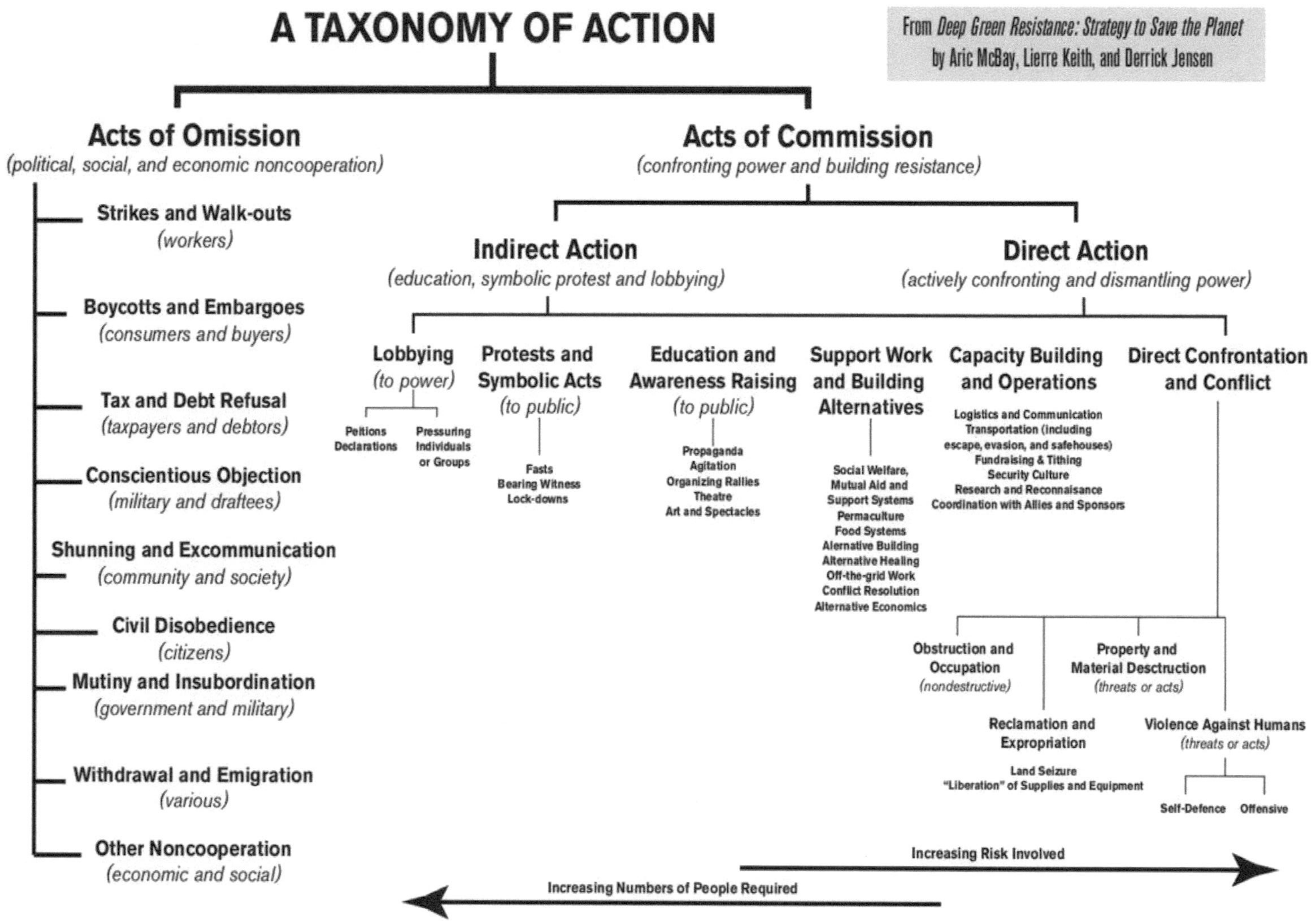

A TAXONOMY OF ACTION

From *Deep Green Resistance: Strategy to Save the Planet*
by Aric McBay, Lierre Keith, and Derrick Jensen

Acts of Omission
(political, social, and economic noncooperation)

- **Strikes and Walk-outs** *(workers)*
- **Boycotts and Embargoes** *(consumers and buyers)*
- **Tax and Debt Refusal** *(taxpayers and debtors)*
- **Conscientious Objection** *(military and draftees)*
- **Shunning and Excommunication** *(community and society)*
- **Civil Disobedience** *(citizens)*
- **Mutiny and Insubordination** *(government and military)*
- **Withdrawal and Emigration** *(various)*
- **Other Noncooperation** *(economic and social)*

Acts of Commission
(confronting power and building resistance)

Indirect Action
(education, symbolic protest and lobbying)

Lobbying *(to power)*
- Petitions
- Declarations
- Pressuring Individuals or Groups

Protests and Symbolic Acts *(to public)*
- Fasts
- Bearing Witness
- Lock-downs

Education and Awareness Raising *(to public)*
- Propaganda
- Agitation
- Organizing Rallies
- Theatre
- Art and Spectacles

Direct Action
(actively confronting and dismantling power)

Support Work and Building Alternatives
- Social Welfare, Mutual Aid and Support Systems
- Permaculture
- Food Systems
- Alternative Building
- Alternative Healing
- Off-the-grid Work
- Conflict Resolution
- Alternative Economics

Capacity Building and Operations
- Logistics and Communication
- Transportation (including escape, evasion, and safehouses)
- Fundraising & Tithing
- Security Culture
- Research and Reconnaisance
- Coordination with Allies and Sponsors

Direct Confrontation and Conflict

- **Obstruction and Occupation** *(nondestructive)*
- **Reclamation and Expropriation**
  - Land Seizure
  - "Liberation" of Supplies and Equipment
- **Property and Material Desctruction** *(threats or acts)*
- **Violence Against Humans** *(threats or acts)*
  - Self-Defence
  - Offensive

Increasing Risk Involved

Increasing Numbers of People Required

Before we proceed, let's keep our overall mental model of strategy fresh by invoking this simple perspective: "Conceptually, strategy is simple.

- First understand the context: where are we, what are our problems, what are our opportunities, strengths?
- Then, develop the goal(s): where do we want to be?
- Identify the priorities.
- Figure out what actions are needed to get from point A to B.
- Finally, identify the resources, people, and specific operations needed to carry out those activities."

Deep Green Resistance

How *can* we figure out what actions are needed?

Assessing Strategic Options

We shouldn't choose a campaign or tactic at random, or because it seems cool, dramatic or romantic. That's a losing proposition, and although you may occasionally stumble on the best one, your odds aren't great. If there's one thing we need to do in resistance, it's to fight smart. We need to be able to assess our options in a way that maximizes our chances of succeeding. Here are three perspectives on choosing a Strategic Option.

<u>Perspective #1: Situational Factors.</u> The best type of action (campaign or tactic) is, most importantly, one that addresses what you are trying to accomplish. Before you rush into your action planning, reflect on your context and purpose.

First of all, what is your strategic or tactical aim? Here are some possibilities:
- Shut down operations.
- Cause a ruckus or distraction.
- Publicize or popularize an issue.
- Ridicule a target person, organization, or concept.
- Protect and resist.
- Disrupt and dismantle harmful forces.

Have you reflected on your collective's mission? Have you done a SWOT analysis based on that? Probably, if you've been interactive in your reading (or you're experienced in planning). Your efforts will serve you well in choosing a campaign or tactic category from the list above, for example. In particular, for this perspective, you will want to attend to Opportunities and Threats form the SWOT analysis. These are

266

critical factors to get your head around. This is a good start to your critical thinking about strategic options. However, we can and should bring more decision factors to the table if we are to make the wisest, most effective decisions regarding how to build our resistance.

Perspective #2: "Fast, Cheap, Good: Pick Two." I'm generally of the opinion that glib statements are more often than not incomplete or wrong, but I'll make an exception in this case. If you've worked in an organization of any size, you may have been exposed to this pithy slogan. At the risk of ruining the punchline such as it is, I'll explain. We often don't have enough money, time, or expertise to produce the "products and services" we need, the way we need them. So, we're forced to prioritize our desirables, such that the best we can reasonably hope for is something that is either:
- Fast and cheap, but not good;
- Fast and good, but not cheap; or
- Cheap and good, but not fast.
None of these outcomes is ideal, is it? This is the reality we need to plan in.

Maybe you need a centerpiece for your campaign to publicize the dangers of deep-sea mining. Corporate goons are gearing up to engage in test mining efforts soon, and you need to get that initial piece out to the public to garner resistance to the threat. In this example, you might need to choose between:
- A professional film or video;
- A press release;
- A speech to be made at the City Council; or
- Videotaped comments you upload to a social media platform.

Which of these can you choose? **If time is the most critical** factor, and you don't have a lot of money, you might choose a poorly made film or one of the other options. **If you have money but no time** and quality is important, you might choose the first option, but know that it will cost you. See how this goes? It's not complicated, but it's a good touchstone for you to rely on as you lay out or chose your options.

You can't always get what you want, as the saying goes, but if you try you can get what you need. Make sure the campaign or tactic type you choose reflects the reality of the real world:

You need to choose your options in a world of limits.

<u>Perspective #3: Intrinsic (to the Action Itself) Factors.</u> Reflecting on the characteristics of the tactics or campaigns themselves can offer us insight as to which are desirable in a given strategic context. Your SWOT is useful here once again, in a complementary way to what we used it for in Perspective #1. Here, our focus is best turned to Strengths and Weaknesses (internal factors, you will recall).

Here are some factors you may want to incorporate into your analysis:

Fit with your Strengths / Weaknesses	Effectiveness
Ease of setup / use	Cost / resources required
People required	Exposure (as a function of
Durability	mobility, e.g.)
Versatility	Repeatability
Risk (Physical / Legal)	

Let's try a couple of examples:

Slash Piles. I love slash piles. They're likely not going to tax your Strengths or exacerbate your Weaknesses. They're easy to set up and use. They generally only require one or two people to put in place. They're effective if they serve to block narrow transportation channels, e.g., with few alternative paths nearby. Little to no cost in most cases. They do stand exposed, but **you** don't have to. Quite repeatable if you have twigs, branches, or trash nearby. Low risk from a physical standpoint, and legally less risky, if you're not around displaying your work.

You might **not** want to use a slash pile if you need something that is durable, though, or will withstand efforts to remove or destroy it. It's also not terribly versatile, and its use is pretty limited regarding appropriate circumstances.

Petitions. A friend of mine told me about a wine tasting she attended years ago. As the attendees worked their way through the offerings, one of them asked, "So, how do you feel about rosé?" Without missing a beat, the merchant replied, "Well, it's gotten a lot of people to try wine." So it goes with petitions. In most case, their main value is that they have gotten people to "try activism". Petitions might be available to many Communities, even those with few resources, or few Strengths. They're generally easy to set up, but not always. Ideally, they can be implemented with only one comrade. Also, they don't cost much if anything.

The main drawback is that they are not effective for the most part. I hope you can prove me wrong, but that's been my experience. This comment brings us back to an important lesson – **a tactic or campaign which is not generally seen or experienced as effective, regardless of other benefits it might confer, is not worth your time.** In that regard, maybe your end-stage strategic planning, when it comes to choosing specific tactics or campaigns, should include research into what has worked for other Communities. This is a theme we'll return to shortly.

Failing that, your longer-range plans should include tests of your possible tactics. Over time, you will have information about what works for your purposes and what does not. And that takes us all the way back to the iterative Strategic Planning Process.

A Note on Valve Turners. I love them for what they have done to bring attention to the fragility of the oil and gas infrastructure and what might be required to substantially disrupt it. I also applaud their courage and love of the living world. I only wish their choice of tactic was different. How could you improve on what the Valve Turners did?

—————————

I talk again and again about thinking critically with respect to Strategy and Community. This list of considerations above gives you another framework you can use to think deeply about exactly what you want to do in material resistance. Try this as a discipline – make it a practice. You don't have to be "mechanical" about it. By using the list above as a touchstone a few times, you will have internalized a mental map of what will be useful and what will not. **Even better, having a grasp of these criteria allows you to adapt and create your own tactics and campaigns!**

> *"Conceptually, the work of a saboteur is just a matter of looking for weak links from a security perspective and ways of exploiting them in the simplest, least expensive and most repeatable way possible."*[181]

The Taxonomy of Action provides a valuable touchstone for Community Leaders to help create and implement a strategy to Protect and Resist. It's well organized and incorporates critical parameters into the model it represents. It's also substantially comprehensive with respect to the range of actions it includes. It's with respect and deference, then, that I offer a bit of complementarity to the Taxonomy. Specifically, I comment on several approaches, from our CPR perspective:

- Legal Action
- Civil Disobedience / NVDA
- Looting, Rioting
- Violence
- Humor

---

[181]   Att. to Max Wilbert

One Over-emphasized, and Three Under-emphasized Strategic Options

Legal Action for Resistance

The US likes to style itself as a "nation of laws". Apparently that's supposed to serve as comfort, pride, and reassurance. While I can't argue with the premise, I'll argue the consequence.

Assuming the premise is true, it follows that nation states that tout their reliance on "The Law" could theoretically be forced to adhere to legal strictures that protect a living planet, should those particular laws exist. To the extent those laws do not yet exist, legal procedures could theoretically fill that vacuum. On the other side of the coin, violators of laws protecting life and the natural world could be punished either through lawsuits, arrest, or administrative sanctions. Finally, Communities could pursue legal autonomy, so they could draft and enforce their own laws focused on the environment, social justice and the like. In this sense, legal approaches could be offensive or defensive.

Let's see how this ideal plays out in reality.

Exhibit A: CELDF. One model for pursuing the legal approach was developed by the Community Environmental Legal Defense Fund (CELDF):

"...we are not a typical environmental organization. We assist communities to develop first-in-the-nation, groundbreaking laws to protect rights – including worker, environmental, and democratic rights, and rights of nature. CELDF provides free and low cost legal services, grassroots organizing, and education, to communities, states, and countries facing injustice. We help them to assert their rights to fight the harms they face."[182]

A Major thrust of CELDF's work centers on the Rights of Nature:
According to their website, CELDF is assisting civil society, indigenous peoples, communities, and governments to advance laws and policies for the protection of Nature and the environment. This includes providing legislative and policy drafting, legal research, public engagement and education, ongoing support during global crises, and trainings.

CELDF and similar organizations boast that the Rights of Nature movement is gaining momentum around the globe, and considers this movement a boon to the protection of the living world. Communities in the US and Ecuador have also worked with CELDF to establish the first global laws protecting Nature, again according to the CELDF website. CELDF is working in India, Nepal, Australia, Cameroon and other countries to establish similar laws.

---

[182]   https://celdf.org

CELDF members are committed to protecting the environment and enabling Communities to seek autonomy in drafting laws and other mechanisms to protect their environs. Their philosophy is often self-described as revolutionary in this regard, and to some extent that may be true. While early returns offer a glimmer of promise, my experience and that of other activists suggests less cause for optimism. Let me explain.

<u>Exhibit B: Colorado River Rights of Nature Suit.</u> In 2017 I joined six other activists as Plaintiffs in the first-ever federal lawsuit seeking personhood and rights of nature for the Colorado river and its ecosystem. The suit, *Colorado River v. Colorado*, was to be heard in Federal Court in Denver, Colorado. To garner and demonstrate support for the suit, we organized a demonstration at the Courthouse on the day an initial hearing was scheduled. The court postponed the hearing at the last minute.

Long story short, the suit was amended two months after initial filing. Initially, the suit was vacated (ruling on it was delayed to give the state time to review the amended complaint). However, the Colorado Attorney General (AG) filed a motion to dismiss, and threatened sanctions against our attorney, "for the unforgivable act of requesting rights for nature."[183] The AG cited Rule 111 of the Federal Rules of Civil Procedure, for knowingly presenting false or unwarranted claims to the court. The Court granted the AG Motion to Dismiss without waiting for a response, and issued an Order directing the Amended Complaint be dismissed with prejudice, meaning it cannot be filed again.

This vindictive judgment is typical of how the State reacts when challenged on their relationship with corporate interests, and when movements advocate for the living.

We lost this attempt to protect our river's ecosystem. But we learned a lesson: Without a finding in favor of such complaints, **existing environmental laws will fail to protect the river, fail to protect the human and natural Communities** dependent on the river, and allow a fundamental contradiction, antithetical to American citizens' right to life, to persist.[184] (Emphases added)

> *"Filing a lawsuit, however, is nothing more than an attempt to persuade a judge to do the right thing. We attempted to persuade a federal judge- who spends most of her time isolated from reality behind the walls and under the roof of a courthouse and who most likely lacked the time to let the river expand the judge's sense of self – to recognize the river's rights to exist, flourish, regenerate, and naturally evolve.*

---

[183] Will Falk (2017), personal communication

[184] Attributed to Will Falk, as incorporated in: Gibson, F. (2018). Rights on Nature for the Colorado River: A Case Study. Presentation and Workshop for the 2018 Bioneers Conference, Boulder, CO.

We never had control over what happened in the case. This lack of control has become all too familiar in the environmental movement. "[185]

A comrade supporting the lawsuit offers a perspective that hits home, given our discussion of resistance tactics:
"Even the most aggressive litigation strategy only buys time.
This is where the individual must compound her / his impact by organizing.
This conclusion is appallingly difficult for most of us on the 'left' to absorb —
that we must function as a collective force, taking orders and
doing our duties, to successfully confront power."

I couldn't agree more. In fact, one Premise of Communities that Protect and Resist says that CPR Collectives are critical survival platforms.

<u>Exhibit C: Protect Thacker Pass Campaign.</u> The Colorado River tale is a story that gets repeated too often among Communities that struggle to protect their land and waters. Such is the case for those acting to protect Thacker Pass from the destructive effects of lithium mining. I introduced that campaign earlier, but it's instructive to renew our acquaintance. Since the previous story went long, I'll summarize the context, and you won't be surprised to learn how the campaign is progressing.

Briefly, the lithium craving boosted by the "green energy" wave is manifesting as an imminent threat to the lands of western Nevada, including to critical Sage-grouse habitats in the remote Nevada-Oregon borderlands. The proposed Thacker Pass lithium mine would destroy thousands of acres of essential land, and engulf sacred lands of local indigenous tribes.

Unsurprisingly, the government greased the skids for corporate interests. Bureau of Land management (BLM) officials fast-tracked an Environmental Impact Statement for an immense open pit lithium mine sought by Lithium Americas at Thacker Pass. According to a recent report, BLM glossed over the mine's death blow to wildlife and to the region's tiny springs and dwindling groundwater, and downplayed mine pollution. Meaningful Tribal consultation was forsaken for this mine that would desecrate a place of great cultural significance. The BLM has dug in its heels, defending the mine to the hilt.[186]

A representative for local indigenous tribes has represented them in court, and filed a motion to stop the destructive mining and its related procedures. Judge Miranda Du

---

[185]   Falk, W. (2019). How Dams Fall: On Representing the Colorado River in the First-ever American Lawsuit Seeking Rights for a Major Ecosystem. Little Bound Books.

[186]   Fite, K. (2023). The Lithium Frenzy is an Ecological Catastrophe for Oregon's High Desert. Counterpunch, February 10, 2023. https://www.counterpunch.org/2023/02/10/the-lithium-frenzy-is-an-ecological-catastrophe-for-oregons-high-desert/ Accessed February 24, 2023.

ruled largely in favor of Lithium Nevada and the BLM in a prior consolidated case involving claims brought in 2021 by environmental groups, a local rancher, and two Native American tribes.

As of this writing, the tribes have, through their lawyer, filed another lawsuit. And while the tribes and their activist supporters in the Protect Thacker Pass campaign continue their impassioned defense of the land, the outlook is not rosy. It never is in circumstances where we try to defend the land and waters using the legal system established by the dominant culture. From the lawyer representing several tribes in the Thacker Pass Campaign:

"The judge issued her decision in the Thacker Pass case yesterday. She ruled against us. It's really important that everyone remember that law is a limited tactic – especially in public lands mining cases where the law presumes corporations have a right to mine. No lawsuit in public lands mining cases can achieve permanent protection for Thacker Pass. Lawsuits can delay construction and cause investors to think about pulling their money out, but it is likely that there will come a time when there simply is no legal tactic left for us to use to fight the Thacker Pass lithium mine."

"If we're going to truly protect Thacker Pass, we're going to have to do more than file lawsuits and litigate in court. We cannot rely on the government or a judge to protect Thacker Pass. We'll have to do it ourselves."

Will Falk[187]

The lesson should be clear: Legal strategies can delay the devastating effects of industrial civilization, but as we saw, they are only delaying tactics or publicity-gaining measures. If we were to apply our criteria for campaigns and tactics to legal avenues, we'd find little to recommend them: They're costly, rarely fit with a Community's Strengths, effective only in the short term (and so they are not durable), difficult to set up unless you're a lawyer, occasionally non-repeatable, and can result in legal exposure. So while they do not require large numbers of people to implement, and are versatile to the extent they can be used in a variety of contexts, I would not pin my hopes of Community defense solely on legal remedies.

The legal system is an extension of the power of the State, and exists solely for that purpose. It is the means by which it maintains and wields power. We therefore should not confuse what is legal with what is just.

---

[187] Will Falk, Attorney. https://www.facebook.com/ProtectThackerPass

"…crime is not some transcendental fact of life against which the police nobly battle but is rather the thing identified by the state and the police as a post facto explanation for the repression they already carry out on behalf of society's rulers."

Osterweil[188]

<u>Exhibit D: "Property Rights".</u> Should the reader still suffer from the illusion that the law can help us Protect and Resist, I'll play one more card – **Eminent Domain.**

Eminent Domain is the power the American government reserves for itself to take private property and convert it into public use. And by "public" they mean whatever serves the government and corporate partnership. The Fifth Amendment to the US Constitution provides the government may only exercise this power if they provide just compensation to the property owners. The government has repeatedly cited the Takings Clause (Fifth Amendment) as justification for taking private property without the landowner's consent.

This practice has occurred since the early days of America, and in theory the government is restricted from taking private property except when required for the "public good". Unfortunately, compensation is generally insufficient or inappropriate, even if the underlying principle of Eminent Domain wasn't immoral and corrupt on its face.

Even if we accept the premise of Eminent Domain as reasonable and fitting, it doesn't guarantee any measure or form of justice, and in fact is rarely if ever intended for that end. Eminent Domain is easily and readily abused. For example, a Supreme Court decision in 2005 severely undermined the protections afforded by the Takings Clause and greatly expanded the government's power to seize private property. According to Reed (2015): In *Kelo v. City of New London*, the Supreme Court held that "economic development" constituted a "public use" that justified the taking of private property through eminent domain. According to this decision, the government can utilize eminent domain to seize your property whenever the government deems it necessary for "economic development." At least we know now what is really meant by "public good".[189] Here is perhaps the most egregious example of this practice:

> *"Familiar with its spiritual significance, the U.S. government included the Black Hills in negotiating the Treaty of Fort Laramie in 1868. In exchange for halting attacks on railroads and settlers, the government promised the Sioux tribes "the absolute and undisturbed use and occupation" of roughly half of present-day South Dakota. Six years later, an expedition led by Lt.*

---

[188]   Osterweil, V. (2020). In Defense of Looting: A Riotous History of Uncivil Action. New York: Bold Type Books.

[189]   Reed, T. (2015). Eminent domain abuse violates private property rights.
https://thehill.com/blogs/congress-blog/246691-eminent-domain-abuse-violates-private-property-rights Accessed Feb 25, 2023.

Col. George Armstrong Custer discovered gold. In 1877, with a gold rush in full swing, Congress claimed the land through eminent domain."

If your home for generations was razed to make room for an interstate highway, and you received "fair market" compensation from the government, would that satisfy you, or make you whole? I don't think so. Substitute "tribal lands" for "home" and "pipeline" for "highway", and you'll get the same result.

> *"Nowhere is this struggle [for colonized (stolen) land] more pronounced than in the Black Hills of South Dakota. The Supreme Court said in 1980 that the area, sacred to Native people for 12 centuries, was taken in such egregious fashion that the government owed the Sioux tens of millions of dollars in compensation.*
> *But members of the Sioux…have steadfastly refused the award, which is now worth over $1 billion. Generations of systemic poverty – and broad disparities in health, education, and criminal justice outcomes – cannot be repaired with money, they say."*[190]

Our neoliberal, capitalist society thinks everything is for sale, and that money compensates for any injury or loss. We know this to be untrue.

Even Thomas Linzey, co-founder of CELDF, waxes pessimistic about the capacity for the current system of law to protect Communities:

> *"In many ways, the current system of law views local laws as unenforceable unless affected corporations agree to abide by them. If a corporation should decide that it does not want to abide by a local law, there are … ways it can nullify it.*
> *… for community rights to become a reality, we must nullify and then overturn the legal doctrines that currently allow a relatively small number of people who control corporate decision making to override our communities.*
> *…This will require millions of people and thousands of communities across this country to openly disobey those key legal doctrines — including corporate "rights" and state preemption — in the name of their constitutional right to local, community self-government.*
> *…it is that process of problem-solving that is giving birth to a new army of community leaders who understand that **dismantling the corporate state is a prerequisite towards being able to protect their own communities.***
> (Emphasis added.)

---

[190] Gass, H. (2023). When $1 billion isn't enough. Why the Sioux won't put a price on land. https://www.csmonitor.com/USA/Society/2023/0628/When-1-billion-isn-t-enough.-Why-the-Sioux-won-t-put-a-price-on-land

Nothing less than a mass movement of people, out from under the spell woven by the unholy alliance of a corporate few and their legislative lackeys, will be able to change the basic elements of a system. "[191]

There's not enough time for the legal system to evolve, voluntarily or otherwise, into a planet-friendly institution. Dismantling the corporate system is similarly useful but time-intensive. Community leaders might consider these approaches, but I'd prefer those that might have a more proximal and material effect on the collective's ability to survive and thrive.

Let's spare each other any further journey into a property rights morass, and keep our focus, which is that the legal system protects the powerful, corporate interests, and the dominance of the state. The moment an existing law interferes in a material way with the government-corporate alliance or constricts commerce enough to create real discomfort, it will be struck down, revised or ignored. There is no cure for this state of affairs other than dismantling it and its related systems. Instead, we should observe and serve natural law and the needs of the living planet, rather than the vagaries of a legal system that serves property and the dominant culture.

———————————

As a coda and segue to consideration of other strategic options, I cite Howard Zinn, from *Disobedience and Democracy: Nine Fallacies on Law and Order*.[192] The title of that work serves as a spoiler, but to work our way gradually in that world, here are a few tidbits.

A major theme of Zinn's: *"law is congealed injustice"*. Among his "Fallacies":
- *The rule of law has an intrinsic value apart from moral ends.*
  Fallacy, all right. The law protects government-corporate interests, instead of the needs of a living planet.
- *The person who commits civil disobedience must accept his [sic] punishment as right.*
  Forget that – do your duty to save your Community or your planet, and then **run** to do so another day.
- *Civil disobedience must be absolutely non-violent.*
  To believe this is to limit yourself to measures that either are neither powerful nor effective in protecting, resisting or dismantling systems of oppression and destruction. A living planet deserves all measure of resistance. We'll talk more.

---

[191] Linzey, T. (2015). The Myth of Community Rights: Self-Governance has a Corporate Ceiling. In These Times. https://inthesetimes.-com/article/the-myth-of-community-rights Accessed July 13 2023.

[192] Zinn, H. (2012). From Disobedience and Democracy: Nine Fallacies on Law and Order. Haymarket Books

"Until American citizens can overcome this idolization of law, until they begin to see that law is, like other institutions and actions, to be measured against moral principles, against human needs, we will remain a static society in a world of change, a society deaf to the rising cries for justice – and therefore, a society in serious trouble."[193]

If the legal system provides no relief for Communities who want to protect their land and waters, or their members, what is left? We need to consider "extra-legal" options in planning for our collectives to build and leverage their power to Protect and Resist.

———————

Direct Action (DA)

DGR's Taxonomy of Action is an excellent framework for categorizing and understanding the strategic options available to those who would resist. It should be your main reference for the end stages of your Community's strategic planning. My intent here is to use the Taxonomy as a point of departure to briefly explore the notion of Direct Action (including Non-Violent Direct Action), and later to shine a light on strategic options that do not get the attention they might. We need to fight as smart as we can, and that philosophy behooves us to not leave any stone unturned in the search for campaign or tactical options. If I'm lucky, I will have left you considering more possibilities than you might have otherwise.

A wide variety of actions in DGR's Taxonomy are outlined under their rubric of Direct Action, including: Support Work and Building Alternatives; Capacity Building and Operations; and Direct Confrontation and Conflict. For the purposes of moving the discussion along, I'd like to concentrate on the last category, and in that context briefly mention Civil Disobedience, although in the DGR Taxonomy that is considered an Act of Omission.

Perhaps the essential philosopher of the DA "Movement" is Gene Sharp, and his 1973 work, *The Politics of Non-violent Action*, informs our discussion of that approach. As is commonly accepted in most corners of resistance scholarship, Direct Action is:

"The process of taking action to achieve a desired goal without having to appeal to an authority figure or powerholder to take care of it for you. Direct action means to take action to change an injustice without asking for power from third party."[194]

---

[193]   Zinn, H. (2012). From Disobedience and Democracy: Nine Fallacies on Law and Order, p. 23
[194]   DGR unpublished presentation

One perspective is that DA uses political, economic, and/or social leverage to attempt to coerce the structures of power to change, up to and including total abdication. Another perspective holds that DA seeks to create such a crisis and foster such tension that a (government, e.g.) that has refused to negotiate is forced to confront the issue. It seeks to dramatize the issue that it can no longer be ignored.

Other facets of DA (From a DGR presentation):
- Actively confronting and dismantling power.
- When a group takes an action intended to reveal an existing problem, highlight an alternative, or demonstrate a possible solution to a social issue.
- A political action aimed at achieving a specific goal or objective and which is carried out directly by a person or group of people without appealing to a higher authority for legitimacy.
- A tactic – a specific type of action that can be used to implement a wide variety of strategies.
- In its purest form DA does not seek to persuade those in power, but to foster and assert the power of those carrying out the action themselves. For example, a resistance group might, rather than petition a politician, block an oil pipeline themselves.

In the Deep Green Resistance philosophy, Direct Action offers a way for movements to build and assert collective power, both to defend Communities and to fight for a world we want to live in.

— — — — — — — — — —

Reflections on the DA Construct. In the interest of considering all resistance options, let me offer an alternative approach to characterizing Direct Action. I do this not to quibble over definitions but to test the boundaries of the construct and in the process encourage activists to consider a wider range of approaches to acting in resistance work.

Here's where we might expand the definition of Direct Action:
> *"DA activities are those undertaken with a clear, obtainable goal of furthering resistance to the dominant culture. These activities are oriented toward materially effecting the opposition's power."*
>
> Will Falk[195]

---

[195] Personal communication

What are the implications of these elaborations? If you subscribe to them, it follows that **two categories of DGR's Direct Action do not qualify as such:**
- Support Work and Building Alternatives (Including Social Welfare, Mutual Aid and Support Systems, Permaculture Food systems, Alternative Healing, Alternative Economics, etc.)
- Capacity Building and Operations (Including Logistics and Communication, Transportation (such as escape, evasion, and safehouses), Fundraising and Tithing, Security Culture, Research and Reconnaissance, and Coordination with Allies and Sponsors).

This revised perspective on Direct Action potentially narrows the scope of tactics Communities might incorporate into a strategic plan. Once again invoking DGR's Taxonomy (the most valuable and comprehensive categorization system), that leaves us with actions comprising Direct Confrontation and Conflict. This includes Obstruction and Occupation, Reclamation and Expropriation, Property and Material Destruction, and Violence against Humans. We'll discuss a couple of these.

While my approach to Direct Action limits the potential array of options Communities of Resistance might otherwise incorporate into related portions of their plans, I'm generally in favor of having as many options as possible. Here's why you might want to adopt this philosophy, though: The options that remain are arguably "stronger" for many CPR collectives, especially those who are not very populous, lack resources, and/or face clear and imminent threats. In that context, options in the revised DA category fit well regarding the criteria of effective tactics I laid out earlier. To wit:
- Such tactics generally require fewer people, can be durable and effective, keep costs and resource requirements low, can be easy to set up and can be versatile.
- In this analysis, such actions should be a good fit with a Community's Strengths and Weaknesses given the assumptions about context above.

These revised DA options do have drawbacks, as any reasoned analysis would reveal. If they were perfect, everybody would use them. Remember, we live in a world of limits and constraints ("Fast, Cheap, Good – Pick Two"). Most notably, they are risky in both the legal and physical senses. And given this, they may not be repeatable.

Here is my "strong view": Risk is the price we pay for choosing actions in the larger revised Direct Action context – we don't have time for actions in the other categories, which are planning-heavy and often require many participants. We'll also never get enough people involved as we need to in order to carry out many of the actions in these categories.

Have you wondered, worried, or stewed over the fact that in the US there still has not been any real large-scale revolutionary activity, given all the scandals, human rights violations, and fascistic policies over the last generations? I have. It's not likely to happen, either, at least not in time to stop the extinction-level damage being done to the planet. Have you ever seen the movie "Reds"? Here's a great quote:
*"Jack dreams that he can hustle the American working man, who's one dream is that he could be rich enough not to work, into a revolution led by *his* party."*
"Eugene O'Neill" (Jack Nicholson)

Until a few years ago, I thought I could cleverly use my knowledge of Social Psychology and Attitude and Opinion science to change the way the populace thought about resistance and saving the living world. Sadly, I'm not any smarter now, but I am less naïve. Our time and resources are severely limited, so we're obliged to make use of the most impactful tactics we can.

My philosophy regarding DA serves as a clue as to the types of strategic options I discuss next - specifically, variants of Property and Material Destruction, Reclamation and Expropriation, Obstruction and Occupation, and Violence against Humans.

_ _ _ _ _ _ _ _ _ _

<u>A Direct-Action Controversy: Destruction of Property.</u> Whether you agree with this approach or not, we can probably agree that destruction of property is a clear form of Direct Action. Unfortunately for the resistance, this action seems to be used less than it could and should, in great measure because of the connotations associated with it.

Our comrades in DGR explore this phenomenon. From one of their presentations:
A major debate centers on whether destruction of property should be included in the realm of violence or nonviolence. This debate can be illustrated by the response to groups like the Earth Liberation Front and Animal Liberation Front, which use property destruction and sabotage as Direct Action tactics. Although these types of actions are often prosecuted as violence, those groups justify their actions by claiming violence is harm directed towards living things and not property.

Use of sabotage as a method can be contrasted with minor property damage that is a small but necessary part of a non-violent campaign methodology, such as breaking locks and fences to gain entry to a site. Some activists believe a doctrine of diversity of tactics can resolve the controversy. U.S. and international law include acts against property in the definition of violence and state that even in a time of war, "Destruction [of property] as an end in itself is a violation of international law".[196]

I include this brief assessment of the notion, not to convince you of its necessity nor to dissuade you. Instead, I do so to arm you with a perspective so that as you consider the forms of action in this chapter, do so with knowledge of their effectiveness as well as what some might label their moral or ethical "baggage".

Let me put this another way. I care little (actually, not at all) how one might pigeonhole destruction of property in the panoply of definitions related to resistance work options. **What I do care about is whether and how such a category of tactics works as part of a resistance strategy.** I'll leave this philosophical chat with what I always use as a touchstone – namely that what we're ultimately trying to do is to build and leverage the power of CPR collectives, to protect the living planet. **That** is what you might use to help balance the scales in your determinations.

Non-Violent Direct Action (NVDA)

Direct Action as a Category of Resistance Options is often lumped in with Non-Violent Direct Action. It's not unreasonable to suggest they are generally used interchangeably, but here are some comments that serve to make a distinction.

From a DGR Presentation: Under this model, non-violent resistance is a technique used to control, combat, and destroy your opponent's power. As Gene Sharp says, "Nonviolent action is a means of combat, as is war. It involves the matching of forces and the waging of "battles," it requires wise strategy and tactics, and demands of its "soldiers" courage, discipline, and sacrifice."[197]

In some cases, nonviolent action impinges upon an opponent's power more directly than would violence. That's because nonviolent action is capable of striking at the sources of the ruler's political power (habit, fear of sanctions, moral obligation, self-interest, psychological identification with the ruler, indifference, absence of self-confidence).

<u>Forms of NVDA.</u> NVDA action is not generally considered verbal, although we will discuss a tactic that is. Instead, NVDA consists of social, economic and political activity and more. One attractive feature of NVDA as a "philosophy of action" is that a wide range of possibilities exist within the overall framework. In fact, the

---

[196] DGR, unpublished Presentation
[197] DGR, unpublished Presentation

possibilities are limited only by the needs of the situation and the creativity of the activists and planners.

Examples include:

Sit-ins	Strikes	Workplace occupations
Blockades	Protests	Hacktivism

NVDA is a cornerstone of many if not most resistance plans. NVDA adherents are legion, and the approach is widely touted for its successes. My intent here is not to dispute the value of DA versus NVDA, but to suggest complementary conceptualizations of DA, and highlight approaches that some consider effective when, e.g., NVDA falls short or is not as successful as often depicted.

NVDA Revisited: Other Perspectives

As we move toward more "militant" approaches to strategic options, we need to leaven what is often an unbridled optimism regarding Gene Sharp's contribution to resistance. There has been interesting analysis in this arena of late.

V. Osterweil's (2020) *In Defense of Looting: A Riotous History of Uncivil Action*[198] offers an interesting overview of the approaches I set out to discuss in the rest of the chapter, while at the same time putting to rest much of the conversation used to prop up NVDA as **the** strategic option of choice for resisters.

According to Osterweil, while the success of the NVDA approach is often touted, such as in descriptions of the American Civil Rights movement, the broader narrative is false and propounded in great measure by liberals.

"…there was no straightforwardly nonviolent civil rights movement.
Nonviolence was a tactic designed at the time to appeal to Northern white liberals for funding and support…. However, away from the cameras, demonstrators and organizers armed themselves."[199]
(Including MLK Jr, whose entourage was heavily armed.)

"… looting is a powerful tool to bring about real, lasting change in society.
The rioters who smash windows and take items from stores… are engaging in a powerful tactic that questions the justice of "law and order," and the distribution of property and wealth in an unequal society."[200]

---

[198] Osterweil, V. (2020). In Defense of Looting: A Riotous History of Uncivil Action. New York: Bold Type Books.

[199] Ibid. p. 150

[200] Escobar, N. (2020). One Author's Controversial View: 'In Defense Of Looting'. npr.org. https://www.npr.org/sections/codeswitch/2020/08/27/906642178/one-authors-argument-in-defense-of-looting

Osterweil is not the only one providing a different perspective.

"Once more: those sites could be shut down using civil disobedience, but unless you have a nonviolent army of thousands, all that you and your 20 friends will accomplish is a morning of symbolic action. But thinking like a resistance, you and your 20 friends could stop mountaintop removal."[201]

Always Be Critically thinking about your choice of tactics.

_ _ _ _ _ _ _ _ _

A Philosophy of Rioting and Looting

I discussed my less-than-sanguine feelings about resisters shielding themselves, their land and waters, and their Communities using the legal system. Rioting and looting are two alternatives that spring from such a rejection of the State's law, seen by many as an instrument of oppression.

Rioting and looting have often gone hand in hand, as Osterweil declares. According to Osterweil, "Rioting" generally refers to any moment of mass unrest or upheaval. Riots are a space in which a mass of people has produced a situation in which the general laws that govern society no longer function, and people can act in different ways in the street and in public.

Rioting is a broader category in which looting appears as a tactic.

Rioting, property destruction, and looting are all tactics, and though they may be more favorable to certain forms of struggle, they can be and have been used to further differential and opposing political goals and agendas.[202]

"I mean the mass expropriation of property, mass shoplifting during a moment of upheaval or riot. That's the thing I'm defending. I'm not defending any situation in which property is stolen by force. It's not a home invasion either. It's about a certain kind of action that's taken during protests and riots."

Per Osterweil, looting is more common among movements coming from below. It tends to be an attack on a business, a commercial space, maybe a government building – taking those things that would otherwise be commodified and controlled and sharing them for free.

[201]   McBay, A., Jensen, D., & Keith, L. (2011). Deep Green Resistance: Strategy to Save the Planet. 7 Stories Press, p. 501

[202]   Osterweil, V. (2020). In Defense of Looting: A Riotous History of Uncivil Action. New York: Bold Type Books, p. 104

In Osterweil's conception, rioting does a number of important things:

- It gets people what they need for free immediately, which means they are capable of living and reproducing their lives without having to rely on jobs or a wage. That's looting's most basic tactical power as a political mode of action.
- It also attacks the very way in which food and other goods are distributed.
- It attacks the idea of property, and it attacks the idea that for someone to have a roof over their head or have a meal ticket, they have to work for a boss, to buy things people just like them somewhere else in the world had to make under the same conditions.
- It points to the way in which that's unjust.
- And the reason the world is organized that way, obviously, is for the profit of people who own the stores and the factories.
- So you get to the heart of that property relation, and demonstrate that without police/state oppression, people can have things for free.

And yet, according to Osterweil, people who consider themselves radical or progressive criticize looting. This "bias" if you will, comes out of mainstream history of the American Civil Rights movement. As alluded to earlier, the popular understanding is that the movement was successful when it was nonviolent and less successful when it was focused on Black Power. Osterweil's thesis is that it's a myth we get taught from the first moment we learn about the Civil Rights movement - that it was a nonviolent movement, and that that's what matters about it.

This perspective doesn't stand up to a more radical orientation on that period in history. Nonviolence emerged in the 1950s and 1960s during the Civil Rights movement, (in part) as a way to appeal to Northern liberals. When it did work, as with the lunch counter sit-ins, it worked because Northern liberals could flatter themselves that racism was a Southern condition. Those two factors combined to make nonviolence/NVDA a seemingly effective tactic. But even under those conditions, Freedom Riders and student protesters were often protected by armed guards.

---

[203] Ibid. p. 152

Earlier I introduced the "controversy" that occasionally labels destruction of property as "violence". More from Osterweil:

> *"One thing about looting is it freaks people out. But in terms of potential crimes people can commit against the state, it's basically nonviolent. You're mass shoplifting. Most stores are insured; it's just hurting insurance companies on some level. It's just money. It's just property. It's not actually hurting any people.*
>
> *A discussion of rioting and looting often leads to a bit of hand-wringing among resistance members. The argument generally centers on the assumption that these actions are actually forms of violence. These arguments fail to make the distinction between violence against property, like smashing a window or stealing something, versus violence against a human body.*
>
> *We [e.g., Osterweil] object to violence on some level. But it's a broad category. It can mean breaking a window, lighting a dumpster on fire, or the police murdering a black person. That word is not strategically helpful. The word that can mean both those things cannot be guiding me morally.*
>
> *Ultimately, what nonviolence ends up meaning is that activists don't do anything that makes them feel violent. Getting free is messier than that. We have to be willing to do things that scare us and that we wouldn't do in normal, 'peaceful' times, because we need to get free.*
>
> *'We need to argue for and defend every tactic that might help us overturn this miserable world of white supremacy, anti-Blackness, [patriarchy], capitalism, empire, and property.'"*[204]

–––––––––

Debating whether one form of action (like looting and rioting) is actually violence nudges us dangerously close to philosophical nit-picking. Instead of engaging in the exercise of assigning categorizations, let's instead focus on the specific acts we can engage in as Resistance Community leaders. We do this, of course, by engaging in a disciplined strategic planning process, as I've described throughout the book. That process will lead to a consideration of **relevant actions** that fit our aims, strategic context, and Strengths and Weaknesses. We can leave the labels to those who have the time and distance to assign them.

That was a bit glib of me, for sure. But in the face of the threats to the living planet, which we are dedicated to dismantling, our first consideration is whether our approaches will **work**. After that, we can explore our personal morality. Since we are

---

[204] Ibid. p. 249

not likely to commit to actions we find immoral or distasteful, I have to concede you might need to pay heed here, and prioritize your values, at least.

At the risk of oversimplifying, your reflections should attempt to answer questions like, "What am I willing to do to resist, protect and defend?"
If you have to this point hesitated to add to your pool of resistance options, you might feel the urge arising shortly.

– – – – – – – – – –

Violence: A Closer Look

Maybe you've heard of this quote from Barry Goldwater, American Politician and war-mongering archconservative:
> *"Extremism in the defense of liberty is no vice.*
> *And moderation in the pursuit of justice is no virtue."*[205]

I'd be inclined to agree with this, if Barry and I shared the same definitions of liberty or justice, which we don't. But that's not the point. Instead, Maybe this works for us:

Violence in the defense of a living planet is no vice.
And moderation in the pursuit of just and sustainable Communities is no virtue.

We've talked around the notion of violence to this point. Let's look at it more directly.

> *"Given the bleak future of a depauperate earth that business-as-usual promises, what shape does direct action take and how extreme should that action be?*
> *In what circumstances is sabotage justified, if ever? If Greta Thunberg's 'fairy tale of eternal economic growth' condemns future generations to apocalyptic suffering, what duty do we have to oppose that noxious and ultimately homicidal economic system? What kind of sacrifice will that entail, now, today? What are we willing to risk for the safety and security of the generations of tomorrow?"*
> Christopher Ketcham[206]

I do not advocate the gratuitous use of violence in resistance. We'll look at factors you need to consider before you choose to go down this path. But once again, you need to think long and hard about what's at stake for your Community and your planet, and how you can and should resist with what you have available to you.

---

[205] Acceptance Speech as the 1964 Republican Presidential candidate.
[206] Christopher Ketchum / Kickstarter What it means when you turn your rifle against techno-industrial civilization [downloaded Aug 8, 2022]

<u>More General Observations and Principles re: Non-violence.</u> Part of your calculus in choosing to use or eschew violence would profitably begin with a review of non-violence. In simple terms, here's what you might take away.

First, non-violence does not work, at least not as often or as fully as we've been told. We reviewed the arguments in this behalf in the last section.

> *"Pacifism as a strategy of achieving social, political, and economic change can only lead to the dead end of liberalism."*[207]

Conversely, violence does work, more often than we have been told.

> *"One reason violence is used so often by those in power is because it works. It works dreadfully well. And it can work for liberation as well as subjugation."*[208]
>
> *"The vaunted career of Gandhi exhibits characteristics of a calculated strategy of nonviolence salvaged only by the existence of violent peripheral processes."*
>
> *"without the spectre, real or perceived, of a violent black revolution at large in America during a time of war, King's nonviolent strategy was basically impotent in concrete terms."*
>
> *"...there simply has never been a revolution, or even a substantial social reorganization, brought into being on the basis of the principles of pacifism. In every instance, violence has been an integral requirement of the process of transforming the state."*[209]

Nonviolence in its strong form is virtue-signaling, and at its worst, is racist to boot.

> *"Hence, while the Mahatma and his followers were able to remain 'pure', their victory was contingent upon others physically gutting their opponents for them."*[210]
>
> *"In displacing massive state violence onto people of color both outside and inside the mother country, rather than absorbing any real measure of it themselves (even when their physical intervention might undercut the state's ability to inflict violence on nonwhites), pacifists can only be viewed as being objectively racist."*[211]

---

[207] Mead, E. in the preface of: Churchill, W. (1998). Pacifism as Pathology. Oakland, CA: AK Press, p. 33
[208] Ibid. p. 25
[209] Ibid. p. 54ff
[210] Ibid. p. 55
[211] Ibid. p. 85

"It is instructive that practitioners of armed struggle from the Third World context are also quite vociferously condemned when they are audacious enough to carry violence into the very industrialized nations objectively responsible for their colonization."[212]

The consideration of violence in resistance comes not from a stance of hate, but rather one of love and compassion.

"...the true revolutionary is guided by a sense of love rather than hate,
and 'to love, one must fight'"[213]

Che Guevara

There's also a rational, strategic perspective on choosing violence.

"With all the world at stake, it is long past time we put all our options on the table."
Derrick Jensen[214]

Derrick adds that: This is not to argue for blind, unthinking violence, but instead against blind, unthinking non-violence.

"It has always seemed clear to me that violent and nonviolent approaches to social change are complementary."[215]
"The most vicious and violent ruling class in the history of humankind will not give up without a physical fight....
The question is not whether to use violence...but only when to use it."[216]

A few years ago, Arundhati Roy was interviewed by The Guardian. Roy admitted that guerrillas use violence, generally directed against the police and army, but sometimes causing injury and death to civilians caught in the crossfire. She was asked whether she condemns that violence.

"I don't condemn it any more," [Arundhati Roy] says. "If you're an adivasi [tribal Indian] living in a forest village and 800 CRP [Central Reserve Police] come and surround your village and start burning it, what are you supposed to do? Are you supposed to go on hunger strike? Can the hungry go on a hunger strike? Non-violence is a piece of theatre. You need an audience. What can you do when you have no audience? People have the right to resist annihilation."[217]

---

[212] Ibid. p. 120
[213] Che Guevara, quoted by Michael Lowy, in Pacifism as Pathology, p. 122
[214] Jensen, D. in the preface of: Churchill, W. (2007). Pacifism as Pathology. Oakland, CA: AK Press, p. 4
[215] Ibid. p. 18
[216] Mead, E. in the preface of: Churchill, W. (1998). Pacifism as Pathology. Oakland, CA: AK Press, p. 34
[217] Roy, A. (2011). 'They are trying to keep me destabilised. Anybody who says anything is in danger'
https://www.theguardian.com/books/2011/jun/05/arundhati-roy-keep-destabilised-danger

If your choice to incorporate violence into your strategic resistance plan is a rational one (as it should be), we need at least a few considerations to use as touchstones.

When should a Community use violence as a strategic option to Protect and Resist? Aside from the general considerations embedded in the quotes above, there are factors you and your Community members need to reflect on, in a deep and serious way. I'm probably being overly cautious in advising you to deliberate the use of this tactic more than with the others, mainly because of the great risks involved (which, as you know, is one of the criteria by which we weigh tactics in general).

If violence is even on your radar as a potential choice, you'd do worse than to use the following elements to focus your decision.

When/why **should** your Community engage in violence? Some considerations:
- Desperation / failure of every other action or tactic implemented.
- To intimidate those who want to oppress, poison, destroy.
- To lessen the power of the dominant culture.
- To eliminate a clear and present danger. For self-defense or protection. (Perhaps our previous discussion changed your perspective on this question.)
- To draw attention to your Community or cause, including sharpening social and political distinctions.
- To effect political change, to directly deny behaviors you see as evil, unethical, or extremely damaging.

When/why **shouldn't** your Community want to engage in violence? Considerations:
- Grave legal consequences.
- Loss of public support.
- Martyr syndrome making a hero out of the target of the violence.
- Mobilization of opponents.
- Loss of moral high ground.
- Personal beliefs about violence.
- Risk of escalation of violence which further threatens your Community.

Andrea Dworkin[218]

_ _ _ _ _ _ _ _ _ _

Let's change the mood a little, while maintaining our focus on Strategic Options.

Weapons of Crass Destruction: Humor in Resistance

One thing you might notice when you do our environmental scans (SWOTs, e.g.) is that you don't think you have much in the way of assets with which to resist. **You always have something to fight with, individually and collectively. When you have nothing else, use your wits. Fortunately, Humor is also a weapon of resistance.**

"Nothing undermines authority like holding it up to ridicule."

Clandestine Insurgent Rebel Clown Army[219]

I introduced humor earlier, as a way to build the ability to sustain involvement and effort in resistance campaigns (as part of the EDS model). But humor can be a resistance tactic in and of itself.

Humor means everything that causes amusement, from a joke, story, play, skit, movie or book, to a way of acting or a slogan in a demonstration. It can be based on irony, satire, parody, or ridicule.

The humor I'm talking about is political, directed against oppression, and encourages critical reflection about how society is and how we want it to be.[220] You might think of humor as a mere complement to more material work, but there is more to it than that,

---

[218] Dworkin, A. I Favour Violence: Andrea Dworkin. DGR News Service Dec 31, 2020
https://dgrnewsservice.org/resistance/direct-action/violence/i-favour-violence-andrea-dworkin/
[219] Sorenson, M. (24 Feb 2008). Humor as a Serious Strategy of Nonviolent Resistance to Oppression. Wiley Online Library. https://onlinelibrary.wiley.com/doi/full/10.1111/j.1468-0130.2008.00488.x
[220] Ibid.

in great measure because it functions in more ways than Sorenson delineated. Gene Sharp mentions the possibility of using humorous skits and pranks as a method of NVDA, although not in any aspect of his theory. That's too bad, because humor has a history I think he would appreciate.

Let's reintroduce the topic by citing two recent successes of political resistance associated with the prominent use of humor. The Serbian Otpor movement helped bring down Slobodan Milošević in October 2000. Otpor's success was mainly psychological – the populace were able to challenge the climate of fear and political apathy prevalent in Serbia during the 1990s. This change in the psychological mood was a major achievement and a fundamental factor in creating enough opposition to Milošević's rule.[221]

In the span of a few weeks in April, two longtime North African dictators - Abdelaziz Bouteflika in Algeria and Omar al-Bashir in Sudan – were toppled by nonviolent movements. Less understood and examined is the special, disarming role humor can play in propelling nonviolent movements and defeating oppressive structures.[222]

Yes, humor works. And we should incorporate it into our resistance, if for no other reason than that a life of radical Community building and protection without humor is just a bit less meaningful, isn't it?

The Functions of Humor in Resistance
<u>Humor Facilitates Outreach and Mobilization.</u> Humor can attract members: It becomes more fun to be involved, and it brings energy, something Otpor discovered. It especially worked to attract young people and students, although the increase in membership was an unexpected side-effect of the use of humor[223]. "Experienced" (older) activists and Community leaders, take note.

"Humor, and other low-risk tactics, are key to attracting more people to a movement and expanding participation. Higher-risk tactics like labor strikes and mass demonstration can put protesters in danger in a way a joke on social media cannot."

Note the reference to risk in discussing an action type.

Gallagher & Navone assert that attracting more participants is ultimately the most critical variable in the success of any nonviolent movement. While I might quibble here, there certainly is tremendous value in gathering large numbers of resisters, given

---

[221]   Ibid.

[222]   Gallagher, A., & Navone, A. (2019). Not Just a Punchline; Humor and Nonviolent Action; How Comedy can Provide Relief and Promote Resistance in Authoritarian Environments. US Institute of Peace. www.usip.org.

[223]   Sorenson, M. (24 Feb 2008). Humor as a Serious Strategy of Nonviolent Resistance to Oppression. Wiley Online Library. https://onlinelibrary.wiley.com/doi/full/10.1111/j.1468-0130.2008.00488.x

the type of strategy you want to implement. Again, recall the "Sustain" function in the EDS model of campaigns.

"Sometimes a simple joke or two can go a long way in building momentum."[224]

"Making fun of those in power is a necessary pre-revolutionary phase."
Derrick Jensen

<u>Humor Facilitates a Culture of Resistance.</u>
"[Humor] protected people's self-respect and gave the population some sort of control in an otherwise uncontrollable situation. The jokes also served to break down isolation and create a solidarity and group identity within the population. Because so many people shared the jokes, their very existence contradicted the Nazi propaganda that people who did not join them would stand alone.... The jokes also provided an image of nation-wide solidarity that vitally assisted the resistance effort."
George Orwell.[225]

At the personal level, self-irony and joking about one's own shortcomings are considered to have the greatest impact on self-liberation through humor.

Humor can also be used to articulate grievances. In Algeria, protesters co-opted logos and slogans from international brands to express their displeasure with Bouteflika's attempt to run for a fifth term. "Look at your Rolex, it's time to go," read one sign. Another used a fake Microsoft message: "Your 5.0 system needs to be rebooted."[226]

"Men are afraid that women will laugh at them.
Women are afraid that men will kill them."
Margaret Atwood

<u>Humor Serves as a Healing Practice.</u> Practitioners of NVDA, or those who can't or won't implement violence, looting, rioting or the like in their resistance plans, take note. From Gallagher & Navone: Living under and resisting authoritarianism places immense stress on a population. Nonviolent movements can turn violent as a result. But humor can help keep the peace. Laughter can be a pressure-relief valve – releasing excess steam. Laughter relaxes an individual and shifts tendencies away from violence. That's why Iraqi TV turned to comedy when ISIS bore down on their

---

[224] Gallagher, A., & Navone, A. (2019). Not Just a Punchline; Humor and Nonviolent Action; How Comedy can Provide Relief and Promote Resistance in Authoritarian Environments. US Institute of Peace. www.usip.org.

[225] 'Each Joke is a Tiny Revolution' George Orwell, quoted in: Gallagher & Navone. Humor as a Serious Strategy of Nonviolent Resistance to Oppression https://onlinelibrary.wiley.com/doi/full/10.1111/j.1468-0130.2008.00488.x

[226] Gallagher, A., & Navone, A. (2019). Not Just a Punchline; Humor and Nonviolent Action; How Comedy can Provide Relief and Promote Resistance in Authoritarian Environments. US Institute of Peace. www.usip.org.

country. Activists wanted to combat the public's fear of ISIS ideology through satirizing the group.

It's why South African comedians used stand-up comedy to heal after apartheid. "They watched us because they saw hope in the show - hope to challenge long-standing taboos and authority, whether that came in the form of a beard, or a tank, or a codger demanding, 'Respect your elders.'"

Tension in conflict, even nonviolent conflict, can take its toll on those involved. Humor offers an effective mechanism through which movements can assuage fears.

<u>Humor Turns Oppression Upside Down.</u> Do you know what a "piss-take" is? Essentially, it's when someone teases or makes fun of someone or something – mocking at the expense of others. The point is that humor can be used in a targeted way to "take the piss" out of a person or group. When it works, three things happen more or less simultaneously:[227]

- The humor used is confrontational; it provokes, mocks, or ridicules, which escalates the conflict and puts pressure on the oppressor.
- Although an increased pressure raises the chances of repression, paradoxically the use of humor reduces fear within the resistance movement.
- Humor reduces the oppressor's options for reacting in a way he can later justify.

> *"The best way to drive out the devil, if he will not yield to texts of Scripture,*
> *is to jeer and flout him, for he cannot bear scorn."*
>
> Martin Luther

> *"The devil…that proud spirit…cannot endure to be mocked."*
>
> St. Thomas More[228]

Apparently even religious figures know the value of a good piss-take.

> *"[Humor] was something like the main thing that brought [Milošević] down because people were afraid, there was fear everywhere around and if we are going to change something, the main idea was to make fun of the things that make them afraid ... to make people less afraid by using humor."*
>
> Sorenson[229]

---

[227] See Sorenson, M.J. (24 Feb 2008). Humor as a Serious Strategy of Nonviolent Resistance to Oppression. Wiley Online Library. https://onlinelibrary.wiley.com/doi/full/10.1111/j.1468-0130.2008.00488.x

[228] More, T. (1553). Dialogue of Comfort Against Tribulation, Book 2, sec. 16.

[229] Sorenson, M.J. (24 Feb 2008). Humor as a Serious Strategy of Nonviolent Resistance to Oppression. Wiley Online Library. https://onlinelibrary.wiley.com/doi/full/10.1111/j.1468-0130.2008.00488.x

It's a simple logic; it is more difficult to be afraid of someone when you laugh at him.

Turning oppression upside down is different from the other two functions of humor because it directly challenges the relationship with the oppressor.

Gallagher & Navone use "Upending Power Dynamics" in a related sense: Overthrowing an authoritarian regime requires eroding its pillars of support, the organizations and institutions that help a regime maintain power – security forces, media organizations, the business sector or civil servants. Humor is a particularly effective tactic undermining a regime's pillars of support. It disrupts dominant discourses and challenges power "by disrupting the language and symbols used by those in power to represent reality in a particular way and providing alternative interpretations of that reality."[230]

*"Authoritarian leaders and regimes rely on projections of unshakeable power –
using fear to maintain control. No wonder they hate jokes. Humor is fundamentally
about disruptions. The point of a joke is to break with the expected;
to upend the status quo. For governments who rely on unquestioned authority,
the disruptive nature of humor poses a unique threat.
It's assertive but not violent, earnest but not serious."[231]*

— — — — — — — — —

*"Our strategy should be not only to confront empire, but to lay siege to it.
To shame it. To mock it. With our art, our music, our literature,
our stubbornness, our joy, our brilliance, our sheer relentlessness."*

Arundhati Roy[232]

<u>Practical Implications Regarding the Resistance use of Humor.</u> As heartening as it might be to spend time basking in the world of jokes and piss-taking, we need to bring ourselves back to material issues. Humor can be part of your strategic plan, but for it to be most effective, you need to think about its use in a mindful and planful way.

Molly Wallace brings us back in an elegantly simple way, and presages what we'll offer next. She cautions that first, it may be useful to **conduct an analysis before undertaking an action,** to assess its likely effects on the operation of the dimensions of nonviolent action: dialogue facilitation, power breaking, utopian enactment and

---

[230]   Wallace, M. Why social change needs to be a laughing matter. Waging Nonviolence.org. June 17, 2017. https://wagingnonviolence.org/2017/06/incorporate- humor-civil-resistance/

[231]   Gallagher, A., & Navone, A. (2019). Not Just a Punchline; Humor and Nonviolent Action; How Comedy can Provide Relief and Promote Resistance in Authoritarian Environments. US Institute of Peace. www.usip.org.

[232]   Roy, A. (2003). War Talk. Boston: South End Press.

normative regulation. Which of these will be strengthened and which will be weakened – and are these trade-offs worthwhile and useful for the overall goal of the action? Second, activists should **ask: who is/are the intended audience(s)** for the action, will different audiences be affected or respond differently, and are these responses useful for the overall goal of the action?

What a fortuitous segue! Executing a resistance plan wisely includes the disciplined practice of target selection. We'll turn to that next.

A postscript on choosing a strategic option: Recall our conversation re: the legal option, and the perspectives on that from me, Osterweil, and Zinn, among others. Activist comrades in Nepal provide an insightful perspective on this, and by extension, the larger practice of choosing. For example, violence in Hinduism is not necessarily bad. On the other hand, some view the Nepalese government as repressive. Moreover, there is a general cultural acceptance of all living things as sentient beings. So, what would be an appropriate, fitting option for activists there? Rights of Nature legislation seems to be getting a foothold. And while violence as a tactic might bring about popular support, it might also engender even greater government repression than in other countries (although frankly, that is hard to imagine).[233]

Context Matters.

Focusing Your Strategic Options: Target Selection

Between the options contained in the DGR *Taxonomy of Action,* and the approaches I discussed, you should have quite a range of strategic possibilities, **and** a way to determine what options best fit your circumstances. A complementary analysis you need to undertake, choosing a **target** for your strategy.

Choosing a strategic action is a critical function for resistance leaders, as we discovered. The process involves reflection, research, discipline and creativity, but the result will allow you to employ "what will work best for our circumstances". In addition to choosing **what** to do, you need to choose **where** to do it (or **whom** to do it to).

A Note on Targets *vis a vis* Tactics. Choosing a target (offensive or defensive) cannot be divorced from a consideration of tactics. To try to make this clear, let's introduce a

---

[233] Personal conversation

running example. Assume you're part of the Rebel Alliance. (You are, though we aren't as allied as we should be.) The Alliance considers the Death Star a potential target. Probably a good choice. However, the decision to choose the Death Star has to be done in tandem with a consideration of available tactics – for example, you probably wouldn't choose to file a lawsuit against The Star™, or organize a Non-Violent Direct Action like a general strike of neighboring planets.

The Alliance wants to destroy The Star, or disable it, as part of their larger strategic plan. In that case, sabotage or an offensive is more appropriate. Now, the Alliance might have better lawyers than they do star fighters. In that case, The Star may still be a target, but the "calculations" leading up to a potential target choice would likely provide a different result.

Choosing either or both of *actions* and *targets* is a complementary, mutually influential undertaking. And neither necessarily comes first.

TARGETS <—> TACTICS

Let's begin the where and/or who, then.

CHOOSING A TARGET: REVISING THE CARVER MODEL

A convenient, well-known model for choosing a target is the CARVER model (Criticality, Accessibility, Recoverability, Vulnerability, Effect, Recognizability). This tool was developed by US Army Special Forces in Vietnam to select targets optimally, so resources could be efficiently used. The CARVER approach is a logical way of looking at what one might want to focus on and whether or not the target is possible given your resources.

The model as traditionally presented isn't broke, but we're going to fix it. We're just recasting some of the dimensions so we don't have to do any reverse scoring or such. Make sense? Don't fret – use the model as I offer it here and you'll be ready to go.

Let's use the following "CARVER Table" to illustrate how it can be used, and expanded. First, take a moment to familiarize yourself with the dimension definitions. Thanks to Deep Green Resistance for a fuller description of the dimensions.[234]

---

[234] https://deepgreenresistance.net/nl/strategy-tactics/tactics-targets/target-selection-carver-matrix/

The CARVER Table*

	TGT & TACTIC COMBO 1[235]	TGT & TACTIC COMBO 2	TGT & TACTIC COMBO 3
Criticality. How important is the target to the existence of the force or entity you're trying to resist? *(1 = least critical; 10 = most critical)*	10	10	10
Accessibility. How easy is it to get to the target? *(1 = very difficult; 10 = very easy)*	2	5	9
Recoverability. How easy is it for the target to be repaired? *(1 = very easy; 10 = very difficult)*	10	5	7
Vulnerability. How easy is it to damage the target? *(1 = very difficult; 10 = very easy)*	2	4	6
Effect. How much will striking the target negatively effect the opponent? *(1 = very little; 10 = very much)*	10	1	7
Recognizability. How easy is the target to identify? *(1 = very difficult; 10 = very easy)*	10	10	10
TOTAL	44	35	46

NOTES: "TGT & TACTIC COMBO 1" = Death Star, Physical Attack
"TGT & TACTIC COMBO 2" = Death Star, Legal Attack
"TGT & TACTIC COMBO 3" = Pipeline, Legal Attack
*Numerical values are notional! Leave me alone, Star Wars fans.

At the risk of overthinking this model, I offer potential additional dimensions to the CARVER calculus. Resistance planners, use these or not at your discretion, and add any that help your target analysis fit more closely with your strategic situation.

- **Political Significance.** How likely is it your Target & Tactic COMBO will lead to political opinions sympathetic to your cause? *(1 = very unlikely; 10 = very likely)*
- **Effect on Others**. How likely is it your Target / Tactic will have a negative effect on others not involved in the campaign or action? *(1 = very likely; 10 = very unlikely)*

---

[235]   "COMBO" = "Combination"

<u>Using the CARVER Matrix as Flexible Planning Tool.</u> The developers of the CARVER model assumed the only tactics to be used were those likely to physically destroy or disable the target. However, it's possible to expand our thinking with regard to this analysis. For example, **we can use the CARVER technique to compare tactics as well as targets in the same matrix** (depending on your comfort level with more complex analyses than the typical 2-3-column approach).

Our initial analysis compared attacking The Death Star with physical or with legal means, respectively (the 1st and 2nd scoring columns).
- The target is the same regardless of action type, so the Criticality and Recognizability scores are equal (10).
- However, it's much harder for the target to be repaired after a physical attack than a legal one. Hence the scores log in at 10 and 5, respectively.
- A legal attack is also more likely to be able to access the target (given the Tie Fighter defenses and such), and the Death Star is possibly more vulnerable to attack using legal means than physical, so legal gets slightly better scores in these two dimensions.
- And so on! Do the math, and The Total scores of 44 (TGT & TACTIC COMBO 1) and 35 (TGT & TACTIC COMBO 2) indicate a physical attack is preferred. It also makes for a more entertaining movie.
- Let's say, though, that the only strategic resource available to you is the legal system. In this case, you might want to look for the **target** affording you the best return on your investment. In other words, would your legal dollars be better spent on attacking the Death Star or another target – in this case, a pipeline? Working through the dimensions as we did before, you would arrive at a TGT & TACTIC COMBO 3 score of 46. Compare that to the score for attacking the Death Star using legal means of 35, and you should conclude targeting a pipeline using your legal resources is a better bet than using lawyers (sans guns but with money) to attack The Death Star.

These examples are admittedly goofy, but I hope instructive. I resorted to them because they allow us to discuss a resistance topic without violating security culture guidelines. I hope you'll exercise forbearance!

<u>Further "CARVER" Thoughts.</u>
GIGO. I just made up the numbers for our dimension ratings to illustrate my points. You, though, will want your numbers to be accurate, not based on a gut feel or a hypothetical reaction to a hypothetical situation. **Why? GIGO** – Garbage in, Garbage Out. Bad data lead to bad decisions. If you don't populate your matrix with accurate, reasonable, dimension estimates, you won't get reasonable target estimations on the back end. And that is not a good contribution to your resistance strategy.

How do you get the information to complete the matrix ratings?
- Scouting.
- Intelligence.
- Research.
- Effective group processes for brainstorming, problem solving and the like.

What do you do if you find you can't with any confidence do all the ratings? Consider that you need to do more research or scouting. Depending on the time frame of your plans, targeting can be viewed as an iterative process.

And this is really about the long haul. Targeting specifically, and planning generally, are the disciplines Community leaders and resistance activists need to commit to, practice, and maintain in the forefront of their thoughts and work.

Targets do not have to be physical structures. Let's broaden our thinking a bit when it comes to "what" we could target in resistance work. Targets can be people, businesses and so on. Might you, e.g., target the CEO of a pipeline for some sort of action? Maybe a DDoS (Distributed Denial-of-Service) against a website devoted to fascist propaganda?

Broadening our notion of what a target could be also opens the door to a much wider set of actions. Sabotage works in some settings, sure. But what if the President of your nation is highly susceptible to mockery? Rule in the tactical use of humor for your strategic armamentarium. It's been used before, and serves a wide variety of functions in resistance campaigns, as we've seen.

Targeting can be used for offensive or defensive purposes. The line between these orientations might be blurred at times, but do not limit your plans to either type. Be ready to plan to attack threats to your Community preemptively and **on their turf**, as well as to plan and execute actions to defend your land and life. As before, keep open the widest possible range of strategic and tactical options to maximize your flexibility and effectiveness in resistance planning.

A Final Word re Targeting. In life, success is all about having options, or so it's said. It certainly is with target planning. Expand your view of what targeting entails, and be creative in generating target lists and target actions. You may find your resistance Community is on its way to becoming the feared opponent of the dominant culture you've always envisioned.

"Every resistance victory has been won by blood and tears,
with anguish and sacrifice.
Our burden is the knowledge that there are only so many ways to resist,
that these ways have already been invented, and they all involve
profound and dangerous struggle. When resisters win, it is because
they fight harder than they thought possible."[236]

"We need to fight to win, and that means fighting smart."[237]

— — — — — — — — — —

If this was a University (which it's not), you'd be ready to walk across the stage to receive your diploma. You'd be proud, and you should be congratulated for making it this far. And as with any of the other graduations you might have participated in, you likely also experienced doubt, anxiety or uncertainty, perhaps as, "What now?" or, "What next?" Graduations of whatever form are not endings, they are beginnings. I hope you've been challenged and encouraged to embark on or continue your walk toward Community Leadership, and that I provided enough tools for you to think differently about building and leading Communities, and to plan strategically to help your collective Protect and Resist. There are many actions you can and maybe already have taken in this pursuit.

Still, "What next?"

In graduate school, my professor would not let us graduate without presenting a journal-submission-ready research article. This was to be our entrée to the professional world. I didn't necessarily *like* that requirement, but I sure *appreciated* it. This gave me a running start on my path in that world.

I can't mandate that you do anything of that sort, but you'd be well-advised to do something like it. Think of what you could do, knowing all you know now, to present to your collective that you are capable and committed to the well-being of your Community. Whether you call this a vision, a plan, or a vow, take time to craft something that sustains you, and inspires others to struggle with you.

The final chapter addresses some of your "What next? questions, and can serve as a rough guide for your answer to that question.

[236]   McBay, A., Jensen, D., & Keith, L. (2011). Deep Green Resistance: Strategy to Save the Planet. 7 Stories Press, p. 242
[237]   Ibid. p. 264

Worksheet: Planning the Implementation of Your Strategy

You may not be far enough along in your Community Building / Power Leveraging to have considered or to have chosen specific actions or campaigns, but reflection beforehand can help you do those things more mindfully.

What is your sense of the Intrinsic and Extrinsic factors regarding your Community that will help you evaluate potential actions or campaigns?

I contrasted NVDA with other approaches, like looting, violence and humor. Which of these if any can you imagine incorporating into your strategy?

Which of those resonates most with you? How so?

In addition to the factors that argue for a Community's use of violence, what would you add? Why would **your** Community NOT want to use violence?

Do you have any comedians in your collective? How will you incorporate her / his talents into your Protect and Resist campaign?

What potential targets or tactics (offensive or defensive) are you considering for your Protect and Resist plans?

How comfortable are you in your choices, or your pool of possible targets / tactics? If you're pretty comfortable, congratulations! Now take that to the next level of specificity and begin to put together Action Plans!
- If you've only settled on a tactic, your next challenge is to choose a target.
- If you've only settled on a target but don't have a tactic in mind, well, you know what to do.

If you're not comfortable, what do you need to do? (HINT: Probably gather more data.)

CHAPTER 16

Moving Forward
(You, and Your Collective)

I hope you're convinced that you can be a Community leader or Elder. **I know you can**. However, being or becoming a Community Leader or Elder is not for the dilettante. It's a challenge and a calling that entails a period of commitment and growth, as we investigated in the chapter, "On Being/Becoming…", and elaborated on in the ensuing chapters. Thank you for your dedication to leading in your collectives, and to protecting the living world. I hope this book has provided you with value in your activist work.

If I did my job, you will have learned what you need to develop skills as a Cadre- and Community-builder. I planned an action orientation as an overriding perspective, but skills alone do not make a leader. Effective Community leaders and Elders especially are best when they adopt the values and worldviews I espoused here and there. Recall in particular the Values Chain discussion as an example of how we might frame our values clarification work and articulate what we're all about.

A comprehensive discussion of Radical Community would not be complete without some reliance on theory, which I attempted to provide, both for building a resistance collective and for marshaling its power to greater effect. Theory is needed, in part to frame our thoughts and guide our strategy and building work.

> *"There is nothing so practical as a good theory."*
>
> Kurt Lewin, Pioneer in
> Organizational Psychology [238]

Why? A theory explains how something works, and when you know how something works (like Radical Community, resistance tactics, or humor, e.g.), you can leverage it for material resistance purposes.

Karl Marx:
The object of theory *"is not to understand history, but to change it."*
Later rephrased by Lenin: *"without revolutionary theory there can be no revolutionary practice."* [239]

---

[238] Lewin, K. (1943). Psychology and the process of group living. Journal of Social Psychology 17, 113–131.
[239] Karl Marx, as noted in Churchill, W. (2007). Pacifism as Pathology. Oakland, CA: AK Press, p. 119

"I am suggesting we develop a genuine praxis...action consciously and intentionally guided by theory...."[240]

Earlier I cited the (temporary) fractioning of the Sandinistas as an example of drift. The leader mentioned in that example offered an explanation for that splitting:
"Why did we divide...? Our organization just wasn't prepared for a self-critical process. Few leaders, and even fewer members, had ever had the opportunity to talk about or pay much attention to theory. And there must always be a theoretical process."

Aric McBay[241]

Effective leaders in resistance rely on theory, and not just "theoretically"! the Sandinista quote reminds us, too, of the important role of collective reflection. Create opportunities to do this regularly, whether as part of your Consciousness building and/or in your strategic planning cycles.

As you reflect on what I covered, and as you craft your strategies to Protect and Resist, do so with your expanded consciousness regarding the nature of Community and leadership, and with a sharpened sense of strategy, its possibilities and requirements.

Having possibly "protested too much" regarding the necessity of theory, let me also remark that I hope that the action orientation and focus on best practices in this book serves to demystify leadership for you. Effective leadership, as I mentioned in the first chapter, is in great measure a function of observable behaviors, which you can learn, practice, and master.

— — — — — — — — — —

How to proceed? By way of bringing this book to a close, I again invoke the Janus effect. For us to do the best job of looking forward, we have to look back. Let's do that.

---

[240] Mike Ryan, in Churchill, W. (2007). Pacifism as Pathology. Oakland, CA: AK Press.
[241] McBay, A. (2019a). Full Spectrum Resistance, Volume One: Building Movements and Fighting to Win. New York: Seven Stories Press. p. 208

Looking Back

The best way to begin this retrospective is to invoke our hierarchical model of leadership roles. Being a Community Leader or Elder involves, as you will recall, sets of nested roles, which build on each other to culminate in a mature, wise leader of radical Community.

The Changing Role(s) of Resistance Leader			
Context	Role(s)		
Basic Leadership for Resistance (LFR)	Model / Modeler		
Leading Resistance Cadres (LRC)	Model / Modeler	Professional / Linchpin	
Leading Communities of Resistance (LCOR)	Model / Modeler	Professional / Linchpin	Land Defender / Protector / Elder

Embedded in all these role profiles is an acknowledgment of first principles. The first of these has to do with the nature of leadership:
The art [practice] of mobilizing others to want to struggle for shared aspirations.
Kouzes & Posner

<u>Resistance Leaders</u> do this by embracing the Five Practices:
- Challenge the System [internal and external]
- Inspire a Shared Vision
- Enable Comrades to Act
- Be a Model, and a Modeler
- Encourage and Uplift

<u>Cadre Leaders</u> build effective small "teams" and imbue them with a sense of professionalism. They also function as linchpins between the Cadre and larger collectives.

<u>Community Leaders</u> aspire to become or take on the mantle of Land Defender, Protector and Elder in addition to the previous roles. Among the aspects of this role are another set of critical practices:

- Centering
- Sustaining
- Sharing
- Culture, Spirituality

Another aim of this book is to help comrades **build** and **leverage** the power of Communities that are radical in the authentic sense of that word. We talked about how that might occur. In particular, we discussed cultivating Community characteristics:

- Consciousness
- Comradeship
- Commitment
- Shared Power
- Leadership

Regardless of the leadership role, there is an element of strategy involved. I provided a three-part introduction to that skill, and by now you should have a good grasp of an effective strategy's components and the process of building one from scratch. I discussed how you can leverage your Community Power, by thinking and acting strategically. These touchstones form a solid basis for your work as resistance leader and Community Builder and Elder. Keep them in mind as you frame your current circumstances and chart a way forward.

Looking Forward: What's Next for You

If you've ever flown on a commercial airline, you've suffered through the safety briefing you're required to "listen to". When the briefer describes the oxygen masks that drop down in the event of well, an event, they tell you to don your mask before you try to help others with their masks.

Makes sense. I'd offer similar advice to you as an aspirational or experienced Community Builder or Elder: Before you can help your collective build power and leverage it, you need to work on yourself. You're not much good to your collective if your leadership skills are underdeveloped, you're not clear on your values, or your worldview doesn't center a living planet. So, where do you go from here? Here are simple steps to begin to master your individual leadership self.

FOCUS ON YOUR PERSONAL DEVELOPMENT
Leadership consists of observable and learnable behaviors. You can improve your ability to lead, regardless of how experienced you are.

Leadership development is personal development.

I recommend the avenue you pursue is the process I outlined in that first chapter. Your commitment to that process structures your growth and enables you to develop as a leader better and more quickly than if you left that development to the vagaries of random events, especially if reflection was not part of your development discipline. Equally important, your commitment to this path demonstrates to your Community that you value the collective and are willing to invest in its long-term benefit. You also gain trust from comrades and greater confidence that you are or will be ready to take on a leadership role in the collective.

Maintain a broader perspective on your personal leadership unfolding. One unique aspect of leadership development compared to "training" is that it focuses, not merely on skills work, but on **Attitudes** toward the notion of leadership itself, and **Values** concerning relationships with others and our place in the world. Reacquaint yourself with the Chapter titled, "ON BEING / BECOMING…", especially the section on the Chain of Values. Remember and reflect on the "why" and "how" you are a Land Protector. This perspective is a critical complement to the more skills-oriented development path you also commit to.

Reliance on leadership skills without healthy, life-affirming values and a related worldview is merely manipulation.

Reflect, too, on what you're willing and able to do, to help your Community Protect and Resist.

In any case – do more development! If you rely on this book alone for all your learning, you'll be shortchanging yourself. Look for other opportunities to learn, to lead, to try things out. The Spiral of Experience (Chapter 1), when you recognize it happening to you, can be an exhilarating personal form of evolution. You may not get it all right away, but you'll learn each time. Keep moving on.

BUILD YOUR CADRE
While you're "working on yourself" as a leader, you can embrace the complementary task of working your way through expanding spheres of influence. Build your Cadre, or contribute to a Cadre you're part of by serving in a supportive or co-leader capacity. The primer in the second chapter lays out the basics of this role.

While you're at it, explore how you can advocate for your Cadre (regardless of whatever role you're filling in that group) and serve as a linchpin for them. Help your Cadre succeed by clearing the path for their accomplishment of critical tasks, and by gathering the resources and information they need. Don't wait to be named a leader. Do what you know needs to be done.

Remember, Cadres serve a critical role in accomplishing the on-the-ground work in resistance. They function in the "sweet spot" between what an individual can do (which is generally not nearly enough) and the Community, the basic self-sufficient and sustainable unit of resistance.

Equally important, Cadres can help you with the ultimate leadership challenge of building your collective. They are the trusted agents, the Core of the collective-building work. They can also serve as the literal and figurative foundation of the collective you're working to build. In this regard, Cadre serve both short-term roles (the on-the-ground resistance planning and action) and long-term roles (helping you lay the groundwork for your Community building and strategic planning / implementation).

A gentle suggestion: Don't skip the step of building a Cadre before tackling Community-building. Your Cadre comrades can make all the difference in how well, how easily, and how quickly your collective-building goes.

BUILD YOUR COMMUNITY
This is the central focus of the book, and what we aspire to accomplish. We have a model to work with, examples to learn from, and questions to reflect on to clarify thinking and values. I'd be remiss, though, if I haven't provided you with enough material to leave here with a critical takeaway: **A plan**. Your plan answers the "What next?" question we grappled with at the end of the last chapter. Make your plan service you and your collective – don't try to adapt your plan development work to any particular protocol or format. This is where you breathe life into it as your vision, plan, or vow – whatever resonates with you and your collective.

How do you use what we talked about to craft your plan? Not so difficult, really. To start, if you've worked earnestly through the reflection questions and the exercises like the Community Walk, you will already be 85% done (as in, most of the way there).

How so? For my part, I've tied the concepts and models in the book to actionable items wherever possible. When in doubt, refer to the Five Characteristics model of a Radical Community. I haven't counted, but last time I looked there were dozens of actionable items you can integrate into a plan to build your collective and leverage its power.

You also know how to construct **Action Plans** and think strategically. Use your newfound skills to author a vision and mission if your collective hasn't already.

Use your strategic thinking skills to put together a strategic or tactical plan for your collective or campaign.
- Get feedback on your work from trusted agents.
- Start a dialogue or conversation about what you see, what you feel, and what you believe is a way forward for your collective.
- Make this a repeating process.

LEVERAGE YOUR INDIVIDUAL POWER
We in the resistance don't generally think of ourselves or our movement as powerful. In some measure, that's because our power is for the most part latent. It's lying dormant in ourselves, our comrades, and our collectives. Wake it up, shake it up, and do what you're called to do. It's your responsibility, and your honor.

Looking Forward: What's Next for Your Community

Apart from our environmental analysis, which informs our strategy, and our discussions about building a Radical Community, we haven't talked much about how our collectives might take their place in the larger world. Other than protecting and resisting, or dismantling the dominant culture, what can we say about the roles and expectations of the Radical Community?

To introduce this discussion, let's agree to agree that reviving Radical Communities, that Protect and Resist, isn't just a good idea – the practice is key to our survival. They are key to dismantling the dominant culture. They are also key to "seeding" the planet with just and sustainable social forms after Collapse, as our CPR Premises lay out. But they may not be able to do what they need to if they're working in isolation.

DeFilippis et al. describe six propositions for Communities to engage in the struggle for social change. Their ideas are relevant to our focus, and their propositions serve as an excellent frame for our final conversation. These propositions can be your "takeaways" from the topics we explored throughout this book. We should find parallels to what we have discussed. How can we provide an overall review and guide for thinking about and steering our Communities into the future?

Understand, Celebrate, and Enact the Importance of Community

The history of grassroots organizing and social movements in the US and elsewhere provides a collective memory of efforts that successfully challenged oppression and injustice. Tap into this stream of resistance memory and activism, and learn about this history. A good place to start might be *American Insurgents,* by Richard Seymour (2012)[242], or *Deep Green Resistance,* by McBay et al. (2011).[243]

Know this: Communities are out there, working for radical change. To maximize our power, we need to understand that this base of "movement potential" exists, and tap into it, as I discuss below. An understanding and appreciation of this tradition also helps counter the feelings of isolation and hopelessness that so often plague the resistance activist. Equally important, your knowledge of resistance collectives and movements throughout history allows you to envision your collective's future more effectively, and to plan for ensuring it.

We are not alone. But we can do a better job of linking up.

I've explained the necessity of cultivating Community Consciousness. It is important in its own right, but building local Communities based on a sense of solidarity and belonging is also an essential step in creating a broad social movement that has strong local roots. Look beyond the traditional boundaries of your Community to create or join a base from which larger movements can develop. And campaigns can grow, too, so consider your campaign(s) as seed(s) that can take root in other Communities and with other activists.

Organize Beyond Your Community, too

Although we are Community Builders and Land Defenders first, we would do well to understand that our work also transcends Community. DeFilippis et al. talk about working **"within a place", but not just "about a place".** We work within our Communities, but we understand the threats and issues we oppose are widespread. We need to advocate and agitate for resistance that is also widespread.

Local work is the starting point, but not the ultimate goal, or it shouldn't be - not as long as our aim is dismantling the dominant culture. We are oppositional. We need to address and confront issues and problems within our respective collectives *and* create linkages beyond the local. Otherwise, we will not be able to address the large-scale problems *or* our local problems, in any lasting way.

---

[242] Seymour, R. (2012). American Insurgents: A Brief History of American Anti-Imperialism. Haymarket books

[243] McBay, A., Jensen, D., & Keith, L. (2011). Deep Green Resistance: Strategy to Save the Planet. 7Stories Press

This view is not unique to DeFilippis et al. Chris Hedges (2023) recently posted on a similar theme. *There Are No Permanent Allies, Only Permanent Power,* albeit concerned with a more mainstream political focus, bears repeating:

"If we do not build left-right coalitions…we will be impotent in the face of corporate power and the war machine."[244]

I've had discussions that remarked on the fact that the political spectrum (at least in the US) is not well represented by a straight line, with the far left on one end and the far right on the other extreme. Whether this construct is better conceived as a horseshoe or something else entirely seems beside the point for our purposes. In fact, we should probably ignore the political spectrum entirely since it does not serve us in resistance work and distracts us with abstract navel-gazing which does not lend itself to planning or material action.

Instead, focus on shared values and interests, and their manifestations in issues, perceived threats, and/or campaigns. Only then will we be able to grow the aggregate power we need to make the radical changes to the dominant culture so necessary to saving the living world. Just as we built Power **within** our Community, we need to do so **across** Communities and interest groups. This is where "Collaboration within, conflict without" meets "Organize beyond Community".

Let's suspend our worship of ideological purity long enough to ally with those who can help us win in important ways, and to build momentum needed to continue the fight. Would it be useful to ally with arguably otherwise conservative activists in Pennsylvania fighting against fracking in their valley? You know the answer – yes. Unfortunately, we don't see that happening enough, or sustainably enough. Let's make it a point to look for these opportunities to be pragmatic in our resistance, and keep our eyes on the short-term **and** the long-term goals. But let's also be mindful of maintaining boundaries. There may be some groups with which you just cannot collaborate, or whose cooperation might damage your movement or collective substantially.

Again from Chris Hedges:
"We will not topple corporate power and the war machine alone. There has to be a left-right coalition, which will include people whose opinions are not only unpalatable but even repugnant, or we will remain marginalized and ineffectual. This is a fact of political life. Alliances are built around particular issues, …, which often fall apart when confronting other concerns."[245]

---

[244]   Hedges, Chris. (2023). There Are No Permanent Allies, Only Permanent Power. The Hedges Report. (Substack). https://chrishedges.-substack.com/p/there-are-no-permanent-allies-only Accessed March 22, 2023.
[245]   Ibid.

You'd think this sort of lesson was widely known, but the resistance doesn't act as if it were. It may be widely known but it surely is not widely practiced. If this book helps you see that, there's a small victory. If you know this but still avoid cross-collective collaboration, this may be a special reflection opportunity for you. What needs to be different for your collective to build power with those who do not share your world view in its entirety? And what can you do to change that?

Resistance is About Conflict and Power
This notion should be fresh in your mind from our just-completed strategy section. This theme, that we need to generate and maintain as many resistance options and tools as possible, can't be underemphasized.

Radical change is necessary for things to get better. And for things to get better, conflict over power must be a key orienting direction of Community organizing. This doesn't mean all your activities are confrontational, but that conflict is part of your analysis, your overarching strategy, and tactics to obtain desired results. But do not confuse the external with the internal. We collaborate within and oppose without.

"Power concedes nothing without a demand. It never did and it never will."
Frederick Douglass

DeFilippis et al. explain that conflict is expressed in several ways:
It defines who the opposition is. In their approach that means determining who benefits from the current set of power relations, and who's therefore in a position to deliver the changes demanded. It **also** means **understanding what's necessary** to mobilize against those who are in positions of power. We know this from our study of resistance history and our discussions about targeting and the CARVER model.

Conflict is **expressed through the analysis of social issues**. Political education and analysis are key parts of your activities. This is in great measure what we mean by Community Consciousness, right? Especially at the local and regional levels, ask questions about who benefits and why when issues are confronted. The larger threat of the dominant culture, **that** we already have a handle on.

Conflict is built into our practices not only through **direct confrontational** relations with powerholders but also through creating **alternative practices** that challenge dominant ones. What makes a Community radical in general (and matriarchy specifically, e.g.,) challenges the current order, and with good reason – these non-patriarchal practices make industrial civilization impossible to maintain.

The challenge for Community builders and Elders is to sustain the directly confrontational stance over time - to keep the vision over the long term. An equally difficult challenge is to maintain your Community's integrity over the long haul. If you practice the Community-building discipline I outlined in this book, your chances of success are greatly enhanced. Don't avoid conflict – lean into it. It's the only way to make change. **Maintain your collective anger over what has been done to society, to justice, and to the planet. It's legitimate and important.**

Unite Your Community's Work with Social Movement Efforts

Community organizing and social movements are often part of the same overall struggle. Social movements often start out as local struggles, and then evolve into movements much greater than the sum of their parts.

"… local organizing gives birth to, galvanizes, and sustains social movements..."[246]

In turn, "larger-scale interventions fuel local efforts, providing more power, sparking and giving confidence to an oppositional imagination, legitimizing claims and grassroots work, and sustaining and galvanizing community efforts." The flip side, of course, is that "Problems ensue when community and movement efforts ignore each other."[247]

Build connections with existing, broader social movements. Create a mutually beneficial power-enhancing dynamic. Perhaps the Rights of Nature movement can help your Community secure autonomy for local waters, even if for a finite amount of time. Use that interlude to create yet more alliances, leverage your power, and plan for more effective resistance strategies for the back end. You can pursue a similar strategy with global or national radical feminist groups, Deep Sea mining resistance collectives, the American Indian Movement, or well-known antiwar groups. Research movements which reflect or complement your organizing work. **Get connected, and stay connected.**

Emphasize Critical Analysis and Political Education

From the authors: To be part of a wider, broader, longer-term movement for social change, Communities need social analysis and to disseminate it through political education (i.e., the relationships between Community, corporatism, and the state). This practice can help provide the fuel for resistance.

We know the importance of Consciousness to an effective radical Community, and we saw examples of others who felt the same, such as the Black Panther Party. Readers

---

[246] DeFilippis, J., Fisher, R., & Shragge, E. (2010). Contesting Community: The Limits and Potential of Local Organizing. New Bruns-wick: Rutgers University Press. p. 175
[247] Ibid.

of this book are highly likely to share a radical worldview which includes a "Deep Green" orientation and an understanding that dismantling industrial civilization are imperatives. We also know this worldview must be shared among members of our collectives, and that we must foster critical thought based on these principles.

DeFilippis et al. remind us of this, and offer a further implication – that critical analysis and political education in our respective Communities also enables us to demand more than what neoliberalism offers in terms of solutions. In our (radical) view, our hard-won awareness allows us to see that rejecting the dominant culture out of hand is a key to our ability to effectively resist. It also may provide us with a stronger *a priori* connection with larger movements (a key initiative for the authors), enabling us to see more clearly whom we might ally with, and conversely providing a self-penned "Letter of Introduction" to members of those larger movements, clearing the way for membership or alliances.

However, we need to move beyond mere awareness and critical thought in an insular fashion. If we don't **"name our radical politics"**, we undermine a longer-term and more fundamental social change (and doom ourselves to the short-term, pragmatic and reactive).

We need the courage and confidence to name our politics and **name the problem**. Doing so gives birth to an even greater level of confidence in the righteousness of our struggle and our ability to contribute materially to it. Try it! Go public with your politics and demands. I talked way back in the first Chapter about "Finding Your Voice". Doing that for yourself creates power for you as the individual leader. Doing that at the Community level brings about the same clarity, commitment, and confidence for your collective.

Giving voice to your politics also emboldens other collectives, by showing them they are not alone in their rejection of the dominant culture and their subsequent resistance to it. Resistance is a lonely, isolating endeavor, and the dominant culture wants to keep it that way. Make connections and search others out to aggregate power, and to build sustainability and perseverance.

– – – – – – – – – –

So – Encourage critical reflection in your Community. Beyond what we just discussed, this will convey a broader, long-term perspective on organizing. Take the long view, and commit to long-term building and resistance work. Recall the seven generations perspective, and the Janus effect. They will help you see and move beyond the issue or crisis of the week.

"building power for the long term requires informed and critical leaders and members within the community. Learning and education in the Community are often ignored, or education is limited to specific skills....

A balance between organizing, mobilizing, and education can lift the necessity of always looking for the next issue and help build critical, analytic leadership. This in turn can radicalize the program of [the Community], as the base itself gains confidence in its ability to build a critical consciousness."[248]

Make (and Break) History.

"...history is made by ordinary people in multiple ways and at multiple scales –
not merely the powerful, but by those who challenge their received world."

Communities that Protect and Resist's first Premise is that such collectives are the primary resistance collectives. From our blog:

"Communities provide a fundamental unit of opposition.... [The] dominant culture
has atomized our collectives / families and blunted joint resistance efforts by
invoking the guileful, divisive ideology of neoliberalism. We advocate for a return to
class consciousness, collective struggle and the wielding of power
available only to united groups committed to each other."[249]

De Filippis et al. share this view. They see the "local geographic or cultural community" as the "dominant means and the primary locus of contemporary history making".[250] The primary locus is the local. I half-jokingly use the phrase, "World domination one Community at a time". What I'm really talking about is worldwide resistance-building, one Community at a time.

Building radical Communities and leveraging their individual and aggregated power is our best chance to save the living world. We know we have to do it, and we have the tools to begin this work. But keep in mind how difficult the struggle has been and how quickly opportunities are closed by those in power. Let's inoculate ourselves against the challenges and persist, with our eyes open.

"people make history when they challenge the existing power and
when the times are right."[251]

---

[248] DeFilippis, J., Fisher, R., & Shragge, E. (2010). Contesting Community: The Limits and Potential of Local Organizing. New Brunswick: Rutgers University Press, p. 180

[249] https://ctpr.home.blog

[250] DeFilippis, J., Fisher, R., & Shragge, E. (2010). Contesting Community: The Limits and Potential of Local Organizing. New Brunswick: Rutgers University Press, p. 180f

[251] Ibid. p. 183

The times are never "right", and if somehow they might be, they don't last long, as the authors acknowledge. But we can't wait. The time cannot get any "more right", so we need to challenge **now**.

"It would do us all well to heed the various lessons of the past,
understand history better, and seek to become the history makers
feared by those who have controlled the forces of history…."[252]

"History" has been the prerogative of and tool for the dominant culture to shape the way we think about the world in general and resistance in particular. Both perspectives work to maintain the social order, which is destroying the planet. We need to take history back.

Instead of making history, maybe better – end history.

– – – – – – – – – –

"those of us who today are organizers, rabble-rousers, activists, and quiet lovers of
justice did not invent this struggle for a more just and humane world.
That fight has been going on for thousands and thousands of years.
In every one of those generations, there have been people like us, creative radicals
and rebels, who believed in and worked for the possibility of justice….

That struggle may at times have been driven underground…but,
it has never stopped flowing."

"None of us here today will live long enough to see the just world of which we dream
come to pass. But it will. All we have to do to make that happen is
to do our work as well as we can, in a way that makes the job run just
a little more smoothly for those who we absolutely believe and know will
come after us, who will carry on the work we have done."[253]

Si Kahn

– – – – – – – – – –

A living planet and just, sustainable Communities need your commitment, your leadership, and your comradeship. You know what to do and how to do it. Let's work together to maximize the effectiveness of all that we each have to offer.

And let's begin now, if not sooner.

---

[252] Ibid. p. 182

[253] Kahn, S. (2010). Creative Community Organizing: A Guide for Rabble-Rousers, Activists, and Quiet Lovers of Justice. San Francisco: Berrett-Koehler, p. 191f

Worksheet: Moving Yourself and Your Community Forward

Where do you feel you fit currently in the "hierarchy" of leadership roles? Do you, for example, feel more confident in becoming or continuing as an Elder? Reflect on what that entails for you.

I talked in this chapter about the six propositions for Communities to engage in the struggle for, e.g., social change. Where is your collective in that "unfolding"? What do you need to concentrate on more than you have? What is going well for you?

Have you named your radical politics or nature? How often and clearly does this happen in your Community?

Whom can you count on as your collective's allies? What collectives can you reach out to, who DON'T share all your values, but who can add to your collective power for resistance?

Bibliography

Alinsky, S. (1971). Rules for Radicals: A Pragmatic Primer for Realistic Radicals. New York: Vintage Books.

Anderson, E. (1999). What is the Point of Equality?. Chicago Journals: Chicago University Press.

Aymenn Jawad Al-Tamimi, A. J., 2018. The Internal System of the Communes in Rojava. Cooperation in Mesopotamia. https://www.aymennjawad.org/2018/04/the-internal-system-of-the-communes-in-rojava

Bandura, A. (1977). Self-efficacy: Toward a unifying theory of behavioral change. Psychological Review, 84(2), 191-215.

Behling, O. Employee selection: Will intelligence and conscientiousness do the job? The Academy of Management Executive; Feb 1998; 12, 1; ABI/INFORM Global pg. 77

Bloom, J. & Martin, W.E. (2013). Black Against Empire: The History and Politics of the Black Panther Party. Berkeley: University of California Press.

Briand. M.K. (und.). A Practical Guide to a Community that Works.

Bridges, W. (2003). Managing Transitions: Making the Most of Change (2nd Ed.). DaCapo Press.

Briy, A. (2020). Zapatistas: Lessons in community self-organisation in Mexico. In OpenDemocracy.net. https://www.opendemocracy.net/en/democraciaabierta/zapatistas-lecciones-de-auto-organización-comunitaria-en

Cab, A. (2020). Confessions of a Former Bastard Cop. https://medium.com/@OfcrACab/confessions-of-a-former-bastard-cop-bb14d17bc759

Carter, M. (2012). Kingfisher's Song: Memories Against Civilization. Shelbyville, Kentucky: Wasteland Press.

Calvert, G., "In White America," speech, reprinted in Guardian, March 25, 1967.

Chomsky, N. (2002). Understanding Power: The Indispensable Chomsky. New York: The New Press.

Churchill, W. (2007). Pacifism as Pathology. Oakland, CA: AK Press.

Conley, J. (2023). Rail Company Claims East Palestine Water Is Safe After Funding "Sloppy" Testing https://truthout.org/articles/rail-company-claims-east-palestine-water-is-safe-after-funding-sloppy-testing/

Copelan, C. (2018). Snake Valley celebrates Tenth Annual Water Festival August 31 – September 3rd in Baker, Nevada. High Desert Advocate. https://www.coyote-tv.com/2018/08/29/snake-valley-celebrates-tenth-annual-water-festival-august-31-september-3rd-in-baker-nevada/ Accessed Dec 30 2022.

Coughlin, F. (2014). The Humility of Love: A Lesson from Chiapas. In Deep Green Resistance News Service Nov 6, 2014. https://dgrnewsservice.org/resistance-culture/indigenous/humility-love-lesson-chiapas/

Curphy, G. & Hogan, R. (2012). The Rocket Model: Practical Advice for Building High Performing Teams. Tulsa, OK: Hogan Press.

Dadsen, M. Building huts the old way to get Aboriginal culture 'strong' for future generations. https://www.abc.net.au/news/2020-06-14/traditional-aboriginal-huts-being-rebuilt-along-tasmanian-coast/12353032 Accessed Dec 30 2022.

De Padua, Anthony & RABBITSKIN, Norma. Working with Indigenous Leadership and Indigenous Environments. Chapter in Leadership and Influencing Change in Nursing (Joan Wagner, Ed.) 2018. University of Regina Press. Retrieved Aug 20 2023 from https://leadershipandinfluencingchangeinnursing.pressbooks.com/chapter/chapter-3-working-with-indigenous-leadership-and-indigenous-environments/

Deal, T., & Kennedy, A. (1982). Corporate Cultures: The Rites and Rituals of Corporate Life. Reading, MA: Addison-Wesley.

DeFilippis, J., Fisher, R., & Shragge, E. (2010). Contesting Community: The Limits and Potential of Local Organizing. New Brunswick: Rutgers University Press.

Denchak, M. (2018). Flint Water Crisis: Everything You Need to Know https://www.nrdc.org/stories/flint-water-crisis-everything-you-need-know

Duckworth, S. & Gibson, F. (1996). Building Trust. In Coaching Workshop, developed for OppenheimerFunds.

Dugoni, Bernard L.; Ilgen, Daniel R. (1981). "Realistic Job Previews and the Adjustment of New Employees". The Academy of Management Journal. 24 (3): 579–591.

Eldred, S. M. (April 3, 2022). The Native American History of Lacrosse. MplsStPl (online mag). https://mspmag.com/arts-and-culture/native-american-history-lacrosse/ Accessed Dec 30 2022.

Emanuele, V. (2020). Winning Requires Vision, Strategy and Numbers. https://www.counterpunch.org/2020/07/28/winning-requires-vision-strategy-and-numbers/

Emanuele, V. (2018). Musings on Organizing. https://dgrnewsservice.org/resistance/strategy/musings-on-organizing/, Accessed Mar 22, 2022.

Engler, M., & Engler, P. This is an Uprising: How Nonviolent Revolt is Shaping the Twenty-First Century. New York: Nation Books.

Escobar, N. (2020). One Author's Controversial View: 'In Defense Of Looting'. npr.org. https://www.npr.org/sections/codeswitch/2020/08/27/906642178/one-authors-argument-in-defense-of-looting

Falk, W. (2019). How Dams Fall: On Representing the Colorado River in the First-ever American Lawsuit Seeking Rights for a Major Ecosystem. Little Bound Books.

Fite, K. (2023). The Lithium Frenzy is an Ecological Catastrophe for Oregon's High Desert. Counterpunch, February 10, 2023. https://www.counterpunch.org/2023/02/10/the-lithium-frenzy-is-an-ecological-catastrophe-for-oregons-high-desert/ Accessed February 24, 2023.

Gallagher, A., & Navone, A. (2019). Not Just a Punchline; Humor and Nonviolent Action; How Comedy can Provide Relief and Promote Resistance in Authoritarian Environments. US Institute of Peace. www.usip.org.

Gardner, John W. On Leadership. Highlighted summary of the book, published by Free Press. Accessed August 2020.

Gass, H. (2023). When $1 billion isn't enough. Why the Sioux won't put a price on land. https://www.csmonitor.com/USA/Society/2023/0628/When-1-billion-isn-t-enough.-Why-the-Sioux-won-t-put-a-price-on-land

Gibson, F. (2018). Rights on Nature for the Colorado River: A Case Study. Presentation and Workshop for the 2018 Bioneers Conference, Boulder, CO.

Gibson, F., & Pason, A. (2003). Levels of Leadership: Developing Leaders Through New Models. Journal of Education for Business, Vol 79, Issue 1.

Goettner-Abendroth, H. (2007). The Way into an Egalitarian Society. https://www.hagia.de/fileadmin/user_upload/pdf/the_way.pdf

Goettner-Abendroth, H. (2012). Matriarchal Societies: Studies on Indigenous Cultures across the Globe. New York: Peter Lang Publishing.

Goettner-Abendroth, H. (und). Matriarchal Politics and Matriarchal Manifesta: The Vision of an Egalitarian Society and How We Will Achieve It. Unpublished Manuscript/

Gozdz, K. (1993). Building Community as a Leadership Discipline. In Michael Ray and Alan Rinzler (eds.) The New Paradigm in Business: Emerging Strategies for Leadership and Organizational Change. New York: J.P. Tarcher / Perigee

Guerrero, S. (June 5, 2020). Oakland farmers band together to help feed frontline protesters amid demonstrations. Sfgate.com. https://www.sfgate.com/food/slideshow/Oakland-based-farms-help-feed-frontline-203265.php?fbclid=IwAR34n3dZYFCV6ZHAxEcCvm2qIEEsWpM6ArUjOCLs2RYZgKHh0V0Yf8g79HY (Accessed Jan 1, 2023)

Hedges, C. (2018). The Coming Collapse. In Truthdig.com. https://www.truthdig.com/articles/the-coming-collapse/?fbclid=IwAR11zKIgXIeaEKxaxdCdC4bNbW5vX-7OLzxWKV6x_6m7dQJE15Ep8t59cc8 [Accessed Nov 12 2022]

Hedges, C. (2023). There Are No Permanent Allies, Only Permanent Power. The Hedges Report. (Substack). https://chrishedges.substack.com/p/there-are-no-permanent-allies-only Accessed March 22, 2023.

Hernandez, E. (1998). Assets and Obstacles in Community Leadership. Journal of Community Psychology, Vol. 26, No. 3.

Hughes, R., Ginnett, R., & Curphy, G. (2002). Leadership: Enhancing the Lessons of Experience (4th Ed.). McGraw-Hill.

Human Rights Watch (2019). Canada: Blind Eye to First Nation Water Crisis https://www.hrw.org/news/2019/10/02/canada-blind-eye-first-nation-water-crisis

Jensen, D (2016). The Myth of Human Supremacy. Seven Stories Press.

Jensen, D., Keith, L., & Wilbert, M. (2021). Bright Green Lies: How the environmental movement lost its way and what we can do about it. Monkfish publishing

Johnson, A. (March 14, 2022). In Brazil, Indigenous Ka'apor take their territory's defense into their own hands.
Mongabay. https://news.mongabay.com/2022/03/in-brazil-indigenous-kaapor-take-their-territorys-defense-into-their-own-hands/ [Accessed Nov 21 2022]

Kahn, S. (2010). Creative Community Organizing: A Guide for Rabble-Rousers, Activists, and Quiet Lovers of Justice. San Francisco: Berrett-Koehler.

Kar, R., Watkinson, A., & Nelson, B. (2022). How to Steer a Drifting Culture. https://www.gallup.com/workplace/397034/steer-drifting-culture.aspx

Kenny, C., in Carolyn Kenny and Tina Ngaroimata Fraser (Eds.). Living Indigenous Leadership: Native Narratives on Building Strong Communities. (2012). Vancouver: UBC Press

Kenny, C. (1998). "The Sense of Art: A First Nations Perspective." Canadian Journal of Native Education 22, 1: 77-84.

Ketcham, C. Kickstarter What it means when you turn your rifle against techno-industrial civilization. [Downloaded Aug 8 2022].

Kidder, R. (1994). Shared Values for a Troubled World: Conversations With Men and Women of Conscience. Jossey-Bass.

Kotter, J. What Leaders Really Do. Harvard Business Review. (May-June 1990).

Kouzes, J., & Posner, B. (2012). The Leadership Challenge: How to Make Extraordinary Things Happen in Organizations (Fifth Ed.). San Francisco: Wiley.

Lawrence, P., and Lorsch, J. (1967). "Differentiation and Integration in Complex Organizations" Administrative Science Quarterly 12, 1-30.

Leonard, L. (Feb 4, 2021). Returning to the Roots of Community Resilience in Hawaiʻi. yesmagazine.org. https://www.yesmagazine.org/environment/2021/02/04/hawaii-local-agriculture-food-security Accessed Jan 1, 2023.

Lewin, K. (1943). Psychology and the process of group living. Journal of Social Psychology 17, 113–131.

Linzey, T. (2015). The Myth of Community Rights: Self-Governance has a Corporate Ceiling. In These Times. https://inthesetimes.com/article/the-myth-of-community-rights Accessed July 13 2023.

Madaus, S. (2019). 6 Matriarchal Societies That Have Been Thriving With Women at the Helm for Centuries. Town and Country Mag. https://www.townandcountrymag.com/society/tradition/g28565280/matriarchal-societies-list/

Martin, N. (2021). When Seas Burn and Governments Do Nothing, Community Action Is the Only Way. The New Republic. https://newrepublic.com/article/162909/gulf-pemex-fire-pipeline-community-action?fbclid=IwAR0_mXN9SI9Fqvn10ZMX2pQi3TZdIxlFSTxJw5-frpwJsVDsOWIa1Xz7iHg

Mattesich, P. & Monsey, B. (1997). Community Building: What Makes it Work. Saint Paul, MN: Amherst H. Wilder Foundation.

Matusak, L. (1997). Finding Your Voice: Learning to Lead…Anywhere You Want to Make a Difference. San Francisco: Jossey-Bass

McBay, A. (2019a). Full Spectrum Resistance, Volume One: Building Movements and Fighting to Win. New York: Seven Stories Press.

McBay, A. (2019b). Full Spectrum Resistance, Volume Two: Actions and Strategies for Change. New York: Seven Stories Press.

McBay, A., Jensen, D., & Keith, L. (2011). Deep Green Resistance: Strategy to Save the Planet. Seven Stories Press.

Merin, M. (2019). School is a Riot. In Mink, John (Ed.). Teaching Resistance: Radicals, Revolutionaries, and Cultural Subversives in the Classroom. Oakland, CA: PM Press.

More, T. (1553). Dialogue of Comfort Against Tribulation, Book 2, sec. 16.

Morse, S. (1998). Five Building Blocks for Successful Communities. In F. Hesselbein et al. (Eds) Communities of the Future. San Francisco: Jossey-Bass.

Murphy, P., & Cunningham, J. (2003). Organizing for Community Controlled Development: Renewing Civil Society. Thousand Oaks: Sage Publications.

N., Sam M.S., "CULTURAL DRIFT," in *PsychologyDictionary.org*, April 7, 2013, https://psychologydictionary.org/cultural-drift/ (accessed November 15, 2023).

Osterweil, V. (2020). In Defense of Looting: A Riotous History of Uncivil Action. New York: Bold Type Books.

Putnam, R. (2000). Bowling Alone: The Collapse and Revival of American Community. New York: Simon and Schuster.

Rebrii, A. (2020). Zapatistas: Lessons in community self-organisation in Mexico. In opendemocracy.net, 25 June 2020, 8.53pm. https://www.opendemocracy.net/en/democraciaabierta/zapatistas-lecciones-de-auto-organización-comunitaria-en

Reed, T. (2015). Eminent domain abuse violates private property rights. https://thehill.com/blogs/congress-blog/246691-eminent-domain-abuse-violates-private-property-rights Accessed Feb 25, 2023.

Rost, J. (1993). Leadership for the Twenty-First Century. Westport, CT: Praeger.

Roy, A. (2011). 'They are trying to keep me destabilised. Anybody who says anything is in danger' https://www.theguardian.com/books/2011/jun/05/arundhati-roy-keep-destabilised-danger

Roy, A. (2003). War Talk. Boston: South End Press.

Sandel, M. (2009). Justice: What's the Right Thing to Do? New York: Farrar, Straus & Giroux.

Seymour, R. (2012). American Insurgents: A Brief History of American Anti-Imperialism. Haymarket Books.

Shaffer, C., & Anundsen, K. (2005). Creating Community Anywhere: Finding Support and Connection in a Fragmented World.Dillon Beach, CA: CCC Press.

Sharma, M. (2017). Radical Transformational Leadership: Strategic Action for Change Agents. Berkeley, CA: North Atlantic Books.

Silverstein, S. (2021). Accountable Leaders Learn to Spot Cultural Drift. https://www.soundwisdom.com/blog/accountable-leaders-learn-to-spot-cultural-drift

Sorenson, M. (24 Feb 2008). Humor as a Serious Strategy of Nonviolent Resistance to Oppression. Wiley Online Library. https://onlinelibrary.wiley.com/doi/full/10.1111/j.1468-0130.2008.00488.x

Strand, K., Marullo, S., Cutforth, N., Stoecker, R., & Donohue, P. (2003). Community-Based Research and Higher Education. San Francisco: Jossey-Bass.

Surrusco, E. (2021). These Women Environmental Leaders Are Fighting For Their Communities. https://earthjustice.org/article/these-women-environmental-leaders-are-fighting-for-their-communities Accessed Feb 12, 2023

Theodori, G. (und.). The Community Activeness/Consciousness Matrix: A Tool for Community Development. Webpage downloaded Feb 28, 2020. https://www.shsu.edu/~glt002/Outreach%20articles/Theodori %202004%20community%20activeness%20consciousness%20matrix.pdf

Tuckman, B. (1965). The Developmental Sequence in Small Groups. Psychological Bulletin 63. 384-399.

Ulrich, D. (1998). Six Practices for Creating Communities of Value, Not Proximity. In F. Hesselbein et al. (Eds). Communities of the Future. San Francisco: Jossey-Bass.

Wacziarg, R., & Desmet, K. (2018). Are Americans Drifting Apart Culturally? https://www.promarket.org/2018/07/12/americans-drifting-apart-culturally/

Wallace, M. Why social change needs to be a laughing matter. Waging Nonviolence.org. June 17, 2017. https://wagingnonviolence.org/2017/06/incorporate-humor-civil-resistance/

Wilbert, M. & Thompson. D. (2015). Presentation on Organizing, Deep Green Resistance Conference.

Wood, R., & Bandura, A. (1989). Social cognitive theory of organizational management. Academy of Management Review, 14(3), 361-384.

Zinn, H. (2012). From Disobedience and Democracy: Nine Fallacies on Law and Order. Haymarket Books

----

Fred Gibson, PhD, is co-founder of Communities that Protect and Resist. An environmental and social justice activist, he's lived in Colorado, USA off and on since 1970, and has witnessed the native beauty and biological diversity of the Rockies Front Range, as well as its ongoing destruction. He is determined to reverse that trend.

Fred has worked as an organizational psychologist and leadership scholar, coach, and practitioner for over 40 years. He offers his experience to build effective leadership and organizational capacity to groups that resist the destruction of the planet. His experiences in the military, business world and academia provide useful perspectives on organizing and leading.

Although relatively new to activism, Fred has participated in resistance work in various forms, including the Castle Rock Prairie Dog campaign in Colorado, support efforts in Oak Flat, Arizona, Standing Rock, North Dakota and the Great Basin, Nevada, and the Philippines.

Photo courtesy of Max Wilbert

In addition to helping grow CPR as an organization, Fred teaches courses to activists and Community leaders. To register for one of these courses or to get more information, please contact him at ctpr@protonmail.com

— — — — — — — — —

Boris Wu, Msc, is a radical environmentalist, social rights activist and permaculture farmer. With the books he publishes with his press BabylonApocalypse.org he wants to inspire and encourage dissidents to break through an increasingly narrow public discourse and spread the seeds of decisive resistance and radical social change.